Safeguarding Children
Across Services

Caring for Abused and Neglected Children

Making the Right Decisions for Reunification or Long-Term Care

Jim Wade, Nina Biehal, Nicola Farrelly and Ian Sinclair

Jessica Kingsley *Publishers*
London and Philadelphia

First published in 2011
by Jessica Kingsley Publishers
116 Pentonville Road
London N1 9JB, UK
and
400 Market Street, Suite 400
Philadelphia, PA 19106, USA

www.jkp.com

Library of Congress Cataloging in Publication Data
Caring for abused and neglected children : making the right decisions for long-term care or reunification / Jim Wade ... [et al.].
    p. cm. -- (Safeguarding children across services)
  Includes bibliographical references and index.
  ISBN 978-1-84905-207-8 (alk. paper)
  1. Abused children--Long-term care. 2. Custody of children. 3. Child welfare. I. Wade, Jim.
  HV873.C37 2011
  362.76'88--dc22

British Library Cataloguing in Publication Data
A CIP catalogue record for this book is available from the British Library

ISBN 978 1 84905 207 8

Printed and bound in Great Britain

Caring for Abused
and Neglected Children

Safeguarding Children Across Services Series
Series editors: Carolyn Davies and Harriet Ward

Safeguarding children from abuse is of paramount importance. This series communicates messages for practice from an extensive government-funded research programme designed to improve early recognition of child abuse as well as service responses and interventions. The series addresses a range of forms of abuse, including emotional and physical abuse and neglect, and outlines strategies for effective interagency collaboration, successful intervention and best practice. Titles in the series will be essential reading for practitioners with responsibility for safeguarding children.

Carolyn Davies is Research Advisor at Thomas Coram Research Unit at the Institute of Education, University of London.

Harriet Ward is Director of the Centre for Child and Family Research and Research Professor at Loughborough University

other books in the series

Safeguarding Children from Emotional Maltreatment
What Works
Jane Barlow and Anita Schrader McMillan
ISBN 978 1 84905 053 1

Recognizing and Helping the Neglected Child
Evidence-Based Practice for Assessment and Intervention
Brigid Daniel, Julie Taylor and Jane Scott with David Derbyshire and Deanna Neilson
Foreword by Enid Hendry
ISBN 978 1 84905 093 7

Adolescent Neglect
Research, Policy and Practice
Gwyther Rees, Mike Stein, Leslie Hicks and Sarah Gorin
ISBN 978 1 84905 104 0

Safeguarding Children Across Services
Messages from Research
Carolyn Davies and Harriet Ward
ISBN 978 1 84905 124 8

of related interest

Good Practice in Safeguarding Children
Working Effectively in Child Protection
Edited by Liz Hughes and Hilary Owen
ISBN 978 1 84310 945 7
Good Practice in Health, Social Care and Criminal Justice Series

Safeguarding Children Living with Trauma and Family Violence
Evidence-Based Assessment, Analysis and Planning Interventions
Arnon Bentovim, Antony Cox, Liza Bingley Miller and Stephen Pizzey
Foreword by Brigid Daniel
ISBN 978 1 84310 938 9
Best Practice in Working with Children Series

Contents

List of Tables and Figures

Acknowledgements

Wse owe a debt of gratitude to the great many people who helped to make the study upon which this book is based possible. Our project was funded under the government's Safeguarding Children Research Initiative, jointly sponsored by the Department for Children, Schools and Families (now Department for Education) and the Department of Health. We are very grateful for this assistance and, in particular, to Dr Carolyn Davies, our research liaison officer, for her invaluable help and encouragement throughout the project. The findings are ours alone, but we hope the messages they convey will have continuing relevance for the new coalition government's efforts to strengthen safeguarding policy and practice.

The study could not have taken place without the commitment and support of managers, social work practitioners and administrators working within the seven participating local authorities. Administrative staff made our lives easier by being very well organized and efficient. Team managers and social workers made us welcome, helped us to access children and birth parents and responded to our persistent requests for information with patience and good humour. Their cooperation was grounded in a strong desire to improve outcomes for looked after children. We are indebted to the schools that agreed to take part in the study, to the children's teachers who completed questionnaires about the children in their care and especially to the children and parents who allowed us to collect information about them and, in a small number of cases, to spend time talking to us about their experiences.

A number of people helped us with data collection and deserve our thanks. In particular, the children's social work case files were analysed by a dedicated team of auditors, all of whom were highly experienced social workers. Special thanks therefore go to Judi Armitage, Caroline Barber, John Corden, Mayank Joshi, Alison Kirkbride, Ruth McKenna, Karen Schiltroth and Lindsay Thompson.

Special thanks also go to members of our Research Advisory Group who provided consistent advice and support throughout the project and provided insightful comments on drafts of the final report. We would therefore like to thank Dave Basker, Carolyn Davies, Elaine Farmer, Jenny Gray, Christine Humphrey, Olive Stevenson and Lindsay Thompson for giving us their valuable time and expertise. It was much appreciated.

Finally, we are grateful to Lisa Parmiani, who worked with us as a researcher in the early stages of the project, and for the specialist help provided by administrative staff in the Social Policy Research Unit at the University of York. The financial and administrative infrastructure they provide enabled us to focus entirely on the research task. Thanks especially to Dawn Rowley for her skill and patience throughout the project and in proofreading and formatting these chapters.

A Note on Terminology

Children in care

The Department for Education website defines 'children in care' in the following way:

The term 'children in care' refers to:

- all children being looked after by a local authority, including
  - those subject to a care order under section 31 of the Children Act 1989 and
  - those looked after on a voluntary basis through an agreement with their parents under section 20 of the Children Act 1989.

(www.education.gov.uk/help/atozand glossary/)

This is how we have chosen to use these terms throughout this book. We move interchangeably between describing children as 'looked after' or 'in care' and, when referring to the system within which they are cared for, between the 'looked after system' or 'care system'. We do this to enhance ease of reading and also because they are used interchangeably in everyday language by young people, practitioners and families.

Where we refer specifically to children on 'care orders' or children trialled at home through 'placement with parents', this is made explicit in the text. Otherwise the reader can assume that we are referring to looked after children as a whole.

Throughout the text we contrast reunions that occur through 'placement with parents' (with a continuing care order) with children 'discharged' home (those who leave the care system to return home without a care order in existence). We therefore have a 'placement with parents' group and a 'discharge' group.

Children's services

Where reference is made to children's services in the course of the book, the term is used to denote the 'social care' aspect of these services.

1

Introduction

This book reports findings from a study of children who entered the looked after system for reasons of abuse or neglect. It focuses on the care pathways of these children and compares the progress and outcomes for those who remained looked after with those who returned home.

Separating maltreated children from their parents and either returning them home or, alternatively, providing them with long-term care are amongst the most serious interventions made by children's services. The decisions associated with separation and return are very difficult ones for social workers, in collaboration with other professionals, to take. They are also decisions that have long-term and potentially damaging implications for the children and families concerned. What happens to children as a result of these decisions lies at the heart of this book. By knowing more about how things turn out for maltreated children who go home in comparison to those who remain in care, about when and in what circumstances the prospects for reunification appear good and about the planning and support that is needed to improve the chances of success, it may be possible to improve this decision making and, it is to be hoped, the outcomes for children who go home. This comparison of pathways and outcomes can also tell us something more about the strengths and limitations of substitute care for maltreated children and about the potential for some children to settle and fare relatively well in long-term foster and residential placements.

In undertaking this research, we have sought answers to a number of interrelated questions:

1. How do the care pathways of maltreated children compare to those of children looked after for other reasons? Are these children more or less likely to remain looked after, return to their families or go on to other forms of permanent placement through adoption, residence or (more recently) special guardianship?

2. Where there appear to be differences in these pathways, how might these differences be accounted for? What, for example, appears to be the balance between the characteristics of the children and their families and the local authorities in which they live in explaining these differences?

3. Within the maltreated group, which children are more likely to go home and which are more likely to remain within the system?

4. What appear to be the main factors that are taken into account when the key decision to reunify (or not reunify) a maltreated child is made? How does this planning process vary and how are these decisions supported in the early stages of reunion?

5. What are the longer-term consequences of these decisions up to four years later, on average? How do the progress and outcomes of children who went home compare to those who stayed in care with respect to their safety, stability and psychosocial well-being?

6. What can we learn from the past and present experiences of children and their families and from the interventions they receive that help us to understand differences in outcome that are identified? How might this knowledge help to strengthen decision making in the future?

For practical reasons, it is not possible to report on all of these findings within the covers of one book. We will therefore focus here on the maltreated group and on detailed comparisons between children who went home and children who did not (questions 3–6). This will provide a sharp focus on decision making, experiences and outcomes. Findings on comparative care pathways and the influences upon them (questions 1–2), which drew primarily on analysis of large-scale administrative data held by local authorities, will be published separately in due course through journal papers. However, reference will be made to these findings where they seem especially relevant to the central arguments in this book.

The study was commissioned as part of the government's research initiative on safeguarding children. Initiatives to improve child well-being, to promote the welfare of children and to protect those suffering or at risk of harm have been central to government policy and legislation in recent years. *Every Child Matters*, enacted through the Children Act 2004, established five broad outcome areas that were considered important to well-being in childhood and later life – being healthy, staying safe, enjoying and achieving, making a positive contribution and achieving economic well-being (Department for Education and Skills 2004). It also established a national framework for local programmes of change to be led by local authorities and their partners and a performance framework against which progress could be judged. *Care Matters*, which informed the Children and Young Persons Act 2008, focused on improving the quality of care and the substantive progress and outcomes of children in the looked after system (Department for Education and Skills 2007).

The *Every Child Matters* programme originated, at least in part, from the findings of the inquiry into the death of Victoria Climbié on the failure of services to safeguard her adequately (CM 5730). In 2006 (and revised in 2010), the publication of *Working Together to Safeguard Children* provided statutory guidance for social workers and other professionals with responsibility for safeguarding children, with important emphasis on cross-agency communication and collaboration (HM Government 2006, 2010). However, and despite these initiatives, the development of consistent high-quality safeguarding practices continues to be elusive, as the Laming Report following the tragic death of Baby Peter made clear (Lord Laming 2009). Amongst a range of recommendations, the report emphasized the need for greater strategic coordination, for improvements in the recruitment, training, management and supervision of frontline social workers, for reduced and better-managed caseloads and for all agencies with a safeguarding role to have clear duties and responsibilities to work together and share information. These recommendations were accepted by government (Department for Children, Schools and Families 2009b).

Subsequently, in 2010, the coalition government instigated a fundamental review of the child protection system undertaken by Professor Munro. In commissioning this review, the Secretary of State for Education set out the three principles which would underpin the new government's approach to reform in this area: early intervention, trusting professionals and removing bureaucracy, and greater transparency and accountability (Munro 2010). The ensuing Munro review of child protection applied a systems approach to its analysis of the child protection system. At the time of writing, it had yet to report its final recommendations.

Findings from research have also informed the development of safeguarding policy and practice, and the balance of this chapter will provide a brief summary of some aspects of research on child maltreatment and on the reunification of children as these relate to our key research questions. This will help to set the scene for the chapters that follow where these findings will be discussed in more detail.

Defining maltreatment

From a research perspective, the findings from studies of child maltreatment tend to vary according to the definitions of physical, sexual, emotional abuse or neglect that are used and according to the research methods that have been employed – including sampling, data collection strategies and measures (see Cawson *et al.* 2000). Definitions may also vary across cultures and over time, as attitudes about what constitutes maltreatment change (see Creighton 2004; Department of Health 1995).

Historically, some forms of child maltreatment have received greater research attention than others. Despite the fact that emotional abuse and neglect are the most pervasive forms of maltreatment, they have tended to be the most under-researched and the least well understood (Horwath 2007; Iwaniec 2006). Horwath, writing about child neglect, links this to problems of defining what constitutes appropriate standards of child care, perspectives about which may vary according to culture, faith and social class beliefs, and to the lack of theoretical frameworks that can inform neglect research. Iwaniec suggests that researchers and practitioners may also shy away from emotional abuse because its signs are not immediately visible and its consequences for children's emotional and behavioural development may be more readily (but perhaps wrongly) attributed to other causes (p.24). These are not small matters, as a failure to reach consensus about different forms of maltreatment may have implications for the reporting of cases and for the potential of early intervention strategies.

Defining child maltreatment is therefore complex. *Working Together to Safeguard Children* provides descriptions of the behaviours which may constitute physical, sexual and emotional abuse or neglect, although these do not always correspond with those that have been employed in research studies (HM Government 2010, pp.37–39). The features of physical abuse that are described include hitting, shaking, throwing, poisoning, scalding or otherwise causing physical harm to a child and also includes the fabrication or inducement of child symptoms of illness by a parent. The description in *Working Together* of sexual abuse is similarly broad. It includes forcing or enticing a child to take part in or view sexual activities, including prostitution, irrespective of whether the child is aware of what is happening or not.

Emotional abuse and neglect are yet more difficult to define. Emotional abuse has been described as a constituent element in all forms of maltreatment but also as occurring as a distinct form (Iwaniec 2006). It generally refers to a relationship rather than an event, may not involve physical contact and may involve acts of either commission or omission (Glaser, Prior and Lynch 2001). It describes situations where parents either fail to respond to their child or react in a hostile or dismissive manner, making children feel unloved and unwanted (Howe 2005). It does not primarily refer to isolated events, as it is the relationship that is abusive, and while emotional abuse may exist along a continuum from less to more severe, these behaviours need to be repetitive and sustained over time (Iwaniec 2006). The absence of specific incidents or moments of crisis in emotional abuse and neglect cases has contributed to difficulties in identification, reporting and intervention by agencies (Horwath 2007).

Researchers have developed typologies of emotional abuse to capture the range of behaviours that are likely to inflict psychological and developmental harm on children. These have typically included spurning (degrading or rejecting), terrorising, isolating, exploiting or corrupting, denying emotional responsiveness and failing to provide for the psychological, medical or developmental needs of the child (see Iwaniec 2006, pp.28–30, for a discussion of these typologies). *Working Together* (2006) describes the behaviours associated with emotional abuse and its effects in these broad terms (see p.38).

Definitions of child neglect have also been contentious. Emotional abuse and neglect tend to co-occur and both address physical and psychological dimensions of child development. For this reason, researchers have confirmed the importance for practitioners of keeping these two aspects of maltreatment in mind in child protection work through the concept of psychological maltreatment (Glaser 2002). Stevenson suggests that the definition provided in *Working Together* offers a workable consensus by addressing the physical and psychological dimensions of neglect, its chronicity and the potential for prenatal neglect – through, for example, maternal substance misuse (Stevenson 2007). *Working Together* (2010) describes neglect as the persistent failure to meet children's physical or psychological needs in a manner likely to impair their health or development – including their need for food, clothing and shelter; failing to protect them from harm or danger or by ensuring adequate supervision; or by failing to ensure access to appropriate medical care or treatment (p.39). It also addresses emotional neglect through failure to address children's basic emotional needs.

In this study, we have classified the forms of maltreatment experienced by children through the descriptions recorded on children's case files by social workers. We assume these descriptions had been informed by government guidance, but cannot guarantee it. The file audit was undertaken by experienced practitioners in our local authorities. The *Working Together* (2006) guidance was used as a framework to assist them to make judgements about maltreatment from the evidence on file, although some variance in interpretation is possible.

Occurrence of maltreatment

Measuring the extent of child maltreatment also presents problems. National statistics are collected on the number of children who become subject to a child protection plan each year. For the year ending 31 March 2009, the total was 37,900 children (Department for Children, Schools and Families 2009c). These statistics show that neglect is the most common recorded category of maltreatment (46%), followed by emotional (27%), physical (13%) and sexual abuse (6%). However, measures of maltreatment based on national or local administrative systems measure only the incidence of maltreatment that is referred and investigated. Statistics of this kind may tell us less about actual incidence and more about operational assumptions and decision making within the safeguarding system (Stevenson 1996).

Prevalence studies offer an alternative method for understanding the extent of child maltreatment. The largest prevalence study in the UK, which has recently been repeated with publication due in 2011, was that conducted by Cawson and her colleagues (2000). They surveyed a random probability sample of 2869 young adults aged 18–24 years about experiences of childhood maltreatment. The researchers divided experience of physical abuse into 'serious', 'intermediate' or 'cause for concern' based on an assessment of young people's responses. On this basis, one-quarter of the sample (24%) were considered to have experienced some form of physical abuse (with 7% rated as 'serious'). In relation to sexual abuse, 4 per cent were assessed as having been sexually abused by a parent, carer or relative, 11 per cent by other known people and 4 per cent by a stranger or someone just met. Neglect was divided into 'absence of care' and 'lack of supervision'. Seventeen per cent of young people were rated as having experienced some 'absence of care' (with 6% rated as 'serious') and 20 per cent some supervisory neglect (5% rated as 'serious'). Emotional maltreatment was difficult to estimate. Assessment was made across seven dimensions (similar to the typology presented above) to provide an overall score with a midpoint cut-off for assessing maltreatment. On this basis, just 6 per cent of young people were assessed as having crossed the threshold for maltreatment, although a further 6 per cent were at or just below it.

Not only is the co-occurrence of different forms of maltreatment quite common (Howe 2005; Stevenson 2007), but these are often interwoven with a complex range of quite deep-seated family difficulties. It is the interaction of these multiple adversities that may increase the risk of poor outcomes for children (Rutter 2000; Rutter, Giller and Hagell 1998). Parental substance misuse, domestic violence and violent offences have been found to cluster together in families and to be strongly associated with maltreatment (Cleaver et al. 2007; Glaser et al. 2001). Parental mental health problems have also been associated with maltreatment, although perhaps more clearly in relation to emotional maltreatment than to physical abuse or neglect (Cleaver, Unell and Aldgate 1999; Hunt, Macleod and Thomas 1999). Parental learning disability has also been associated with physical and emotional neglect, quite commonly as a result of parents not realizing what they should be providing. Where learning-disabled parents do neglect their children, studies point to the likelihood of intrusive interventions with a high proportion of children being removed from home (see, for example, the discussion in Horwath 2007, p.106). Finally, while most attention is given to younger children, we need to be mindful that adolescents are also likely to experience maltreatment. Although fatalities and serious injury may be less common for this age group, young people are more likely to place themselves at risk through running away, truancy, self-harm, substance misuse and offending (Rees and Stein 1999).

It is this constellation of difficulties that can confuse, or even overwhelm, child protection practitioners attempting to identify and assess needs and develop appropriate intervention strategies. In particular, emotional abuse and neglect rarely sit comfortably with a 'forensic model' of investigation based on discrete incidents and episodes (Stevenson 2007, p.8). There is evidence that child protection investigations are less likely to be conducted without the presence of an event or injury and, where this is lacking, that cases are more likely to be closed without provision of services (Buckley 2000; Platt 2006). Even though a delayed response to neglectful behaviour may prove very harmful to a child, studies have shown that family assessments in cases of emotional abuse and neglect have tended to be low-key, maintaining this focus on risks and incidents rather than on the developmental needs of the child (Wilding and Thoburn 1997).

The complex nature of family difficulties also makes it more difficult for practitioners to maintain a focus on the child's needs (including, perhaps, their need for a compensatory environment) while responding to parent problems (Brandon *et al.* 2008; Horwath 2007). In these circumstances, emotional maltreatment and its effects may not be recognized. For example, a recent study of maltreatment referrals in an American city found that while 50 per cent of a sample of 303 children had experienced emotional abuse, this had been identified by agency staff in only 9 per cent of cases (Trickett *et al.* 2009). Practitioners may also become accustomed to low standards of parental care in families, with the result that the need for decisive action to safeguard a child may not be recognized until an incident occurs that prompts a reassessment (Ayre 1998; Stevenson 1996). These judgements may also be reinforced by negative perceptions amongst social workers and allied professionals about the quality of care provided in the looked after system.

Admission to the looked after system: thresholds and outcomes

Given these perspectives, thresholds for admitting children to the care system tend to be high (see Brandon *et al.* 2008). A recent study profiling care proceedings cases brought before the courts, for example, found that the vast majority of these children had been known to children's services for over one year beforehand and 45 per cent for five or more years (Masson, Pearce and Bader 2008). Even where proceedings were unplanned in response to a crisis, almost three-quarters (72%) had been known for at least one year. Despite evidence of relatively long-term social work involvement, the findings suggested that many cases had not been 'open' or active throughout this time and that only a later serious deterioration prompted an approach to the courts. While family difficulties may be 'held' for quite long periods of time, its unpredictability means there is always potential for child protection crises to erupt suddenly. Furthermore, even where these cases are brought before the court, it is not uncommon for courts to reject applications for care and to require local authorities to continue managing the situation through family support services.

Recent studies have also highlighted how thresholds for admission to care vary considerably between local authorities (Dickens *et al.* 2007; Sinclair *et al.* 2007). Decision making is therefore not consistent across local authorities. Studies have also pointed to the way that local authorities vary in their use of different placement resources. Sinclair and colleagues' (2007) study found significant variation by local council in the likelihood that children, once they were looked after, would be reunified, remain fostered or go on to adoption. These differences were found to have less to do with the characteristics of children and families and much more to do with differences in the local councils themselves. Similar variations have also been found in studies of kinship care (Farmer and Moyers 2008), adoption (Biehal *et al.* 2010) and special guardianship (Wade, Dixon and Richards 2010). As later chapters will make clear, differences in local authority decision making and in the pathways that flowed from them were also evident in this study.

Decisions about whether children should or should not enter the care system have also been affected by widespread concerns about the relatively poor outcomes attained by looked after children. In this respect, care has often been viewed as 'a last resort', rather than as part of an integrated service continuum linking preventive and reunification services. Concern about poor outcomes has been long-standing. The looked after system has had great difficulty providing stability and continuity in relationships for young people (Jackson 2002), in offering adequate compensation for children's educational disadvantages and, for those who do remain long-term, in supporting their transition to adulthood (Biehal *et al.* 1995; Dixon and Stein 2005; Wade and Dixon 2006). Perhaps especially in residential settings, it has not always managed to keep young people safe (Farmer and Pollock 1998; Sinclair and Gibbs 1998; Wade *et al.* 1998), although our awareness of the potential for maltreatment in foster settings is also growing (Biehal *et al.* 2010).

While children's undoubted educational and behavioural difficulties often antedate their arrival into the system, entry to care may also offer relief for some children and opportunities for a fresh start. For example, there is evidence that those children who fare better educationally and go on to be economically active tend to be female, to have been looked after for a longer time, most often in foster settings, and to have had fairly settled care careers and active encouragement from adults around them (Biehal *et al.* 1995; Dixon *et al.* 2006; Robbins 2001). This suggests that the care system, given the right ingredients, can make a positive difference to outcomes for children and young people.

Reunification of looked after children: predictors of return

Since the Children Act 1989, greater emphasis has been given to supporting children in their families and, if separation is considered necessary, on returning them to their homes as soon as it is considered safe to do so. Although, in keeping with this philosophy, the flow of children entering the care system over subsequent years has (until recently) tended to decline, the number of children looked after at any point in time has increased due to a trend for some children to stay longer.[1] The major reason for this increase almost certainly lies in the higher proportion of children looked after for abuse or neglect (around 61% in 2009 and 2010) who cannot easily be returned home (Biehal 2006; Gibbs, Sinclair and Stein 2005).

Most children who go home tend to do so quite quickly, the vast majority within two years of entering care (Bullock, Gooch and Little 1998; Bullock, Little and Millham 1993; Packman and Hall 1998). Children placed for reasons of abuse or neglect, however, have been found to return home more slowly than those placed for other reasons (Cleaver 2000; Davis *et al.* 1996; Fanshel and Shinn 1978; Landsverk *et al.* 1996). There is also evidence that

---

1   Department for Children, Schools and Families (2009), *Children Looked After in England (including Adoption and Care Leavers) Year Ending 31 March 2009* (available at www.education.gov.uk/rsgateway/DB/SFR/s000878/index.shtml). However, the flow of children into the looked after system has recently increased from 23,300 starts during 2007–2008 to 27,800 during 2009–2010, a pattern influenced by (amongst other things) the tragic death of Baby Peter in 2007.

those placed for neglect are more likely to remain looked after than those placed for either physical or sexual abuse (Grogan-Kaylor 2001; Wells and Guo 1999), and that this may relate to social workers making active reunion plans for those cases offering a better chance of success (Barth *et al.* 1987; Farmer and Parker 1991). Although neglected children return at a slower rate, it is nonetheless likely that most will go home at some stage (George 1990).

Although the evidence is far from conclusive in some areas, the likelihood of return appears to have some association with the characteristics of children. Children in middle childhood (aged four to 12 years) may be more likely to return home than very young children or adolescents (see Biehal 2006). Children with learning impairments appear especially likely to remain longer in care (Berridge and Cleaver 1987; Cleaver 2000; Davis, Landsverk and Newton 1997). This may also be the case for some children with emotional or behavioural difficulties, perhaps especially those with 'externalizing' rather than 'internalizing' difficulties (Glisson, Bailey and Post 2000; Landsverk *et al.* 1996).

There is also evidence of variation according to the composition of families and the nature of parent problems. It is not surprising to find that families with relatively fewer problems and more emotional resources are more likely to be reunified than those with more complex interrelated problems, such as substance misuse, domestic violence, offending or chronic mental health or emotional problems (Fraser *et al.* 1996; Rzepnicki, Schuerman and Johnson 1997). In the US, poverty and poor housing conditions have also been identified as background factors associated with a slower rate of reunification (Barth *et al.* 1987; Fraser *et al.* 1996; Jones 1998; Smith 2003).

The motivation and determination of parents and children for reunion, often in the absence of clear social work planning, and their willingness to change and adapt have also been found to be important influences on return (Bullock *et al.* 1998; Farmer and Parker 1991; Sinclair *et al.* 2005). Children may often return to changed family circumstances, and one UK study on reunification found that younger children placed for reasons of abuse or neglect generally fared better after return home when there had been no or only a few changes in the household and least well when changes involved additional children (Farmer and Parker 1991). However, children who go home have often been found to have a number of subsequent moves between parents, relatives and family friends (Bullock *et al.* 1998; Farmer and Parker 1991).

In general terms, studies have consistently pointed to a lack of planning for reunion, to limitations in the post-reunification support that is provided and to the degree to which reunion occurs through happenstance, especially for older children (Bullock *et al.* 1993; Department of Health and Social

Security 1985; Farmer and Parker 1991; Farmer, Sturgess and O'Neill 2008; Millham *et al.* 1986; Sinclair *et al.* 2005). Purposeful social work planning and activity directed towards reunion, assessments that lead to clear goals and targets in relation to the changes that are needed, provision of social work and specialist services to support those changes and planning that is inclusive of children and families have been identified as important features of positive reunification practice (Aldgate 1980; Biehal 2006; Cleaver 2000; Farmer and Moyers 2008; Stein and Gambrill 1977).

Outcomes of reunification

This study is concerned with an assessment of the risks and potential for reunifying looked after children with their families where prior maltreatment has been present, through a comparison with children who do not return home. Although no previous UK research has systematically compared these two groups, what evidence there is suggests that reunification cannot be viewed as self-evidently a safe policy, that risks need to be weighed carefully in individual cases and that outcomes of return home for children are at best mixed.

Reunions frequently do not last. Studies have found that sizeable minorities of reunified children have experienced home breakdown and that most of these children subsequently re-entered the looked after system (Bullock *et al.* 1998; Farmer and Parker 1991; Farmer *et al.* 2008; Packman and Hall 1998; Rowe, Hundleby and Garnett 1989). Concerns have also been raised in the literature about the risks of children 'oscillating' in and out of the care system as repeated attempts at reunification are made (Bullock *et al.* 1993). Farmer and colleagues' (2008) study of a reunified sample of 180 children, for example, found that only 36 per cent of the children had not experienced a disruption at home and that 35 per cent had experienced two or more.

Amongst children who go home, it is not surprising to find that the risk of re-abuse or further neglect through poor parenting appears higher than it is for those who do not go home (Barth and Berry 1994; Ellaway *et al.* 2004; Runyan and Gould 1985; Terling 1999). In one fostering study, re-abuse after return also predicted a worsening of children's mental health (Sinclair *et al.* 2005). Re-abuse rates vary according to sampling and length of follow-up. However, recent studies have found that approaching one-half of children in reunified samples of varying duration were thought to have been exposed to further maltreatment (Brandon *et al.* 2005; Farmer *et al.* 2008; Sinclair *et al.* 2005).

A small number of studies have also found that children who return home tend to fare worse in relation to a wide range of outcomes when compared to those who remain looked after. Amongst young children, those at home may be less likely to thrive (King and Taitz 1985) and more likely to display poor emotional well-being or 'disturbance' (Hensey, Williams and Rosenbloom 1983). In relation to older children, those reunified have been found to have significantly more emotional problems, self-harming and risk behaviours, including substance misuse and offending, than those who remained in care (Sinclair *et al.* 2005; Taussig, Clyman and Landsverk 2001). In contrast, children who spend a relatively long time in care appear less likely to become involved in delinquency (Minty 1987; Zimmerman 1982). Educational performance may also suffer. Sinclair and colleagues' (2005) research on foster children found evidence that, against a measure of educational performance and participation, those who returned home and those in residential care showed no improvement when compared to those fostered or adopted.

Although the existing comparative evidence is limited, it does suggest that decisions to return children home, perhaps especially maltreated children, should be taken with considerable care if family reunions are to be given the best possible chance of success. It also suggests that there may be a balance to be struck between the relative merits of care or home in individual cases. Of course, these decisions may not always be firmly in the control of social workers and their professional colleagues. Older children may vote with their feet and crises may emerge to unsettle planning. There may also be little merit in keeping children in the system if they really do not accept the need to be there, if they yearn to be with their family, experience several placement breakdowns and eventually return by default. It is these decisions and their consequences for the progress of children that will form the substance of this book.

The structure of the book

The book is structured chronologically and traces the experiences of 149 children who had entered the system for reasons of abuse or neglect; some went home again while others did not. Chapter 3 describes the children's admission to care, the types of maltreatment they had experienced and the background factors that contributed to them entering the care system. Chapters 4 through to 7 move forward to the period when the decision for them to go home or not was made. These chapters draw on evidence from case files and interviews with parents and children to examine how the children were getting on in care and the range of parent problems about which social work concerns persisted. They consider the assessment and planning that surrounded this key decision, identify the range of factors that were taken into account when making it and consider how this decision was supported over a subsequent period of six months. Finally, we look at what factors best predicted who would go home and assess initial outcomes for both the *home* and *care* groups at the six-month stage.

Chapters 8 through to 11 draw on survey responses from social workers and teachers and interview material from parents and children to assess the comparative progress of these groups of children at follow-up. We consider how the *home* and *care* groups were faring with respect to their safety, stability and overall well-being and identify factors associated with their relative progress. Chapter 12 draws together the main findings from the study and highlights some important messages for policy and practice that flow from them. First, however, it is necessary to describe how the study was undertaken.

2

Study Design

This chapter provides a brief outline of the study design, sampling and methods of data collection and analysis. This will help to situate the findings that are presented in subsequent chapters and to make sense of how these findings were derived. We have attempted to keep technical information to a minimum.

The study builds on an earlier large-scale study of pathways for looked after children conducted by Ian Sinclair and colleagues (2007) at the University of York. The *Pursuit of Permanence* study was conducted in 13 local authorities and collected information on all 7399 children who were looked after at some point during 2003–2004. Some 60 per cent of these children had entered care for reasons of abuse or neglect. Although this study employed a range of mixed methods, it relied primarily on local council administrative data to track the careers of these children over a period of one year and on information drawn from social workers for children looked after at some point in the second half of that year. In addition to the tracking data, some information was also collected on children's histories. The present study was conducted in seven of these local authorities and has collected further information on all 3872 children who had been in their care at that time and who had therefore been included in the *Pursuit of Permanence* study.

These local authorities were selected on the basis of their willingness to undertake further research tasks, the quality of their information systems and their size – to ensure that sufficient numbers of children were available to achieve our projected sample size (3500 to 4000 children). They were also selected to ensure a good distribution of local authorities by type and location. The sample included two London boroughs, two unitary authorities, two metropolitan districts and one shire county. They were also spread across four different regions of England from London to the North-East.

For reasons of cost and practicality, the study was based on a longitudinal 'catch-up' design. This approach also enabled us to take advantage of the information already collected on these children from the earlier York study.

The design included quantitative and qualitative components and the different stages of the project were phased as the information we needed became known.

Phase 1: *census study* (n=3872)

The *census study* provided for a three-year follow-up (on average) of placement patterns for *all* 3872 children who were looked after at some point in the year 2003–2004[1] in the seven authorities. The information collected included one year's retrospective data on the children gathered during the earlier York study (and some information on their earlier careers) and a further two years' data on the comings and goings of these children into and out of the looked after system.

The *census study* was based primarily on information available from local authority information systems, although this was supplemented by questionnaires provided by social workers for a proportion of these children (2435) and information from social work managers collected during the course of the *Pursuit of Permanence* study (Sinclair *et al.* 2007).

The *census study* enabled us to compare the pathways of maltreated children to those of children looked after for other reasons. Within the maltreated group (n=2291), these data were used to examine factors associated with whether these children returned home or stayed within the looked after system and the reasons for these differences (insofar as we were able to judge from the information available) and to trace patterns of stability and change over the follow-up period. Although the extent of centralized information collected by local authorities is restricted, it was sufficient to understand:

- the characteristics of children (age, sex, ethnic origin)
- important aspects of their care careers (age at first entry, reasons for this admission)
- the main contours of their pathways over the follow-up period (number and types of placement, changes in legal status, admissions and discharges from the system and the reasons for these).

The *census study* sample also provided the sampling frame for our more detailed *survey* phase. Although findings from the *census study* will not be presented fully here, some key findings will be given where they provide important context to data generated through the surveys and interviews.

---

1   The census date chosen in negotiation with each local authority varied slightly during the course of this year (2003–2004), ranging from 31 May 2003 to 31 March 2004. The end point of the census follow-up therefore varied from 31 May 2005 to 31 March 2006.

Phase 2: the surveys (n=149)

The surveys provided much more detailed information about a sub-sample of 149 of these maltreated children. All of these children had entered the looked after system at some point between mid-2001 and early 2004, although not necessarily for the first time in their lives. A proportion of these children had returned home before the end of the *census* follow-up and the remainder had continued to be looked after.

The sample was selected according to certain criteria:

- All children had an admission to care during a two-year period between June 2001 and March 2004.

- In all cases, abuse or neglect had been a primary reason for this admission.

- It was intended that approximately one-half of the children should have returned home before the end of the census follow-up period and one-half should have remained looked after (although they may have moved elsewhere subsequently). This precise split was ultimately not achievable.

- All were aged 0–12 years at the relevant admission and were, therefore, aged 3–15 years at 1 January 2007, the date at which survey sample recruitment began.

In addition to these criteria, we were also looking for a reasonable spread of cases across the local authorities. The age criterion was applied because we intended to collect information from each child's current school teacher. Given the known tendency for looked after children to leave school early, it was therefore important that all children would be likely to be in pre-school or compulsory school provision at final follow-up.

Once these criteria were applied, the sampling frame that was available to us is shown in Table 2.1.

Table 2.1 Survey sample frame by local
authority and *home/care* groups (n)

Local council	*Home* group	*Care* group	Overall total
Area 1	113	107	1064
Area 2	72	36	730
Area 3	37	33	362
Area 4	26	16	331
Area 5	36	50	914
Area 6	26	14	241
Area 7	8	8	230
Total	318	264	3872

The recruitment process began at the start of 2007, continued into 2008 and was based on a random selection (within stratified cells) of those eligible within each local authority area. Ethical considerations raised by some of our local authorities shaped our approach to sample recruitment. Some were rightly concerned about providing us with personal details of parents and children before they had been provided with an opportunity to give their consent. As a result of these discussions, the surveys were conducted anonymously (using just the same child ID codes). Parent and child consents were sought using an 'opt out' procedure, as the survey did not require their direct participation. However, we did need permission to collect information from case files, social workers and teachers. This approach inevitably led to a complex and very elongated recruitment process; one that relied heavily on the cooperation of social workers and administrative staff to pass on all recruitment materials and to encourage the participation of children and birth parents.

Across all areas, 270 children and parents were approached. This resulted in an achieved survey sample of 149 children. However, as shown in Table 2.2, its distribution by area was more uneven than we had originally intended.[2]

---

2   This was close to our original projected sample of 154.

Table 2.2 Final survey sample by local authority
and *home/care* groups (n)

Local council	*Home* group	*Care* group	Total
Area 1	13	15	28
Area 2	13	15	28
Area 3	13	13	26
Area 4	5	9	14
Area 5	11	15	26
Area 6	12	11	23
Area 7	1	3	4
Total	68	81	149

The attrition rate was higher than we had expected. Well over two-fifths of the children/parents (45%) that we approached had to be withdrawn from the study and, on each occasion, a new case had to be selected. Reasons for withdrawal varied. Two-fifths of withdrawals involved children or parents exercising their right to opt out, one-fifth involved families moving away from the area, and smaller proportions included social workers having no knowledge of cases closed some years previously or advising us that the circumstances of the child or family were too unstable or difficult for us to proceed. Overall, these findings point to the difficulties that confront researchers when trying to engage families where maltreatment (and the range of difficulties that surround it) has figured prominently in their histories.

The surveys were designed to help us understand more about how this 'effective decision' to reunify or not was made, what factors were taken into account when making it and to compare the progress of these children six months after this decision (*care* group) or return home (*home* group) and at the end of the follow-up period. Final follow-up took place, on average, four years after this decision had been taken and up to six years after the children's relevant admission to the looked after system.

The *survey* phase included three elements of data collection:

- a case file study of assessment and decision making that led to the decision to stay or return, of social work plans to support this decision and of child progress and social work interventions in the subsequent six months

- a questionnaire survey of social workers to assess the subsequent progress of these children from a social work perspective
- a supplementary questionnaire survey of these children's school teachers to provide a view on children's progress and outcomes from an education perspective.

In outline, the case file schedule collected information on the:

- background circumstances and reasons for the child's admission to care, including the nature of maltreatment experienced and other presenting difficulties
- circumstances and progress of the child at the point of decision making (while still looked after) and the extent of social work concerns about parents at this time
- process by which this decision was made and the child, parent and resource factors that were taken into account when making it
- ways in which this decision was subsequently supported by children's services and other agencies over the next six months
- initial progress and outcomes for the child and family at the end of this six-month period.

The questionnaires to social workers and teachers were designed to capture children's progress and outcomes some four years, on average, after this decision had been taken. The questionnaires covered similar territory, although each version drew on the specialist knowledge of the professionals concerned. They were designed to collect information on the safety, stability and aspects of the psychosocial development of children and included information on:

- the child's placement (including ties with adults, safety, belonging and quality of relationships)
- the child's educational progress (including home–school relationships and educational services provided to the child)
- the child's well-being and social relationships
- interventions and support provided by children's services and other agencies over the follow-up period.

Although the questionnaires were primarily quantitative, space was made available for teachers and social workers to append comments to most questions and to review the progress made by the child, the factors associated with this progress and its relationship to interventions provided. The *survey* sample also provided the sampling frame for the *case study* phase of the research.

Phase 3: case studies (n=12)

The final phase of the study provided information from 12 case studies. The children included were all aged nine or over and all had experienced emotional abuse and/or neglect. Although we had hoped to recruit more children and parents, obtaining informed consent to interview proved challenging. As we did not know the identities of parents and children in advance, all materials had to be routed through children's services and only once written consent had been obtained were we able to make direct contact. Despite taking steps to approach all eligible children and parents in the survey sample (n=97), only nine parents and 11 children agreed to take part within the study timeframe, making a total of 12 case studies.[3] The reasons for withdrawal were various, including:

- refusals by parent or child (37)
- advised by social worker not to approach the family at this time (12)
- the case was closed and no family details were available (11).

In addition, there were a further 23 cases where we were never able to approach the family due to lack of social worker cooperation. Either the social worker was never contactable during the recruitment period or, after an initial conversation, it was not possible to establish whether the research materials had been forwarded or received by the families concerned.

The purpose of the case studies was to understand more about the meanings and significance of family histories, placement and social work interventions for children's experiences and outcomes. Parents were asked to reflect back on the decision-making process that had led to the decision for children to stay in care or return home, their perceptions of and involvement in it and their views on the subsequent support provided to help their adjustment to return or separation. The interviews also explored parental motivation and ambivalence in relation to the children's return, current family circumstances, the progress of the children (at home or in care) and their perceptions of the support received from children's services or other agencies.

The interviews with children explored their experiences of being looked after or being at home, whether and how their views were taken into account when these decisions were made, their perceptions of their own strengths and difficulties in key areas of their lives and their views about the support provided by social workers and caregivers. Where children were

---

3   Only 37 of the children in the survey sample were aged eight or under at 1 January 2007. In addition, 15 children were not approached as they were siblings of children who had been approached for interview.

looked after, the interviews also explored their views about contact with their families and on the support they had received to adjust to life in care.

Survey response rates and sampling bias

Case file information was collected for all 149 children. Information from social workers or teachers on children's circumstances and progress at final follow-up was available for 146 (98%) of the children in the *survey sample*. Social workers provided completed questionnaires for 135 (92%) of these children and teachers for 90 (62%). Overall, therefore, we had a complete data set (from case file, social worker and teacher) for just over one-half (54%) of the children and some information from teacher or social worker on virtually all of them.

As some of these cases involved children who had returned home some time previously, we were concerned about how up to date the knowledge of social workers might be. As it turned out, the majority of social workers who provided information (85%) had seen the children during the previous six months and almost all (91%) had been in touch in the past year. They therefore had a good understanding of the children's circumstances. Twelve children had not been seen by social workers for one year or more, but for four of these children information was provided by their current teachers. We therefore had recent information on most (91%) and knew something about the circumstances of others (98%).

It is, however, important to consider how far the different steps involved in sample recruitment may have introduced a bias to the different samples and whether this carries implications for the findings presented in later chapters.

In carrying out these analyses we considered whether:

- the findings based on the full *census sample* provide a reasonably representative national picture of pathways for maltreated children

- the difficulties involved in recruiting our *achieved survey sample* have introduced systematic differences when compared to our *intended* sample frame.

With respect to the first question, our findings are quite straightforward. Comparisons between the *census sample* (n=3872), the *Pursuit of Permanence* sample (n=7399) and national statistics for 2004 provided by the Department for Children, Schools and Families revealed very few differences, except in one respect. The *census sample* included a higher than average number of minority ethnic children, although this difference had no real effect on the progress and outcomes of these children.

With respect to the second question, the findings were more complicated. The selection criteria adopted and the difficulties in recruiting children did produce some systematic differences. Children recruited to the *achieved* survey sample were on average older, were more likely to have displayed challenging behaviour and were more likely to have had repeat admissions to care when compared to the *intended* sample frame. Once age had been taken into account, however, only a repeat admission was significantly associated with being in the *achieved* survey sample.

What is more, children included in the *home* group were more likely to have had repeat admissions in the past than were those in the *care* group. This particular bias could have increased the apparent 'difficulty' of those who went home when compared to those who did not. In order to check the implications for our analysis of comparative outcomes for the *home* and *care* groups, we checked this key comparison in a regression that included 'repeat admissions'. This analysis showed that children who went home did worse on our overall well-being score at follow-up even when repeat admissions were included in the analysis.[4] It should not, therefore, affect the comparative findings reported later to any great extent.

The differences observed in the *achieved* survey sample are likely to reflect the greater ease of recruiting older children, children in the care system or children who had returned to it after a previous home breakdown and the greater reluctance of parents and children where settled at home to join the study and reopen old wounds. This is therefore likely to have had the effect of making these children appear more 'difficult' than would be the case from a pure randomly drawn sample. While this should not affect later comparisons between the progress of our *home* and *care* groups, it is something to be borne in mind.

Data analysis

Preliminary analysis of data from different aspects of the study (census, case files, social worker and teacher surveys) was undertaken at different stages of the research cycle in order to facilitate sample selections and the phasing of fieldwork. Final analysis drew these elements together and all key statistical variables were analysed using the computer software package SPSS-16:

---

4   Membership of the 'home' group was associated with a significantly worse outcome ($p=0.003$). The other variables in this regression were behaviour problems, behaviour that contributed to the relevant admission and whether or not the child had been living with a stepfather. All these were significantly associated with outcome. Repeat admissions were not ($p=0.086$).

- The census study provided data on patterns of placement, including patterns of stay, return and re-entry, and the factors associated with these different pathways over a period of up to three years.
- Statistical variables from case files provided data (for a sub-sample of 149 maltreated children) on the child, family and service factors taken into account when decisions to stay or return were made and on progress and interventions in the subsequent six months.
- The surveys of social workers and teachers yielded data on: a) the adequacy of placements; b) the safety of children; c) their psychosocial outcomes at follow-up and d) social work interventions over the follow-up period.

Descriptive and multivariate analysis was conducted to identify which groups of children were likely to return or stay, the factors that were taken into account when these decisions were made, the consequences of these decisions for children's progress and outcomes and the relationship between these and interventions by children's services and other agencies. Qualitative data from case files and the surveys shed further light on how and why factors identified in statistical analysis tended to have the influence they did.

Wherever possible, we have used non-parametric tests for bivariate analysis, as these make fewer assumptions (for example, about the distribution of the data), but we have used some parametric tests where these seemed appropriate and there was no non-parametric equivalent. A test result of $p=0.05$ was considered statistically significant (that is, at the 95% confidence level). Reliability tests were used to measure the level of consistency within scales using Cronbach's alpha. All p values, coefficients and sample size indicators for test results are included in the text (or in footnotes) to enable readers to reach their own judgements about the relative importance of particular findings.

Information from the parent–child interviews was transcribed and analysed using the software program Atlas-ti. Qualitative data from the social worker and teacher questionnaires on each child were added to enhance data triangulation. Analysis was undertaken to identify key themes across cases (within and across the samples of 'emotionally abused' and 'neglected' children) to explore how and why child and family histories, placement experiences and support were related to progress and outcomes for children in these cases. The interview data were also used to construct detailed illustrative case study material. However, details of some cases have been changed to protect the anonymity of all participants and all names referred to in the text are pseudonyms.

The children in the *survey sample*

The chapter will conclude with a brief description of the characteristics and family circumstances of the maltreated children in the *survey sample* at the time of their relevant admission to the care system. It will set the scene for our next chapter, which will explore the circumstances surrounding the admission to care of these children in much greater detail.

Age at admission reflected the sampling strategy described above. Ages ranged from one month to 12 years with a mean age at admission of 7.4 years. By follow-up in 2007–2008, therefore, the children's ages ranged from four to 17 years with a mean age of 11.7 years. The selection criteria imposed on the *survey sample* inevitably meant that its age profile was skewed when compared to the larger and much more representative *census sample*. Younger children were under-represented (just 23% were admitted below the age of five compared to 47% in the *census sample*) and children in the mid range were over-represented (52% included in the *survey sample* compared to 32% in the *census sample*). The purpose of the survey was to compare progress and outcomes for children who went home with those who remained looked after. At the younger end, it was therefore desirable to reduce the numbers who may have gone on to leave care through adoption (most of whom are under five years of age) and, at the older end, to reduce the possibility that young people would have aged out of care (or left education). Controlling the age profile of the sample was therefore considered necessary to meet our research aims.

Almost three-quarters of the *survey sample* were reported to be White British (74%), reflecting the proportion in the *census sample* (74%). Amongst those of minority ethnic backgrounds, the largest groups in the *survey sample* were Black African/Caribbean children (14%) and children of mixed heritage (10%). Just four children were reported to have been seeking asylum. No children were reported to have had physical disabilities and just two had a sensory impairment. However, just over one in six (16%) were reported to have had a learning disability and, as we shall see further in Chapter 5, these children were less likely to return to their families within the study timeframe.

Information was also collected on where children were living immediately prior to the relevant admission to care, as shown in Table 2.3.

Table 2.3 Child's carers prior to relevant admission

	Per cent (n)
Both birth parents	21.5 (31)
Lone parent	44 (64)
Birth parent and step-parent	9 (13)
Birth parent and relative	7.5 (11)
Birth mother and other adult	8.5 (12)
Relative	8.5 (12)
Other adult	1 (2)
Total	100 (145)

The vast majority of children were living with at least one birth parent prior to this admission. Most, however, were living with their birth mothers (83%) rather than with their birth fathers (26%). Only eight children (5% of the whole sample) were living with their fathers but not their mothers. Around one-fifth of children living with their mothers were living in households shared with members of their extended family. In roughly one-half of these cases, mothers and children were living with the children's grandparents and, in the remaining cases, with one or more of the mother's siblings.

Around one in ten children had been living with neither birth parent at the time of the relevant admission, the majority of them in informal placements with relatives. Two of these children, however, had been living with non-related adults. One child had stayed with her step-grandmother for a month prior to admission, but had previously been living with her mother and partner. The other was an asylum-seeking child from West Africa who was living with strangers who claimed to have found her wandering the streets.

Summary

This study has built upon earlier research undertaken at the University of York and has examined the care pathways of maltreated children who were in the care of seven local authorities at some point in 2003–2004, with a focus on comparing the progress of those who returned home and those who remained within the system. The study involved a number of phased stages:

1. A *census* study, drawing largely on local council administrative data, followed up a sample of 3872 children for a period (on average) of three years. The pathways of maltreated children were compared to those of children looked after for other reasons and, within the maltreated group, these data were used to identify factors associated with whether or not these children went home, the reasons for these differences and to trace patterns of stability and change (including factors associated with re-entry to the system) over the follow-up period.

2. A *survey* of a sub-sample of 149 of these children. All of these children had been maltreated, were aged 0–12 at admission and while some (81) had remained looked after to the end of the *census* follow-up, others (68) had returned home at some stage. The children were then followed up (retrospectively) for a period of four years, on average, after this key decision (to return or stay) had been made. The survey comprised three elements:

   ○ An audit of children's case files to identify how this 'effective' decision was made, what factors were taken into account in reaching it and how this decision was supported over a period of six months. This was completed for all children.

   ○ A questionnaire survey of social workers to assess the subsequent progress of these children from a social work perspective. This was completed for 135 children.

   ○ A supplementary survey of each child's current school teacher to provide a view on children's progress and outcomes from an education perspective. This was completed for 90 children.

3. Case studies (n=12) comprised interviews with nine birth parents and 11 children. The purpose of these interviews was to understand more about the meanings and significance of family histories, placement and social work interventions for children's experiences and progress at follow-up.

The chapter concluded with a description of the 149 children in the *survey* sample whose experiences at home and in the looked after system will form the substantive focus of this book. Reference will be made to findings from the large *census study* only where they seem especially pertinent to our comparative findings on children in the *home* and *care* groups included in our survey and interview samples.

3

The Children's Admission to Care

In this chapter we describe the maltreatment and associated family problems that contributed to the decision to admit these children to care, comparing the histories of children who subsequently returned home (the *home* group) with those of children who remained in care (the *care* group). We also consider the support provided prior to admission and explore the views of parents and children on the admission to care.

Maltreatment which contributed to the admission

The vast majority (84%) of the children in our *survey sample* were reported to have experienced neglect and for a similar proportion (85%) social workers reported emotional abuse. Neglect and emotional abuse were the most common forms of maltreatment, followed by physical abuse and then sexual abuse, as shown in Table 3.1.

Table 3.1 Evidence of abuse and neglect prior to admission (n=149) – per cent (n)

	Strong evidence (substantiated)	Some evidence (suspected)	Any evidence
Neglect	71 (105)	13 (20)	84 (125)
Emotional abuse	62 (93)	23 (34)	85 (127)
Physical abuse	26 (38)	33 (50)	59 (88)
Sexual abuse	10 (15)	10 (15)	20 (30)

The relative frequency of the different categories of maltreatment for our sample of children admitted to care differs from that for children with a child protection plan, the majority of whom are supported in the community. As we saw in Chapter 1, neglect is the main category recorded for 45 per cent of children with a child protection plan, followed by emotional abuse (25%), physical abuse (15%) and sexual abuse (6%) (Department for Children, Schools and Families 2009c). Findings from a recent study of referrals for maltreatment in an American city suggest that agencies may not always recognize emotional abuse. It identified four sub-types of emotional abuse, which it categorized as spurning, terrorising, isolating and exploiting/corrupting. In an analysis of the case records of 303 children, it found that 50 per cent had experienced emotional abuse, yet this had been identified by agency staff in only 9 per cent of cases (Trickett *et al.* 2009). It is possible that in some cases evidence of emotional abuse emerges following entry to care, which may help to explain the higher proportion reported to have experienced this among our *survey sample*, compared to the proportion among children with a child protection plan.

The vast majority (89%) of the children were reported to have experienced two or more forms of maltreatment, as shown in Table 3.2. In contrast, government statistics indicate that multiple categories of abuse and neglect are recorded for only 9 per cent of children with a child protection plan.

Table 3.2 Number of types of maltreatment
(suspected or substantiated) (n=149)

Number	Per cent (n)
0	1 (2)
1	10 (15)
2	38 (56)
3	41 (61)
4	10 (15)

This difference seems to suggest that children known to have experienced multiple forms of maltreatment may be more likely to be admitted to care. However, it is difficult to know whether the difference between national data on maltreated children in the community and data on our *survey sample* reflects real differences in the children's experiences or simply the manner in which administrative data are recorded in local authorities. It is also possible that once the children had entered care more details had emerged of the maltreatment they had previously experienced.

Two of the children had not directly experienced any maltreatment, according to their social work files. One was considered at risk of abuse due to the physical abuse of siblings and the presence of a Schedule 1 offender in the home. The other was an unaccompanied asylum seeker, a destitute 11-year-old girl found wandering in the streets and therefore clearly at risk of harm. Among children thought to have experienced only one type of maltreatment, the most common type was neglect (seven children), followed by physical abuse (four children).

Although emotional abuse may occur alone, all types of maltreatment are likely to involve some level of emotional abuse (Howe 2005; National Collaborating Centre for Women's and Children's Health 2009). In particular, neglect is frequently accompanied by emotional abuse, and this was true for the children in our study (Stevenson 1996). The majority of children (87%) known, or suspected, to have experienced emotional abuse were also thought to have experienced neglect. Furthermore, among the children considered to have experienced emotional abuse, the majority (62%) were also thought to have experienced physical abuse, although this association did not quite reach significance.[1]

Box 3.1 Case Study: Jonathan

Jonathan was a seven-year-old boy who was living with his mother prior to admission. He had been physically and emotionally abused over a lengthy period and a child protection plan had failed to improve the care he received. He experienced physical abuse by his mother, and had witnessed extreme violence between his mother and her partner as well as injuries to his siblings. There was also strong evidence of neglect as he was given a poor diet, had serious tooth decay and rarely attended school.[2]

Within our sample we identified a number of sub-groups who had experienced different configurations of maltreatment types, as shown in Table 3.3.

---

1 Chi-square tests: emotional abuse by neglect significant at p=0.005; emotional abuse by physical abuse did not quite reach significance at p=0.061.

2 All names used in these case illustrations are fictitious and some details of cases have been adjusted or merged to protect anonymity.

Table 3.3 Evidence of abuse and neglect prior to admission (n=149)

	Per cent (n)
Emotional and physical abuse and neglect	34 (51)
Emotional abuse and neglect	25 (37)
Emotional and physical abuse	7 (11)
Emotional abuse, neglect and sexual abuse	5 (8)

One-third of the children had been subjected to physical and emotional abuse and neglect, a combination that has also been identified in previous research (Trickett *et al.* 2009). These may co-occur where a carer is both violent and neglectful or where one parental figure feels helpless and depressed while the other is prone to anger and aggression. Such unpredictable regimes, which are both emotionally unresponsive and randomly violent, may lead to very disturbed behaviour in children (Howe 2005).

Consistent with previous research, the girls in our sample were more likely to have experienced sexual abuse than were boys (Howe 2005). Seventeen per cent of the girls were reported to have experienced sexual abuse, compared to only 4 per cent of boys.[3] Previous studies have shown that where carers are emotionally detached or abuse alcohol or drugs there is an increased risk that children will be left prey to sexual abuse (Berliner and Elliott 1996). This was the case with Phoebe, who was sexually abused by an adult she had been left with.

Concerns about neglect were significantly more likely to have contributed to the admission decision for the children who remained in care (91% of cases) compared to those who returned home (70% of cases).[4] However, there was no difference between these two groups in the likelihood that 'some' or 'strong' evidence of emotional, physical or sexual abuse had contributed to the decision that the child be looked after. Nor were the children in our *care* group any more likely to have experienced a greater number of types of maltreatment than the *home* group.

---

3   Fisher's exact test significant at p=0.022.

4   Chi-square test significant at p=0.007.

Box 3.2 Case Study: Phoebe

Phoebe was an anxious, withdrawn child who was nearly seven years old at admission. She had been living with her mother, father and her mother's new partner, but the mother had frequent, lengthy and unexplained absences during which she would leave her children with friends and relatives, one of whom lived with a Schedule 1 offender. Her parents were both substance misusers and the child regularly witnessed domestic violence. She was reported to suffer from chronic physical neglect and poor supervision, as she was not consistently fed, was often inappropriately clothed and was sometimes left unsupervised, in charge of her younger sibling. She was also emotionally abused, as she was frightened by the domestic violence that she regularly witnessed and was drawn into parental arguments. She felt anxious and upset by her mother's lengthy, unexplained absences. Her poor school attendance was thought to be due to her anxiety and guilt about leaving her mother.

One study in the US has suggested that decisions about reunification may be related to the severity of the maltreatment experienced. It found that a sample of physically abused children who had experienced less severe abuse were more likely to return home than those who had experienced abuse that was more severe (Barth *et al.* 1987). Our study did not classify maltreatment in terms of its severity, but does distinguish between cases where there was strong evidence of abuse or neglect and those where abuse or neglect were suspected but not substantiated. We found that the group who remained in care included a much higher proportion of children for whom there was strong evidence of neglect compared to the group which returned home (85% within the *care* group compared to 66% within the *home* group).[5] However, this was not the case in relation to other forms of maltreatment.

Other problems which contributed to the admission

Some researchers have argued that an ecological framework is needed to understand the complex interaction of multiple risk and protective factors which may increase the risk of child maltreatment. Belsky, for example, has argued that child abuse and neglect are multiply determined by factors

---

5   Chi-square test significant at p=0.004.

operating at the level of the individual parent or carer (which may make someone more or less likely to be a perpetrator), within the family, the community and in the wider society in which the child and family live, including the beliefs and values that contribute to the perpetuation of child maltreatment (Belsky 1980). Furthermore, differences in the home environment of children may account for variations in developmental outcomes after maltreatment (Egeland, Sroufe and Erickson 1983; Howe 2005).

We therefore examined parental problems and other environmental factors in the child's life that might increase the risk of maltreatment. All of the children in our study had become looked after for reasons of abuse or neglect. However, decisions to separate children from their parents are often informed by a cluster of concerns about their safety and welfare within their families.

Parental problems

Parental drug or alcohol misuse, domestic violence, mental health problems and violent offending are all well-recognized risk factors for child maltreatment (Cleaver *et al.* 1999; National Collaborating Centre for Women's and Children's Health 2009). The maltreated children in this sample were vulnerable in a number of ways. Our *census study* found that children who became looked after for reasons of maltreatment were more likely to have come from families where there were problems of domestic violence and the misuse of alcohol or drugs than were those admitted for other reasons. Among those children in the *census sample* who entered care due to maltreatment, 58 per cent had lived in households where there was evidence of these problems. A significantly smaller but nevertheless substantial proportion of children who had entered care for other reasons (35%) had also experienced parental substance misuse or domestic violence.[6]

Table 3.4 shows that parental substance misuse (63%), domestic violence (64%), inadequate parenting (93%) and, to a lesser extent, parental mental health problems (48%) had contributed to the admission of a majority of the children.

---

6   Chi-square significant at p<0.001, n=2579.

Table 3.4 Contribution of parental problems to
relevant admission (n=149) – per cent (n)*

	No evidence	No contribution	Some contribution	Strong contribution
Parental illness or disability	33 (49)	44 (66)	15 (23)	7 (11)
Parental mental health problems	24 (36)	28 (42)	23 (34)	25 (37)
Parental substance misuse	17 (25)	20 (30)	17 (26)	46 (68)
Parent involved in offending	23 (34)	42 (63)	23 (34)	12 (18)
Domestic violence	19 (28)	17 (26)	28 (42)	36 (53)
Sexual offender in household	42 (63)	37 (55)	11 (17)	9 (14)
Inadequate parenting	1 (2)	5 (8)	12 (18)	81 (121)
Parent's request for care	75 (111)	11 (17)	14 (21)	0
Absent parenting	36 (53)	50 (74)	7 (11)	7 (11)

*Not all rows total 100 per cent due to rounding.

Our *census* study also found that maltreated children were less likely to go home if they had families where there was evidence of substance misuse or domestic violence, but these were relatively weak predictors of return.[7] Among the children in our *survey sample*, those children who remained in care were no more likely to come from families where there was evidence of substance misuse or domestic violence than those who returned home. The

7   Logistic regression predicting children in the *census sample* who did not go home. Maltreated children were less likely to go home if they had families where there was evidence of substance abuse or domestic violence (p=0.031), they were considered by their social worker to be disabled (p=0.042) or they accepted the need for care (p=0.003). However, the local authority and the social work team looking after them were stronger predictors of return.

only clear differences lay in relation to the presence of a sexual offender in the household, inadequate parenting and parents' request for care.

Twice as many children in the *care* group (27%) came from households where there had been a known sexual offender, compared to the *home* group (13%). In contrast, parents' request for care had been a factor contributing to the admission of nearly twice as many of the children who subsequently returned home (34%), compared to those who remained in care (19%). Inadequate parenting made a strong contribution to the admission decision for nearly all in the *care* group (93%) compared to 68 per cent of the *home* group.[8]

Substance misuse, domestic violence and offending by parents (or their partners) frequently co-occurred, as previous studies have also found (Cleaver *et al.* 2007). Virtually all (96%) of the parents involved in offending were also known to have problems of substance misuse, and 58 per cent of those abusing substances had a history of offending. Substance misuse was also significantly associated with domestic violence. In 88 per cent of families where at least one parent (or their partner) had substance misuse problems, there were also concerns about domestic violence. For one-quarter of the children (37), all three of these parental problems coexisted.[9] All of this group were reported to suffer from neglect and, in most cases, one or more other forms of maltreatment too.

Parental problems and type of maltreatment

We found a strong association between parental substance misuse and neglect. The majority (83%) of children who had experienced neglect had a substance-misusing parent. Among children who experienced both emotional and physical abuse as well as neglect, a similar proportion (86%) had a parent with substance-misuse problems.

Children born to substance-misusing mothers are at risk of harm even before they are born. Once they are born, alcohol- or drug-addicted parents frequently find it difficult to be emotionally responsive and meet their needs in a consistent, predictable manner. Where parenting is neglectful, emotionally unresponsive or hostile, a vicious circle may develop whereby children's behaviour may become more impulsive, demanding and disruptive, increasing stress on parents who are already unresponsive or hostile (Howe 2005). This

---

8   Chi-square tests: home or care group by sexual offender in household p=0.006, inadequate parenting p<0.001, parent request for care p=0.007.

9   Chi-square tests significant at p<0.001 for substance abuse by offending, for substance misuse by domestic violence and for domestic violence by offending; significant at p=0.017 for domestic violence by request for care; significant at p=0.017 for substance misuse by both domestic violence and offending.

contribution of substance misuse to maltreatment and to the development of serious emotional and behavioural problems in the children was evident among children in our sample, as shown in the following case illustrations.

Box 3.3 Case Studies: Teresa and David

Teresa was two years old and living with her birth mother and her partner prior to admission. There was strong evidence of substance misuse and some evidence of domestic violence in the home. Teresa was removed due to concerns over physical and emotional abuse, plus neglect. There were unexplained injuries on her body, insufficient food and clothing provided and she was left alone or with very young babysitters, on one occasion for 15 hours. She was withdrawn and had started self-harming, as she was observed biting herself and pulling her hair.

David was a ten-year-old living with his mother and stepfather, both of whom were drug misusers. He was emotionally abused and neglected, as he regularly witnessed domestic violence, his stepfather shouted and swore at him and threatened to kill him, and he and his sibling were left alone at night. His mother was unable to protect him and he had started setting fires.

Domestic violence was associated with emotional abuse, although it is possible that some children were deemed to experience emotional abuse precisely because they were exposed to domestic violence within their families. Most of the children (81%) thought to have experienced emotional abuse also had experience of domestic violence, but there was no association between domestic violence and other forms of maltreatment. As we have seen, most of the children lived with parents who had multiple problems which contributed to the maltreatment they experienced, as in the case of Jane.

Box 3.4 Case Study: Jane

Jane was ten years old and was living with her mother and aunt at the time of admission. There were concerns about drug dealing and prostitution in the home and violence between adult males. Jane and her siblings were reported to be suffering from chronic neglect, as there was poor hygiene in the home, there were no beds or bedding for the children, no cooking facilities, the children were seen in the streets late at night and their school attendance was poor. Physical abuse was also suspected and she was exposed to sexual activity.

Environmental factors

It has long been established that children in care often come from families experiencing material and social deprivation (Bebbington and Miles 1989). For example, the ALSPAC study of a cohort of 14,256 children found that, among children under the age of six, indicators of poverty significantly increased the likelihood that a child's name would be entered on the child protection register. However, the odds that children from families living in poverty would enter care were reduced once parental background factors were taken into account. Four key parental factors increased the risk of maltreatment: age (that is, early parenthood), low educational achievement, a history of mental health problems and a parental history of abuse. The researchers suggested that these parental factors were mediated through the socio-economic environment of these families. They also argued that the association between poverty and child maltreatment may be influenced by referral bias, as thresholds for referral may be lower for young and poor parents (Sidebotham and Heron 2006).

In our study, poverty made a strong contribution to the decision to admit the child to care in only 7 per cent of cases, but poor housing conditions did so in nearly one-quarter of cases (23%). In total, environmental factors including poverty, poor housing or homelessness and the unsafe nature of the home area made 'some' or a 'strong' contribution to the admission decision in just under one-third of cases (48).

Child-level factors

Child-related problems or the child's wish to be removed from home rarely made any contribution to the admission decision. However, the child's behaviour had made a strong contribution to the decision in one-sixth of cases, alongside concerns about maltreatment and parenting capacity.

Child behaviour problems were more likely to be a factor informing the admission decision in relation to older children. These were cited as making a strong contribution to the admission decision for 38 per cent of children age ten or over at admission, compared to 24 per cent of children aged five to nine years (and were not reported in relation to children under five).[10] It is well established that the experience of hostile, neglectful or emotionally unresponsive parenting can lead to the development of behavioural problems in children (see Howe 2005). It is also the case that witnessing domestic violence may increase the risk of behaviour problems in children and, as we have seen, domestic violence made a strong contribution to the decision to admit over one-third of the children in our sample. A national study of the mental health of over 10,000 children found that witnessing domestic violence significantly increased the odds that children would have a conduct disorder, even when other factors predictive of conduct disorder were taken into account (Meltzer *et al.* 2009).

In three cases, the children's own wish to be removed from home made a strong contribution to the decision to admit them to the looked after system. The following cases illustrate the circumstances in which they did so.

Box 3.5 Case Study: Monica

Monica was an 11-year-old who, with her siblings, had experienced severe physical neglect evidenced by their lack of food, urine-soaked bedding, lack of stimulation and general lack of care and supervision. Her home conditions were described as 'appalling' and the children witnessed domestic violence. There was some evidence of substance misuse and her parents were reported to be emotionally uninvolved with the children. They had left them with inappropriate carers and on at least one occasion Monica had been sexually assaulted by a member of her extended family. The children were reported to suffer developmental delay as a consequence of the emotional abuse and neglect they had experienced. The parents requested care and Monica was anxious to leave.

---

10   Fisher's exact test significant at p=0.018.

Box 3.6 Case Study: Brendan

Brendan, age 11, had a statement of special educational needs due to his disability and diagnosis of attention deficit hyperactivity disorder (ADHD). He also suffered from enuresis, displayed sexualized behaviour and there were concerns that he had been sexually abused. Both his mother and his school reported that he had very challenging behaviour and he had been excluded from more than one school. His mother had requested that he be accommodated on several occasions in the past. He was placed under an emergency protection order after an incident in which his mother made a prolonged physical assault on him, encouraged by her partner. Brendan had repeatedly run away from home.

Number and duration of difficulties

The interaction of multiple adversities may increase the risk of poor outcomes for children (Rutter 2000; Rutter *et al.* 1998). We therefore measured the total number of adversities experienced by the children and created a total adversity score ranging from one to 12. Each type of maltreatment experienced by the children and each type of parental problem causing concern at the time of the relevant admission was given a score of one.[11] This measure revealed that the children who remained in care were significantly more likely to have experienced nine or more adversities while those who returned home were more likely to have experienced less than five.[12]

Although a simple count can indicate the multiplicity of difficulties in a child's life, it cannot capture the severity of these difficulties or their duration. The case illustrations in this chapter have given some indication of the severity of the difficulties the children experienced while living in their families. However, as Manly has argued, low-severity maltreatment that is chronic may result in child outcomes similar to those associated with severe abuse. However, there is little agreement in the literature on abuse and neglect on how best to measure severity and little research has focused on this issue (Barnett, Manly and Cicchetti 1993; Manly 2005). In relation to physical abuse, some have argued that the chronic use of physical control

---

11   Adversities included in the score were: emotional abuse, physical abuse, neglect, sexual abuse; parental illness or disability/mental health problems/substance misuse, domestic violence, absent parenting, inadequate parenting, sexual offender in the household.

12   Mann–Whitney U exact test significant at p=0.028.

tactics and day-to-day negative parent interactions with children may have more impact than isolated incidents of severe abuse which may come to the attention of the authorities. In order to understand the effects of abuse on children, episodes of abuse must therefore be understood in the context of chronic difficulties in parent–child relationships and in the wider home environment (Gibbons *et al.* 1995).

There was evidence that the abuse or neglect of a number of the children in our sample had persisted for several years. In 83 per cent of cases (123) there had been evidence of serious problems for at least two years prior to the admission decision. In nearly a quarter of cases, the family had been known to children's services for at least three years and often much longer. In a number of these cases, social workers had initially provided support to older siblings and had known the index child since birth. Sometimes family support services had been provided on a number of occasions over a period of several years. Several families had moved between local authorities and had previously received support in another authority.

In 21 per cent of cases (31), the admission had occurred as the result of a sudden emergency. Half (16) of these children and their families had previously received family support services, but it was unclear how long the others had been known to children's services. In some cases, the admission was precipitated by an incident of physical abuse or, in one case, by a specific incident of domestic violence. A number of the other emergencies resulted from parents' substance misuse or mental health problems. For example, a serious deterioration in their mother's mental health prompted the admission of at least five children, and in one case two children were admitted to hospital after their mother gave them a potentially lethal dose of a drug and also overdosed on it herself. In at least one case, a child was removed on a police protection order after being left with an inappropriate carer, and in another the child was admitted after both parents were remanded to custody.

Provision of family support services

In 79 per cent of cases, evidence on the case files indicated that children and families had received support from children's services prior to admission, frequently in the context of a child protection plan. The provision of family support services or emergency accommodation was no more, or less, likely for children who experienced any specific forms of maltreatment.

For around two-thirds of the children there was clear evidence of the provision of comprehensive support services on their case files, but in the other cases it was unclear what family support services (if any) had been offered. In most cases, parents were provided with support in caring for their children, often including advice on parenting. This was often combined with work on domestic violence or substance misuse problems, as appropriate, and with help with financial or housing problems. Social workers referred many of the parents to specialist services dealing with substance misuse or domestic violence and sometimes assisted in negotiating alternative accommodation with housing providers. Support was provided directly by social workers and also through family centres, family support teams, day care and after-school provision. Case files often contained evidence of multi-agency working involving health/mental health, education, substance misuse and housing support services, although in a small number of cases the file indicated that anticipated support by other agencies, negotiated as part of a child protection plan, had not been provided.

As our study is concerned with children who became looked after, clearly the support provided to these children and families had not prevented the children's eventual admission. There was some evidence on the case files as to why this was so. In nearly one in ten cases, parents' unwillingness to engage with professionals and with the services offered contributed to the admission. In a number of other cases, attempts to help parents address their drug and alcohol problems had been unsuccessful and the children subsequently entered care as a result. In some cases, there was, at most, only limited, or short-lived, change in parenting following the provision of services and a decision was taken that the child's needs would be best met through admission to care.

In some cases, problems had persisted for long periods of time without decisive action by children's services or the courts. There had been repeated referrals for serious neglect by schools, neighbours and others, resulting in the provision of family support, but social workers had not removed the children from home, or courts had not agreed to their requests to do so.

Box 3.7 Case Study: Rachel

For over six years there had been repeated referrals to children's services regarding the neglect of Rachel and her siblings before a care order was granted when she was ten years old, but the children were allowed to remain with their mother at this point. Two months later a medical examination revealed that she had experienced prolific and prolonged sexual and emotional abuse as well as neglect, at which point she was removed from home.

Box 3.8 Case Studies: Paul and George

Nine-year-old Paul had experienced chronic neglect as a result of his mother's drug and alcohol dependency. There had been a number of referrals from the school, neighbours and anonymous sources and Paul had also called the police at times when his mother had returned home drunk and aggressive.

There had been repeated referrals about the neglect of seven-year-old George and his brother, who were repeatedly left alone or with inappropriate carers. Schools and psychiatric services had expressed concerns that they were experiencing emotional abuse and witnessing domestic violence. They were eventually accommodated after it was found that they had been living with two 17-year-old males for five days and that their mother did not know their whereabouts and had not reported them missing.

In some cases, there had been insufficiently strong evidence to remove the children from home or courts had been reluctant to grant care orders, as the following examples illustrate.

Box 3.9 Case Studies: Jack and Harry

Jack was thought to have experienced neglect throughout his life and the local authority had previously attempted to remove him and his siblings from home. An interim care order was only granted after the children's guardian supported their removal.

The maternal grandparents of Harry and his sibling alleged that their mother had hit them with a belt on several occasions. The children confirmed these allegations to the police but later withdrew them because, it was reported, they were fearful of their mother. They were subsequently accommodated when their mother was admitted to hospital following an overdose.

Even in cases of serious and persistent maltreatment such as these, social workers had continued with attempts to support the children in their families.

This is consistent with other research, which has found that professionals may leave children 'bumping along the bottom' in chronically neglectful, emotionally abusive situations, as professionals become acclimatized to low standards of care within a family. In these situations, the need for decisive action to safeguard the child may not be recognized until an incident occurs that prompts a reassessment (Ayre 1998; Stevenson 1996). Negative assessments of the quality of the care system may also reinforce social workers' reluctance to remove children from situations of abuse or neglect (Arad-Davidzon and Benbenishty 2008). Such decisions may also be influenced by thresholds for admission to care, which may vary between authorities (Dickens *et al.* 2007).

Parents' views of family support services

Among the nine parents interviewed, most indicated that they had initially received support from children's services, as attempts were made to avoid taking their children into care. In some cases, parents of children with behavioural difficulties had requested this support. Two parents who blamed the admission on their children's extremely difficult behaviour complained that although family support had been provided, it had not been adequate or had been withdrawn too quickly. It is difficult to know whether the support was indeed too limited or had simply been perceived as such by parents. Certainly, the children in these two families had considerable behavioural difficulties which their parents struggled to cope with. These children had experienced multiple forms of maltreatment and had grown up in households marked by parental mental health problems, domestic violence or substance misuse.

Nadine's father, Ian, felt unable to manage her very challenging behaviour without physical reprimand and threats and had approached children's services for help, as he felt unable to cope. Nadine had experienced head injuries and bruising. Her stepmother had severe mental health problems. It was also suspected that Nadine may have been sexually abused as she had been left in the care of a known sex offender. Family support was provided on two occasions but, according to Ian, he had been told he was coping well enough on his own. Her admission to care was not precipitated by a specific incident, but occurred following the decision (supported by a psychologist's report) that neither of her parents could meet her needs and that she needed therapeutic help.

Stephen's mother also found it hard to cope with his extremely difficult behaviour. Stephen, who was 12 years old at admission, had a learning disability and was reported to have experienced emotional abuse and neglect due to his parents' alcohol problems, drug use, domestic violence and frequent separations. He had been poorly supervised, left with inappropriate carers and attended school only infrequently. His mother felt unable to cope with his very dangerous risk-taking behaviour on the streets and requested help from children's services, who provided parenting support and undertook direct work with Stephen to address his behaviour. However, this support was provided for only three months and the scale of the problems faced by Stephen and his mother appeared too great to be addressed through community-based support. He was accommodated after his mother attempted to forcibly restrain him in his room, in an attempt to protect him from the homeless men he had been associating with on the street. She explained:

> I made sure I wasn't hurting him, 'cause I thought I'm going to prove a point to these people now. I remember ringing back the social services [to tell them how she had restrained him]. She went 'That's abusing your child'. I says, 'I know it is. In your eyes it is. I'm not abusing him. I'm not hurting him. I'm protecting him, so he doesn't get out.'

Joe and his mother, a heavy drug user, had received family support for over two years, as he and his siblings were not fed regularly, missed school frequently and lived in poor home conditions. Their eventual admission to care arose partly as a result of their mother's relationship with a violent partner. Although their birth father had not felt able to care for them at the time, they were subsequently discharged to his care. Joe's father complained that the children should have been removed sooner:

> The children were being completely neglected. There were reports coming back from school that they were going late, Joe was smelling of urine. They weren't being fed properly. They were being left alone all the time. His mum is with somebody who ended up being a big drug dealer...and drugs were more important than the kids... It [admission to care] wasn't done soon enough. This was going on for ages, and, you know, they gave her one too many chances.

Parental views of child's admission to care

Few of the parents interviewed felt that the admission had been justified. For example, the parents of Helen, Becky and Jonathan were critical of the decision to remove their children. Helen's family had been known to children's services for several years prior to her removal, as there had been a number of referrals regarding her mother's physical chastisement of her children and her failure to protect them from her violent partners. Helen's mother had a long history of relationships with abusive partners and had herself experienced both sexual abuse and domestic violence as a child. Both she and her partner were heroin users at the time of admission. Helen was eventually admitted to care after her mother called the police during a violent assault by her partner:

> It happened because he was smacking my youngest. She was only six at the time, bless her... I tried to do something about it and he tried to drown me in the bath...and he kept smacking her, and we could hear her [screaming] and we didn't know whether he were smacking her with a belt... And if she shrugged her shoulders, he used to hit her for shrugging her shoulders and make her stand with her hands on the wall, over the radiator and just... I don't know what he were doing with her at the time.

Children's services had clearly been concerned about Helen's mother's ability to protect her children for quite some time, but she herself felt that she had been unfairly treated and had herself been punished as a result of this specific incident.

> I thought they dealt with domestic violence and things like that, in a better way than what they've dealt with this, because at the end of the day, he went to prison for 13 months and he didn't do 13 months, but yet, me and my kids have suffered five years down the line.

Helen clearly remembered the events of the night in question. When she and her sister were taken to foster carers, she did not fully understand why she was being taken into care and, looking back, felt that social workers should have explained things to her better. Her perception was that her social worker had lied to her:

> At the time, we was thinking, were it us? Have we been naughty? But then she explained to us, 'Oh you're going to live with a lovely lady for about two or three days and then go back to your mum'... and it had been about four or five months when I said 'I thought we were only coming for like two or three days'...and that's when she started the lies and I asked why she lied to us... She'd tell us not to lie but then she'd lie.

Becky's father similarly felt that the removal of his children, after he had physically assaulted his partner, had been unjustified. In his view, the police had been 'after him' because he had been dealing in drugs: 'What do I think about it? I think it was totally wrong. I think it was a conspiracy between the police and the social services.'

Children's services had found strong evidence of physical and emotional abuse and neglect and had provided support services for over a year, including after-school clubs, holiday clubs and day fostering for the children. It was also clear from Becky's own account that the assault which had precipitated her admission had not been an isolated incident of domestic violence, and that she found the violence in the household very distressing.

Jonathan's mother also felt that it had been unfair of children's services to remove her children, arguing that this had been done solely as a result of an apparently isolated incident of domestic violence that they had witnessed. After this incident, a social work assessment concluded that she was on the verge of breakdown and she was asked to agree to her children being accommodated for a period of time. She felt she had no real choice in the matter:

> I said no, but when I sought legal advice, I was told that, even if I didn't agree to it, they could do it in any case, so it was better to agree with them. So I agreed with them, and they were in care for six months.

At the time of interview, four years after the children were returned home, Jonathan's mother still felt that the decision to remove her children had been wholly unjustified and that her children had suffered further through their separation:

> [The social worker] knows that there was no need to remove me kids ... We're not the perfect family. We don't have the perfectly behaved children, but they're not beaten, and they're well looked after... Yes, they witnessed something they shouldn't have witnessed, but the kids were never at risk. That will stay with [him] for the rest of his life that he's been in care. It will stay, and of course he's gonna be angry. I mean, I still get quite emotional now when I talk about it. I can make sense of that. He's 12.

However, it was clear from Jonathan's case file that this had not been an isolated incident, as he and his younger siblings had witnessed domestic violence over a lengthy period of time and had themselves experienced physical violence and neglect. Jonathan had also alleged sexual abuse by a family friend.

In contrast, Laura's mother accepted that the admission had been necessary at the time. Laura was eight years old when admitted to care due to a combination of parental substance misuse, domestic violence, physical chastisement and neglect. She explained: 'I was broken down. I'll be honest with you, I was taking drugs. My partner was taking drugs, but I was in denial. I thought I could cope, I was lying to everybody, but I knew what needed to be done.'

There had been a series of interventions with the family during the two years prior to admission and the children had been on the child protection register for the final six months of this period. Laura's mother understood the effects of her behaviour and accepted that she needed to change in order to care properly for her children. The family had received help from the family support team, but when agreements were not adhered to, the children were admitted to care.

> We had case conferences and everything was [set out]. 'This is what is going to happen. This is what needs to be achieved'...and if I didn't it fell back on myself because I wasn't doing, obviously doing what they asked of me.

Laura subsequently returned home.

Children's views about entering care

Some of the children we interviewed made it clear that they had been relieved to be removed from home. Their accounts give some insight into children's experience of living with abuse, neglect, domestic violence and substance misuse. For example, Becky explained: 'My stepmum and my dad always used to fight in front of me, and I couldn't take it, me or my brothers couldn't take it.' She did not remember feeling anything when she first entered care because she did not understand what was going on. However, looking back, she felt that being in care had been better than living at home with her father and stepmother: 'There was no arguing, no fighting. There was no violence and I felt safer.'

Joe also spoke positively about relief at entering his care placement:

> I didn't really need to worry about anything. I thought everything was fine and just tried to get on with everyone straightaway...it was nice to come here instead of my old home 'cause of the space and everything...it was nice to get away from my mum and my old school that I used to go to as well.

He had felt empowered when his social worker consulted him about whether he wished to continue seeing his mother: 'Eventually, after a while, it was my decision if I wanted to see her or not, and I did for a bit, but then eventually I said, "No", 'cause she didn't treat me properly when I used to live with her.'

Gareth had been similarly reluctant to remain with his mother: 'My mum was getting nicked every day, pissed every day. I wanted to go to school, but when I was with my mum, I didn't want to. If she hit us, I don't do anything at all. With my mum, I would get hit...I hate living there.' His older sister explained:

> My mum's an alcoholic, and she always hit us. They'd take it in turns, who would be the punch bag first and, unfortunately, I always got it, but 'cause I ran away when I was 15, the rest of the kids started getting it then...and probably that's the reason why he went into care...you'd be a punch bag one day, and would be hit with the army belt, 'cause my granddad gave my mum a load of belts, or you'd be pushed down the stairs, and hit with walking sticks. You name it, we all got it.

However, although he did not wish to remain with his mother, Gareth was nevertheless apprehensive about moving to live with an unknown family. Unfortunately, his initial experience of placement was traumatic:

> I was all up for moving out and everything. I'd seen [the foster carers]. I said yeah at first. When they came and packed me stuff and they brought me up here, [the social worker] and me mum got out the car, knocked on the door, 'cause I waited in the car. Changed my mind, locked the door...[the foster carer] got me in the house. I didn't wanna go in, so I was kicking and screaming. [He] pinned me down on the couch and sat on me back, I couldn't move or nothing and I couldn't move 'cause he was that fat. So I hated care.

Gareth was subsequently placed with his older sister.

Helen, who did not accept the need to be in care and was anxious to return to her mother, also described her unhappy experience of foster care:

> She did smell horrible. Her kitchen is just mucky and horrible, and if you didn't eat, like all your tea, you weren't allowed anything to eat for the rest of the night, and you'd be going to bed with nothing, even if you were hungry.

Andrew, however, had a far more positive experience of foster care and felt that it was preferable to his home life. He had previously lived with his mother, a heavy drug user, in a squat frequented by other drug users. He had experienced neglect, did not have a bed to sleep in, did not attend school for long periods and had witnessed incidents of domestic violence. He explained his preference for being in foster care: 'When you're in care and you're getting looked after good and you're getting fed good and you're getting a good bed.'

Children's views of being in care were, not surprisingly, related to whether they accepted the need to be in care and to their experience of foster care. Children who, like Helen, do not accept the need to be in care and are upset by separation may be more likely to feel unhappy about admission to care (Sinclair *et al.* 2005). Unfortunately, both Helen and Gareth's accounts suggest that their anxiety about entry to care was compounded by the experience of poor-quality foster care. However, four of the five children who discussed their entry to care had been relieved to be removed from home and three of them spoke very positively about their experience of care.

It was clear from these accounts that the children had experienced multiple and severe difficulties in their families. Nevertheless, children's services had first attempted to support these children at home and, among the small number of families we interviewed, the admission had been precipitated by a particular event which had proved to be a turning point. Most, though not all, of the parents interviewed felt that they had received insufficient help and that the removal had been unjustified. However, all but one of the children spoke of their relief at being removed from these environments. Although three of the children interviewed spoke very positively about their foster placements, it is concerning that two of them had a negative experience of foster care.

Conclusion

To sum up, the majority of the children had experienced multiple forms of maltreatment, the most common forms being emotional abuse and/or neglect. They had also experienced many other difficulties at home, as many had lived in households where they experienced domestic violence or where parents misused drugs or alcohol or had mental health problems.

Children who had experienced a higher number of adversities in their families (including multiple forms of maltreatment and types of parental problems) were less likely to return home. Despite the seriousness of their difficulties, social workers had tried hard to support them in their families, in many cases for over two years, before admitting them to care. However, children who experienced chronic emotional abuse and neglect, often in a context of parental substance misuse and domestic violence, were sometimes left 'bumping along the bottom' until a particular incident occurred which precipitated the admission (Stevenson 1996). Given the seriousness of the difficulties of many of these children, it is surprising that some were supported at home for so long. This raises questions for children's services and the courts about thresholds for entry to care. Such thresholds are influenced not only by local policy and practice but also by the level of resources available and by attitudes towards the care system.

Summary

The vast majority (84%) of the children in our *survey sample* were reported to have experienced neglect, and for a similar proportion (85%) there was evidence of emotional abuse. Evidence of physical abuse was less common (59% of children) and evidence of sexual abuse even less so (20%). Concerns about neglect were significantly more likely to have contributed to the admission decision for the children who subsequently remained in care and were not reunified with parents.

Most (92%) of the children had experienced two or more forms of maltreatment. The majority of children (87%) known, or suspected, to have experienced emotional abuse were also thought to have experienced neglect.

The majority of the children had lived in households where there was evidence of substance misuse or domestic violence. Many children had experienced both, as 88 per cent of those whose parents misused substances also witnessed domestic violence. Parental mental health problems also contributed to the decision to admit the child in 40 per cent (54) of cases.

Child-related problems or the child's wish to be removed from home rarely made any contribution to the admission decision. However, the child's behaviour had made a strong contribution to the decision in one-sixth of cases, alongside concerns about maltreatment and parenting capacity.

Although a majority of families had received some preventive services prior to entry to care, in a number of cases the abuse or neglect of children had persisted for many years without decisive action by children's services or the courts. In some cases, there had been repeated referrals for serious neglect by schools, neighbours and others, but social workers had been reluctant to remove the children from home (or courts had not agreed to their requests to do so) and had persisted with attempts to support the children in their families. Given the seriousness of the difficulties of many of these children, this raises questions for children's services and the courts about thresholds for entry to the looked after system.

4

The Effective Decision: How Children and Parents Were Getting On

This chapter moves forward to the time of the 'effective decision' for children to remain looked after or return home. It examines how the children were faring at this time within the looked after system and describes the patterns of contact they had with their birth families. It also assesses the extent to which there were continuing social work concerns about the circumstances and parenting capacity of birth parents and the work that had been undertaken to ameliorate any problems. How these child and family factors may have influenced the decision to reunify the children or not will be described in Chapter 5.

When was the effective decision made?

We know from our *census study* that most children who returned home tended to do so quite quickly after admission and that maltreated children were amongst those who were less likely to have left the system within the study timeframe.[1] This is consistent with research findings and national statistics. For example, Sinclair and colleagues' (2007) study of the care system identified that those going home made up two-thirds of those who left the

---

1   Analysis of the *census sample* (using Cox's regression) allowed us to estimate the effect on likelihood of leaving the care system of various variables, including maltreatment. This showed that children's chances of leaving care at least once decreased cumulatively with: a) the length of time they had been continuously looked after (before the census date); b) the older they were; c) the presence of a need code of 'abuse or neglect'; d) a social worker judgement that the child was disabled.

system within one year of admission but only one in five of those who left after a year. We also know that maltreated children, especially those who have suffered neglect, tend to return home at a slower rate when compared to children looked after for other reasons (Bullock *et al.* 1998; Cleaver 2000; Courtney and Wong 1996; Davis *et al.* 1997; see also Fanshel and Shinn 1978; Glisson *et al.* 2000; Harris and Courtney 2003; Sinclair *et al.* 2007).

It was not always easy to discern from the social work files precisely when the key decision was made to return children to their families or to create an alternative pathway for them within the looked after system. It was also not uncommon for plans to be subject to change in light of events. We therefore took the effective decision to be the first care plan that specified a plan for children to be reunified with their families, provided this was followed through and reunification subsequently took place, or where long-term plans for substitute care were first mooted and the children did not return within the two years of the *census* follow-up period.

For our *survey sample* of 149 maltreated children, the period of time between their last admission to the looked after system and this effective decision varied considerably. Overall, this period ranged from a few days to three years. For 15 per cent, the decision was made within one month of admission, for half (49%) within six months and for the majority (78.5%) within one year. However, over one-fifth (21.5%) had remained looked after for one year or more before this decision was recorded on file. The mean length of time from entry to decision was 35 weeks (standard deviation 34.74).

How were the children getting on at this time?

Information recorded on case files was used to assess how the children were getting on at this time while they were all still looked after. We were interested to know how these factors were then weighed in decisions about whether to return maltreated children to their families or not. This will be considered further in Chapter 5.

Table 4.1 presents 14 items gathered from case file records. For the sample as a whole there was positive evidence that most children appeared to be relatively settled in the looked after system, that they were getting on reasonably well with their carers, broadly accepted the need to be with them and had a close tie to at least one adult, whether this was their carer, a family member or another key adult in their lives. The degree to which children appeared to have settled in these ways did not differ greatly according to the length of time they had been looked after on this occasion, although newer entrants were thought less likely to have accepted the need for care.[2] Just over one-third, however, appeared to be presenting quite serious behavioural challenges to their carers (36%) and/or suffering from relatively poor mental and emotional well-being (34%). For around one-half (52%) there was evidence that they wanted to go home and around one-third (35%) appeared to be upset by contact with their families.

Table 4.1 How children were faring at time of effective decision (n=149) – per cent (n)*

	No evidence	Positive	Negative
Child reasonably settled in looked after system	11 (16)	75 (112)	14 (21)
Child accepted need to be looked after	24 (36)	62 (93)	13 (20)
Child and current carers got on well	10 (15)	82 (122)	8 (12)
Child presented few behaviour problems	9 (13)	55 (82)	36 (54)
Child's overall mental/emotional well-being was good	13 (19)	54 (80)	34 (50)
Child had at least one close adult tie	13 (19)	83 (123)	5 (7)
Child was doing well at school	22 (33)	55 (82)	23 (34)
Child had not run away	40 (60)	52 (77)	8 (12)
Child had no difficulties with offending	47 (70)	50 (75)	3 (4)
Child had no difficulties with substance misuse	48 (71)	51 (76)	1 (2)
Child had a number of positive friendships	50 (75)	38 (56)	12 (18)
Child wanted to go home	32 (47)	52 (78)	16 (24)
Child was not upset by contact with key family members	44 (65)	22 (32)	35 (52)
Child did not miss contact with siblings	72 (107)	11 (17)	17 (25)

*Not all rows total 100 per cent due to rounding.

2   Kendall's Tau-b test: p=0.04, t -0.149, n=149.

There were very few reports of children engaging in risk behaviours (running away, offending, substance misuse). Those that did were significantly older, as might be expected.[3] Lack of evidence in these areas was quite high, perhaps reflecting a tendency for these issues only to be recorded if a problem existed. Age was also associated with the degree to which young people were reported to be settled within the looked after system at this stage, with older children being evidently less settled and presenting more problems to carers.[4] However, age had no obvious bearing on whether children wanted to go home ($p=0.72$), whether they had a close tie to an adult ($p=0.38$) or whether they were upset by family contact ($p=0.51$).

The characteristics of children also had some significance. Males were considered more likely than females to be displaying behavioural problems, to have poorer overall well-being and to be faring less well at school.[5] Children with learning disabilities were rather less likely to have accepted the need for care, more likely to have behavioural problems and, although not significant, to have poorer overall well-being.[6] Finally, there was also evidence that White children were faring less well in some respects than those from minority ethnic backgrounds. Compared to dual-heritage children, they were considered less likely to be settled in care and to be getting on well with their carers; they tended to have fewer close ties with adults and friends and to be doing less well at school. These differences were also evident when comparing White to Black and Asian children, although they did not reach significance in relation to adult ties and school progress.[7]

There were also variations in how children were faring in the looked after system according to the forms of maltreatment that had led to their admission. Where neglect had been an ingredient in the admission, there were few significant associations with our 14 measures of progress. However, there

---

3   Mann–Whitney U exact tests for age at effective decision: running away ($p=0.001$, $n=89$), offences ($p=0.05$, $n=79$), substance misuse ($p=0.02$, $n=78$). Older children were also doing less well at school ($p=0.04$, $n=116$).

4   Mann–Whitney U exact tests for age at time of effective decision: settled in looked after system ($p<0.001$, $n=133$), accepted need to be looked after ($p=0.055$, $n=113$), child and current carers got on well ($p=0.01$, $n=134$), behaviour problems ($p<0.01$, $n=136$), overall well-being ($p=0.02$, $n=130$).

5   Mann–Whitney U exact tests for sex: behaviour problems ($p=0.05$, $n=136$), overall well-being ($p=0.02$, $n=130$), school ($p=0.01$, $n=116$).

6   Mann–Whitney U exact tests for learning disability: accepting need for care ($p=0.04$, $n=102$), behaviour problems ($p=0.01$, $n=124$), overall well-being ($p=0.07$, $n=118$).

7   Kruskal–Wallis exact tests for ethnic origin: settled in care ($p=0.02$, $n=133$), getting on with carers ($p=0.01$, $n=134$), overall well-being ($p=0.08$, $n=130$), adult ties ($p=0.05$, $n=130$), close friends ($p=0.01$, $n=74$), school progress ($p=0.05$, $n=130$).

was some evidence that these children were less likely to have wanted to go home (29%) than were others (5%) where there had been no documented evidence of neglect.[8] They were also rather more likely than others to be reported as settled in the looked after system, although this did not reach the threshold for significance (p=0.1). As we have seen, this may reflect a tendency for social workers to have decided rather sooner in these cases that the prospects for a return home were not good and that these children therefore needed to be settled into longer-term substitute placements.

Just over two-fifths of children who had experienced emotional abuse were considered to have relatively poor mental well-being (43%) when compared to other children (15%) (p=0.02, n=130). Where children had allegedly been sexually abused, there was some apparent legacy in the interpersonal domain. There was some evidence that these children were less likely to have positive friendships and were more likely to have run away and to lack a close tie to at least one adult.[9] Physical abuse was associated with a tendency for challenging behaviours. These children were more likely to be presenting behavioural problems, to have relatively poor emotional well-being and to be faring less well at school.[10] However, these findings differed for physically abused males and females. When account was taken of gender, there was evidence of physically abused females experiencing better overall well-being than their male counterparts (p=0.04) and the relationship between physical abuse, behaviour (p=0.03) and school problems (p=0.03) was only significant for males.

Children's contact with birth families

The vast majority of children were in touch with relatives at the time of the effective decision. Almost all (89%) were in contact with their birth mothers, just over one-half (54%) with their birth fathers and three-quarters (75%) with other relatives, including grandparents, aunts, uncles, cousins and siblings. Only eight children were prohibited contact with a relative

---

8   Kruskal–Wallis exact test: p=0.02, n=102.

9   Fisher's exact tests for sexual abuse: number of positive friendships (p=0.012, n=74), close adult tie (p=0.05, n=130), running away (p=0.06, n=89). For example, 47 per cent tended to lack close friendships compared to 16 per cent of other children, and 13 per cent lacked a close adult tie compared to 3 per cent of others.

10 Fisher's exact tests for physical abuse: behavioural problems (p=0.01, n=136), mental and emotional well-being (p=0.01, n=130), not doing well at school (p=0.01, n=116). For example, 49 per cent were reported to have behavioural problems compared to 27 per cent of other children, 48 per cent had relatively poor well-being compared to 24 per cent of others and 38 per cent were not thought to be doing well at school compared to 16 per cent of other children.

at this time. These included contact with birth fathers, maternal uncles and partners of their birth mothers largely due to a continuing risk of physical or sexual violence.

Table 4.2 shows frequency of contact with these relatives for the sample as a whole. In the majority of cases where children had daily contact with 'other relatives' (n=33), they had been placed with them by children's services. In a few of these cases, a birth parent was also living with this relative or had moved back to live with them after the placement had been made. In the remaining cases, siblings were living together in foster or residential care. There were also two instances of birth mothers living with their child(ren) in residential assessment centres organized by children's services.[11]

Table 4.2 Face-to-face contact with birth relatives at time of effective decision (n=149) – per cent (n)

	Daily or live with	At least weekly	At least monthly	Less often	Never	No evidence /not applicable
Birth mother	3 (4)	58 (87)	19 (28)	9 (13)	6 (9)	5 (8)
Birth father	2 (3)	28 (41)	13 (19)	11 (17)	28 (42)	18 (27)
Other relatives	22 (33)	30 (45)	14 (21)	9 (13)	6 (9)	19 (28)

Contact with birth parents did not vary greatly across the sample. With respect to contact with birth mothers, however, where children had experienced a high number of pre-care adversities (p=0.02, t 0.167, n=121) and where there had been failed past attempts at reunification (p=0.05, n=120), there was some evidence that frequency of contact tended to be lower. As Table 4.2 shows, levels of contact with birth fathers was lower than for birth mothers and more than one-quarter of children (28%) had no contact with their fathers at all. There was also some evidence that contact with birth fathers tended to be less frequent for older children (p=0.01, t 0.171, n=122), presumably because fathers drifted from the scene over time or children were better placed to choose with whom they wanted contact. Contact with fathers also tended to be less frequent for dual-heritage children when

---

11   There were a further nine cases of children in daily contact with other relatives where no information was available to explain why this was the case.

compared to either White or Black and Asian children, although this was not the case for contact with mothers or other relatives (p=0.01, n=121).

What were the main social work concerns about birth parents at this stage?

Information was also gathered from case files around the time of the effective decision to identify the range of family problems about which social work concerns persisted. These data are presented in Table 4.3 and suggest that serious concerns persisted in relation to the safety of children, the parenting capacity of families and the willingness of birth parents to cooperate with agencies and, to a somewhat lesser extent, in relation to quite deep-seated parental problems, including substance misuse, domestic violence and offending.

Table 4.3 Birth parent problems at time of effective decision – per cent (n)*

	No evidence of concern	Some concerns	Serious concerns
Chronic ill health or disability	79 (116)	16 (23)	5 (8)
Mental health problems	52 (77)	30 (44)	18 (27)
Substance misuse	45 (67)	24 (36)	30 (45)
Criminal offences	66 (98)	20 (30)	14 (20)
Domestic violence	46 (68)	37 (54)	18 (26)
Safety of child (if returned)	16 (23)	31 (46)	53 (79)
Parent(s) capacity to care and nurture	12 (17)	27 (40)	62 (91)
Parent(s) approach to discipline	27 (40)	35 (51)	39 (57)
Parent(s) supervision of child	28 (41)	24 (36)	48 (71)
Presence of other adult(s) in family home	59 (87)	27 (40)	14 (21)
Parent(s) willingness to cooperate with social workers/other agencies	35 (52)	30 (44)	35 (52)
Impact on child of parental contact or home visits	60 (89)	28 (42)	12 (17)

*Not all rows total 100 per cent due to rounding.

Factor analysis suggested that these 12 items clustered together to form four components of birth parent difficulty. The first component, which we will call *parenting concerns*, loaded heavily on child safety (0.745), parental discipline (0.729), parental supervision (0.693) and capacity to care and nurture (0.601). These factors were highly correlated together and reliability analysis suggested that they were tapping, albeit inexactly, into a meaningful dimension of parenting (Cronbach's alpha 0.763). The second component, which we will call *family contact concerns*, loaded on to parental cooperation with agencies (0.755), impact on child of parental contact (0.734), presence of other adults at home (0.661) and parental offences (0.447). The third component, *parental problems*, loaded on to domestic violence (0.720), substance misuse (0.687), parental offences (0.547) and capacity to care and nurture (0.429). The final component loaded only on to *parental mental health* (0.844).[12]

There was no association between the seriousness of social work concerns at this stage and the age of children (at admission or at this point), gender, ethnic origin, disability or the length of time children had been looked after on this occasion.

It was not surprising to find that the presenting problems that had originally led to the admission of these children were closely linked to the continuation of these and other associated concerns. For example, where parental mental health had contributed to the admission, there was a strong correlation with concerns about parental mental health at this stage and, to a lesser extent, with concerns about family contact and parenting.[13] To give another example, where parent problems contributed to admission (substance misuse, offences, domestic violence), this was closely correlated with concerns about the same parental problems at this stage and with concerns about parenting and family contact.[14] The story was also the same where environmental

---

12 Reliability analysis: Cronbach's alpha for 'family contact concerns' (0.666) and for 'parental problems' (0.602). Parenting concerns accounted for 20 per cent of the variance in the component variables, family contact concerns for 16.5 per cent, parenting problems for 15 per cent and parental mental health for 10.5 per cent. With the exception of mental health, for which the original variable was used, new ordinal variables (0–8 scales) were derived for concerns about parenting, family contact and parental problems for use in the analysis that follows.

13 Parental mental health at admission and social work concerns at effective decision (Kendall's Tau-b tests): parental mental health ($p < 0.001$, t 0.712, n=113); family contact (p=0.02, t 0.180, n=113); and parenting (p=0.07, t 0.141, n=113).

14 Parental problems at admission and social work concerns at effective decision (Kendall's Tau-b tests): parental problems ($p < 0.001$, t 0.574, n=100); parenting ($p < 0.01$, t 0.242, n=100); and family contact ($p < 0.001$, t 0.292, n=100).

factors (poor housing, poverty or an unsafe neighbourhood) had contributed to the admission of children.[15] These findings are perhaps reflective of the complex and multilayered difficulties that often surround families where the maltreatment of children is concerned and of the challenges involved in attempts to reduce these risks for children.

Social work concerns also varied according to the type of maltreatment children had experienced in the past. Where children had experienced physical abuse, there were no significant associations with parental difficulties at this stage. Sexual abuse, however, was associated with concerns about parenting ($p<0.01$, $n=148$) and, although not significant, with family contact ($p=0.09$, $n=148$). This probably reflects worries about child safety, the ability of parents to care for and protect their children and the potential risks of harm to children in contact situations. Where children had experienced emotional abuse, there were again no significant associations. However, there was some evidence of continuing concerns about parenting ($p=0.17$), family contact ($p=0.18$) and parental problems ($p=0.1$). In contrast, the parents of neglected children were the subject of multiple concerns, including parenting, family contact and ongoing parental problems.[16] This may help to explain, as we have seen, why these children were rather more reluctant to return home than were others.

What was being done to address these problems?

In a majority of files (74%), there was evidence of work having been undertaken in an attempt to ameliorate these problems in the period leading up to the effective decision. This evidence was missing from the file in over one-quarter of cases (26%). It would be wrong, however, to assume that no work was being done in these cases, as social work case files are known to be variable in relation to the recordings that are made (Wade, Mitchell and Baylis 2005). However, it is reasonable to assume that less priority was being given to these cases at this stage, even if a higher degree of priority might have been given in the past.

---

15 Kendall's Tau-b tests for environmental factors at admission and parenting concerns ($p=0.01$, t 0.223, $n=85$), family contact concerns ($p<0.01$, t 0.267, $n=85$), parent problems ($p=0.01$, t 0.224, $n=85$). None of the presenting problems that led to admission, with the exception of parental health, was associated with continuing concerns about parental mental health.

16 Neglect and concerns about parenting (Mann–Whitney U exact test: $p<0.001$, $n=148$); family contact ($p<0.01$, $n=148$) and parent problems ($p<0.001$, $n=148$). There were no associations between types of maltreatment and ongoing concerns about parental mental health.

While efforts to resolve parental difficulties were not associated with the particular forms of maltreatment experienced by children, they were predictably associated with length of time looked after. Where a speedier decision had been made relatively soon after admission, children and families were less likely to have received interventions to lessen their difficulties.[17]

Our case file auditors were asked to provide a brief description of the interventions that had been undertaken. Where there was 'no evidence' on file, the most common reason (from a social work perspective) appeared to be a failure of parents to engage with services that had been offered, frequently combined with a perceived failure on their part to recognize the impact of their behaviour on their children.

Box 4.1 Case Study

The limited evidence suggests that the parents were offered support services, but failed to engage with them. They failed to have any insight into their drug habits and seemed to be unable to recognize the impact of their lifestyle on any of their children. (This girl remained in the care of her grandparents.)

In some instances, while services may have been provided in the past, parental problems were now perceived to be intractable and not amenable to change or small changes that had been gained were considered to be insufficient for the child's needs. In other scenarios, the maltreatment of children prior to admission had been so severe that a return home had never been perceived as a viable option. In these cases, any direct work undertaken with parents had ceased some time previously.

---

17   Mann–Whitney U exact test (p=0.03, n=147). While there was evidence of interventions for 57 per cent of those looked after for less than one month, this rose to 91 per cent of those looked after for 12 months or more.

Box 4.2 Case Study

At this point attempts were not being made. Numerous attempts had been made before this child was looked after and in the early stages of care when twin-track planning was still underway.

Core assessment on the mother concluded that she did not have the ability to look after her children or protect them from future harm and did not have the ability to change the problems which caused their removal.

The mother had attended a support group on parenting teenagers, but her attendance had been very erratic. Prior to placement, some very minor changes had been made, like providing lunch for the child and helping with some of the child's laundry, but these changes were not significant enough and were overshadowed by the parents continuing to allow the child contact with their ex-lodger, who had an allegation of sexual abuse made about him in the past.

Plans for the child to return home were never a viable option. The child had experienced sexual abuse and chronic neglect over a number of years.

Although these particular children remained within the looked after system, this was not always the case where there was 'no evidence' of work being done to prepare children and families for reunion. In one-third of these cases, the children did eventually return, amounting to one-fifth (19%) of all those who were reunified. This is broadly consistent with Farmer and colleagues' (2008) study on reunification where one-quarter of the children (23%) were found to have been returned to their families without evidence of work having been done on the problems that had led to the original admission. They also found that, in these circumstances, these problems tended to persist after return.

Where there was evidence that work was being undertaken with parents, the best examples were of multilayered interventions that involved different agencies working together in an effort to address the multiple difficulties that frequently beset families. Although evidence of these kinds of intervention was only available in a small minority of cases, they tended to include written plans or agreements with parents that clearly specified what needed to change, the timescales for achieving these changes and a continuing dialogue with parents about their feelings and the progress that was being made. As the brief illustrations suggest, these interventions were not always successful. Progress was often slow, marginal or even non-existent. Although parents often appeared willing to sign up to agreed packages of support, bolstered by the prospect of having their children returned, maintaining their engagement was very difficult. The lives of parents were frequently chaotic. Attendance and cooperation could therefore be sporadic and often declined over time. In these circumstances, social workers faced difficult decisions about when and how to assess the potential for further change, even though some were assisted by psychiatric assessments, and when a decision for an alternative long-term care plan should be made.

Box 4.3 Case Studies

A written agreement had been negotiated with parents setting out expectations of change prior to return. They both worked with a local drugs agency to reduce and eventually eliminate illegal drug use, while maintaining a methadone prescription. They were required to cease offending that placed them at risk of custody and to regularize their position with the housing authority to allow a move to better accommodation. Parents did not make progress in any of these areas. (Child remained in care.)

Efforts were made to assist the mother to give up alcohol and both parents attended parenting classes. Anger management sessions were undertaken by father. Assessments were made by adult and child psychiatrists to ascertain level of parental functioning and prognosis for change. Foster carers worked hard to reduce symptoms of emotional damage and neglect in the child and he also received 32 hours' support per week at school. (Child remained in care.)

There were clear and agreed expectations for the mother to improve conditions at home. The health service provided support for depression and medication. The mother attended an alcohol support unit and cooperated with all plans. Social worker has concerns that the mother still wants to control rather than stop drinking. (Child went home.)

Overall, there was evidence of a range of services being provided in different cases. Most commonly these interventions included referral to substance misuse agencies to reduce (or eliminate) drug and alcohol dependency and provision of services to promote parenting. Each was evident in around one-quarter of the cases. Parenting classes provided a focus on strengthening the capacity of parents to provide better-quality care, to help them establish and maintain routines and boundaries and to address issues concerning supervision, discipline and the protection of children. Where parents attended regularly, there was some evidence that these services helped to provide conditions that facilitated children's return. Substance misuse services, however, appeared to bring about a positive change less often, especially where parents had a long history of drug and/or alcohol dependency.

Box 4.4 Case Studies

Her parents were referred to a drug and alcohol team specializing in rehabilitation. They had a long history of drug and alcohol abuse and had failed in the past at rehabilitation. This attempt was also unsuccessful.

The mother was offered support at a hostel that specialized in drug and alcohol dependency, but despite this service she continued to abuse drugs and alcohol. (These children stayed in care.)

In some instances, parents refused to engage at all despite repeated offers. In others, they attended for a time but then gradually disengaged from the service and resumed life much as before. It is therefore likely that more intensive and structured interventions are required than are currently common in this area to provide evidence of sustained change before returning children home (see also Farmer *et al.* 2008).

Around one in six parents had accessed housing services, either as part of a strategy to escape an abusive partner or more generally to improve the quality of home conditions necessary for a child to return home. One in seven parents had accessed mental health services as part of a therapeutic programme in relation to their own health or as part of an assessment to gauge their capacity to parent successfully, and small numbers made use of anger management courses, counselling, child care and probation services.

However, there was also evidence in some cases that little in the way of services to parents was being provided at this time. In some instances, there was nothing recorded on case files beyond referrals to other mainstream service providers. In other cases, while planning meetings had been held and assessments undertaken, there was very little evidence of any follow-through into service provision. Some files also revealed a tendency for services to parents to decline once the child entered the looked after system. This appeared more likely in circumstances where the prognosis for the child's return was not perceived to be good.

Alongside services to parents, work was also being undertaken with children at this time. Efforts were being made to help children's reintegration into school, to improve their attendance or to support their efforts to recover lost ground. Foster carers, sometimes supported by specialist agencies, were helping children to improve their hygiene and self-care skills, to strengthen their self-esteem and confidence and to help repair the emotional damage caused by their experiences of abuse and neglect. In this work, some were supported by Child and Adolescent Mental Health Services (CAMHS) and some children were accessing play therapy and other initiatives to help their recovery from traumas suffered in the past.

Had parental problems improved at this stage?

Taking everything into account, therefore, to what extent had parental problems improved by the time of the effective decision? Case file auditors were asked to assess whether, on the basis of recordings by social workers, the presenting problems that had led to each child's relevant admission had improved, stayed the same or deteriorated by this stage. Table 4.4 shows that signs of improvement existed in just one-third of cases, that around one-half had remained the same and that in one in seven cases there appeared to have been a deterioration.

Table 4.4 Had the problems that led to the child's admission to care improved or deteriorated by time of effective decision? (n=149)*

	Per cent (n)
Problems much improved	9 (14)
Problems somewhat improved	24 (36)
Problems about the same	51 (76)
Problems somewhat worse	13 (20)
Problems much worse	2 (3)

*The column does not total 100% due to rounding.

A deterioration of parental problems was not associated with most forms of maltreatment. There was no significant association with past sexual abuse (p=0.33), physical abuse (p=0.26) or emotional abuse (p=0.85). However, lack of improvement or even deterioration was much more likely to have occurred in cases of neglect.[18]

It was nonetheless encouraging to find that a return home was much more strongly associated with an improvement in these problems.[19] Two-thirds of the 68 children who returned went home to 'somewhat' or 'much' improved circumstances (65%), one-third to unchanged circumstances (34%) and just 2 per cent to circumstances that were thought to have deteriorated. This contrasts with those who remained in the system. For just over one-quarter (27%) parent problems were assessed as having deteriorated, for two-thirds (65%) they had remained the same and in only 7 per cent of cases was there evidence that parental difficulties had improved.

In Chapter 5 we will consider in some detail how the effective decision was made, the range of factors that influenced this decision and identify those that were predictive of whether children would return home or remain within the system. Clearly, whether or not home circumstances had changed for the better is one ingredient in this mix. Chapter 6 will draw on qualitative material from our case studies to describe in greater depth the complex circumstances of families at this time and the kinds of changes that had (or had not) taken place to allow children to return home.

Summary

This chapter considered how children were faring in the looked after system at the time the effective decision was made, looked at concerns that existed about children's birth parents at this time and identified what was being done to ameliorate these problems.

For most who returned home (57%), this decision was taken within six months of admission. At this time most children appeared to be relatively settled in the looked after system (75%), to have accepted the need for care (62%) and to be getting on reasonably well with their carers (62%). However, around one-half (52%) wanted to go home.

Sizeable minorities were presenting behavioural challenges (36%) or were suffering from relatively poor mental and emotional well-being (34%). Children who were White, male, older or had learning disabilities tended to be less settled and posed more problems to carers.

---

18   Mann–Whitney U exact test (p<0.001, n=149).

19   Mann–Whitney U exact test (p<0.001, n=149).

Children who had been neglected were less likely to want to return (and were less likely to do so) and appeared rather more settled. Those who had suffered emotional abuse tended to have poorer mental well-being. Those who had been sexually abused tended to lack close friendships and adult ties and those who had been physically abused (especially males) posed more challenging behaviours at home and school.

The vast majority of children were in touch with birth family members at this time. Frequency of contact with birth parents was lower where children had experienced a high number of past adversities, where past attempts at reunification had failed or where children had been sexually abused.

At the time of this decision, 'serious concerns' persisted about birth parents in relation to the likely safety of children (53%), the parenting capacity of families (62%), the willingness of parents to cooperate with agencies (35%) and, to a slightly lesser extent, in relation to quite deep-seated parent problems, such as substance misuse (30%), domestic violence (18%), offending (14%) and mental health (30%). The parents of neglected children, in particular, were the subject of multiple concerns in relation to parenting, family contact and ongoing parent problems.

In most files (74%), there was evidence of some work having been done to reduce these parental problems. Where work was no longer being done, this tended to relate to parental lack of engagement or recognition that positive change could not be made and that return home was no longer a viable option. However, in one-third of these cases the children did eventually return, amounting to one-fifth (19%) of all those reunified.

Where work was being done, the best examples had a multi-agency focus and involved written agreements about what needed to change, timescales for achieving it and a continuing dialogue with parents about the progress being made. Even in these cases, however, progress was often slow, marginal or non-existent.

Ratings of whether the problems that had led to the child's admission had improved, stayed the same or deteriorated at this stage showed that there had been some improvement in one-third of cases (33%), around one-half had remained the same (51%) and the remainder had deteriorated (15%).

It was encouraging to find that a return home was associated with these problems having improved. Two-thirds (65%) of those who went home did so to circumstances that were rated as being 'somewhat' or 'much' improved, one-third to circumstances rated as being the same and just 2 per cent to circumstances that had apparently deteriorated.

5

How the Effective Decision Was Made: Planning and Outcome

This chapter provides a focus on the planning and decision making that surrounded the key decision for children to return home or remain within the system. It explores how these decisions were made and the factors that were taken into account when making them and, finally, identifies those factors that best predicted reunification for this sample of children.

Evidence of planning

The case file audit provided an opportunity to assess the type and degree of planning that surrounded the effective decision. Historically, research in the UK on planning for reunion has highlighted its weakness, emphasizing drift arising from a lack of planning and returns that occurred through happenstance, often arising from the direct actions of parents or children or from placement breakdowns (Department of Health and Social Security 1985; Fisher, Marsh and Phillips 1986; Millham *et al.* 1986b; Rowe and Lambert 1973). Despite subsequent legislative changes, a renewed emphasis on permanency decision making and on proactive social work planning, there remains evidence of inconsistency. More recent studies have also found that the reunification of children was frequently poorly planned and supported (Sinclair *et al.* 2005) and that reunion decision making was seldom free from pressures exerted by children, parents, placements or from legal or management imperatives (Farmer *et al.* 2008).

Purposeful social work planning and activity directed towards reunion, thorough assessments that lead to clear goals and targets in relation to the changes that are needed, provision of social work and specialist services to support those changes and planning that is inclusive of children and families have been identified as important features of positive reunification practice (Aldgate 1980; Biehal 2006; Cleaver 2000; Farmer *et al.* 2008; Stein and Gambrill 1977). Farmer and colleagues' (2008) reunification study highlighted continuing inconsistencies in these respects. Just over one-half of their sample (57%) returned home after a reasonably thorough assessment of their family circumstances and only a similar proportion of families (52%) were rated as having been adequately prepared for their child's return. A multi-agency approach to planning was found to lead to more effective assessments and to parental problems being more adequately addressed (as was providing parents with clear conditions to be met prior to return). Sound assessments also led to better services to help address these problems. Where family circumstances were not assessed at this stage and work not undertaken to resolve problems, these tended to persist into return.

In light of these findings, Table 5.1 identifies some important dimensions of assessment and planning and the degree to which they seem to have been employed for maltreated children in this study. How these dimensions relate to the outcome of the effective decision will be discussed below. Overall, there was evidence from case files of a reasonably good degree of purposeful social work planning for two-thirds of the sample (67%) and of planning that was inclusive of birth families for almost three-quarters (73%). Other dimensions were more variable, especially in relation to multi-professional involvement, although all were considered at least 'to some degree' in the majority of cases.

Table 5.2 identifies the different sources of evidence that were used to inform this decision. This shows that considerable emphasis was placed on written social work reports and observations of parent–child interactions by children's services. However, evidence of use of observations by external professionals was much less common (36% of cases) and it is of some concern to find that written assessments of potential risks to the safety of children if returned home were not evident in many case files (35%), especially where children had been looked after for a shorter period of time (p=0.01, n=149). Furthermore, while written reports from professionals external to children's services were present in over two-thirds of cases (69%), as we saw in Table 5.1, their evidence was assessed as having been central to the decision that was taken in less than one-third of cases (27%).

Table 5.1 The effective decision: evidence of planning (n=149) – per cent (n)*

	Very much so	To some degree	Not at all	Not applicable or missing
Involved purposeful social work planning	67 (100)	26 (38)	7 (11)	0
Was inclusive of the child	50 (74)	36 (53)	15 (22)	0
Was inclusive of relevant birth family members	73 (109)	18 (27)	8 (12)	1 (1)
Took account of other relevant professional opinion	27 (40)	60 (90)	12 (18)	1 (1)
Was based on clear expectations of what needed to change for reunion to take place	50 (74)	26 (38)	11 (17)	13 (20)**
Was based on clarity about timescales for reunion	36 (53)	30 (45)	21 (31)	13 (20)**
Was based on clear expectations about the support that would be available to assist reunification	35 (52)	38 (57)	13 (20)	13 (20)**
Considered potential risk of harm to child and how it might be ameliorated	56 (83)	30 (44)	11 (17)	3 (5)
Included consideration of alternative permanent options for child	50 (74)	31 (46)	20 (29)	0

*Not all rows total 100 per cent due to rounding.

**'Not applicable' here relates to cases where a return home was never really considered to be a practicable option and was therefore not planned for.

Table 5.2 Sources of evidence used in reaching
the effective decision – per cent (n)*

Types of evidence used	Yes	No evidence
Written assessment of risks to safety of child	65 (97)	35 (52)
Written reports by social work personnel	85 (127)	15 (22)
Written reports by external professionals	69 (102)	32 (47)
Observation and assessment of parent–child relationships by social work personnel	79 (117)	22 (32)
Observation and assessment of parent–child relationships by external professionals	36 (53)	64 (96)

*Not all rows total 100 per cent due to rounding.

In a majority of cases, therefore, the core decision was taken by children's services, perhaps supplemented by reports from teachers, health visitors, youth offending, probation or family centre practitioners. However, where written reports were provided by children's guardians, by paediatricians or child psychiatrists, outlining the impact of maltreatment on children, or by adult psychiatrists, assessing the potential for change in parents, these tended to be given more weight in the decision-making process.

Variations in planning

The degree to which the different dimensions of planning outlined in Table 5.1 were central to the decision-making process varied according to the characteristics of the children concerned, the local authorities that were responsible for them and according to whether children were discharged home or went home on a care order.

Child and family characteristics

The degree to which children were included in the planning process varied according to their age and perceived understanding, with older children more likely to have been consulted.[1] Learning-disabled children were also less likely than other children to be fully included in the plans that were being made for them, and planning was also less likely to be based on clear timescales for reunion, on expectations of what needed to change or on

---

1   Kendall's Tau-b test (p<0.001; n=149).

the support that would be available to assist it.[2] Although communication strategies with learning-disabled children are more complex for social workers, it was unfortunate to find that only 25 per cent were considered to have been fully involved compared to 52 per cent of other children. The findings on timescales, expectations of change and support are likely to reflect the fact that fewer of these children had a return home as part of their plans.

With respect to forms of maltreatment, there were no significant differences in overall planning for those children who had suffered sexual ($p=0.35$), physical ($p=0.71$) or emotional abuse ($p=0.78$). However, where children had suffered neglect, assessment and planning was less likely to have been inclusive of their birth families ($p=0.001$, $n=148$) or to have been based on clear timescales for reunion ($p=0.03$, $n=129$).

Where parental problems were perceived to have deteriorated since the admission of children, planning tended to be directed less at reunification and more at finding alternative durable solutions within the looked after system. In these circumstances, birth families and other external professionals were rather less likely to have been included and planning was less obviously based on clear timescales for reunion or on an assessment of the services that would be needed to secure it.[3] This interpretation also tends to be confirmed by the finding that purposeful social work planning was no less likely in cases where parent difficulties had apparently got worse ($p=0.82$) and that consideration of alternative placement options for the child was more likely.[4]

Variation by local authority

Our representative *census* study found that the care pathways of maltreated children varied significantly according to local authority and, within local authorities, to the particular social work teams responsible for their care.[5]

---

2   Mann–Whitney U exact tests for learning disability: planning inclusive of child ($p=0.02$, $n=135$), planning based on clear timescales ($p=0.02$, $n=115$) and on support available to assist reunion ($p=0.01$, $n=115$).

3   Planning and parent problems: planning inclusive of birth families (Kendall's Tau-b, $p=0.01$, t -0.190, $n=148$), other professional opinion ($p=0.02$, t -0.167, $n=148$), timescales for reunion ($p-0.01$, t -0.226, $n=129$), support available ($p<0.01$, t -0.245, $n=149$).

4   Kendall's Tau-b ($p=0.01$, t 0.203, $n=149$).

5   Chi-square significance for effects of local authority on final destinations of children at end of *census* follow-up (still looked after, discharged home, placed with parents, adopted) – $p<0.001$; $n=2291$. Examples of ranges across these local authorities include: still looked after (40–59%); discharged home (9–31%); adopted (5–23%). These effects remained even when account was taken of children's characteristics in regression equations.

Although, as we will see further below, other factors linked to the characteristics of children and their families predicted whether or not children would be reunified, remain in care or move on to adoption, the local authority in which they lived was by far the strongest predictor of permanence pathways. Local authorities, however, were found to have less influence over whether children who went home stayed there or returned to the looked after system following breakdown, or whether those who remained looked after were settled in a stable placement.[6] In these respects, the levers available to local authorities were weaker and outcomes of placement were more dependent on the quality of care and support provided by caregivers, social workers and parents.

The *census* also provided evidence that social work teams exerted an influence on these pathways over and above that exerted by the local authority as a whole. Not only did teams influence these pathways, but they also appeared to have some influence over children's stability at home or in care, most likely through the direct work undertaken with caregivers and parents to support placements.[7]

Our *survey* provided more detailed evidence on variation in planning between local authorities. Although the differences between authorities did not reach significance for every dimension of planning, the pattern of variation was evident in all areas. Those that were significant included purposeful social work planning (with 'very much so' ranging from 50% of cases in the lowest authority to 82% in the highest), inclusion of the child (ranging from 27% to 74%) and birth families (ranging from 56% to 100%) and, perhaps of greatest concern, assessment of potential risk of harm to the child (ranging from 35% to 93% of cases).[8] Although, as we shall see, assessment of child safety proved to be a key feature of the decision as to whether a child would return home or not, evidence of variation in the degree to which local authorities make this a central and recorded component of assessment and planning is a matter of concern.

---

6   Chi-square significance for local authority effects on stability at home (p=0.298) and on placement stability in care (p=0.09).

7   The seven local authorities contained a wide variety of social work teams, making a precise comparison of the effects of teams on children's pathways difficult. Analysis of 11 similar teams in one local authority (all serving similar populations of children under age 11) provided evidence of variation (Chi-square 62.02, with 30 degrees of freedom, p<0.001, n=500).

8   Fisher's exact tests for local authority variation in planning: purposeful social work planning (p=0.03, n=145), inclusive of child (p=0.01, n=145), inclusive of birth families (p<0.01, n=144), risks to child (p<0.01, n=141). To provide an example of the ranges in non-significant dimensions of planning, involvement of external professionals (p=0.32) ranged from 15 per cent of cases in the lowest authority to 39 per cent in the highest, and clear timescales for reunion (p=0.26) ranged from 24 per cent to 54 per cent.

Variation between authorities was also evident in the sources of evidence that were relied upon when making this key decision. Significant differences existed in relation to evidence of use of written risk assessments, use of written reports and observations by external professionals and of social work observations of parent–child interactions. The only evidence source that did not vary by local authority involved provision of written reports by social workers.[9] Furthermore, the differences between authorities were quite large. For example, evidence of risk assessments on file ranged from two-fifths of cases (39%) in the lowest authority to four-fifths in the highest (81%). These differences were also mirrored in the use made of social work observations (46–96%) and of written reports (50–89%) and observations from external professionals (11–69%).

For most of the authorities, this pattern of variation was not consistent. Each authority appeared to have different strengths and weaknesses. In one authority, for example, all cases were assessed as being inclusive of birth family members yet, at the same time, this authority was the least successful at engaging children in the planning process, even though the children they cared for were on average older than in some other areas. While another authority was rated highly for purposeful social work planning, it appeared to be the least successful at involving external professionals in the planning process.

One authority, however, tended to be rated quite poorly by our auditors on planning in most areas, although its differences in practice were not always significant when compared to the other authorities. The brief notes provided by auditors shed some light on this divergence. Around one-half of the cases showed signs of weak planning and control. In some instances, birth parents had simply removed the child from S20 accommodation, despite the evident concerns of professionals, and this situation had been subsequently ratified or, alternatively, was subject to ongoing legal proceedings. Several cases had been subject to drift, without a clear statement of what parents needed to do to bring about reunification, the timescales for achieving change or the services that would be provided to help them. In these cases, the role of children's guardians had often been pivotal in bringing the case back to court in an effort to get planning back on track. Finally, there was some evidence that reunions had occurred by default, either through pressure from parents or children or through being perceived as a temporary or last resort in the context of placement shortages.

---

9   Sources of evidence drawn upon by local authorities (Fisher's exact tests; n=145): written
      risk assessments (p=0.01); written social work reports (p=0.87); reports (p=0.01) and
      observations by external professionals (p<0.001) and observations by social workers
      (p<0.001).

At a broader level, our *census* study identified large variations in the use of placement resources by local authorities. These findings suggest that the pathways of maltreated (and other) looked after children – whether they go home or not or whether they go on to long-term fostering or adoption – are associated less with the characteristics of the children and families concerned than with the policies and procedures of local authorities and of social work teams operating within them. These findings are also consistent with those that have emerged from other recent work on the pathways of looked after children (Sinclair *et al.* 2007) and from studies on adoption (Biehal *et al.* 2010), kinship care (Farmer and Moyers 2008) and special guardianship (Wade *et al.* 2010). At a micro level, the findings on planning shed some light on the ways in which differences in case management, assessment and planning also vary between authorities (and probably within them) when key decisions, such as whether or not to return a maltreated child, are being taken. As such, they add to our understanding of the mechanisms through which these differences in care pathways may come about.

Placement with parents

Findings from our *census* study also highlighted the importance of 'placement with parents' as an important route home for maltreated children. Maltreated children were much more likely than other looked after children to go home on a care order.[10] This in itself is not surprising, as we know that maltreated children are more likely to be on care orders than other looked after children, and that this is a prerequisite for this pathway home (Sinclair *et al.* 2007). What is more striking is that, once placement with parents is taken into account, the proportion of maltreated children who in the end went home was almost exactly the same as the proportion of other looked after children who did so (at 23%). Typically, returning home on a care order also tended to occur later in the child's care career than was the case for those discharged home and this had some implications for the planning process.

Amongst those in the *survey* sample who went home on a care order, assessment and planning for this group of children was also significantly stronger. Although only 19 children in the *home* group returned through placement with parents (and we therefore should be cautious about these findings), the differences compared to those maltreated children who were simply discharged home were significant for all dimensions of planning, with

---

10   Chi-square for linear association 12.58, df=1, p<0.001, n=3872.

the exception of involvement of professionals external to children's services (p=0.91).[11]

Box 5.1 Case Studies

The Department, both birth parents and the child were all very careful about this decision and worked together to ensure a smooth and gradual return to the mothers care. The extended family were in full support of this plan. The decision was made over time, and was a well-planned, clear and supported decision, discussed and monitored at the child's reviews, in social work supervision and in multi-agency meetings and discussions.

There seems to be a lot of support systems and agencies in place in preparation for the children's return home. The mother attended a family centre for support with routines and boundaries. Therapeutic work was undertaken with the children, including play therapy, and the family centre remained involved for help with communication between the mother and her children.

The plan was to return the child to his mother's care gradually, starting with overnight stays and eventually to returning the child to his mother's full-time care. The intention of the social worker at this point was to continue to monitor all aspects of this family, to continue to work with the mother, to offer appropriate support and to monitor and assess her care of the child.

Planning for those placed with parents probably reflects, at least in part, the greater parental control that local authorities could exercise through the sanction of a court order. However, in around two-fifths of these cases there had been a substantial change in home circumstances. In some instances, the child returned to their birth father (and not the mother with whom they had been living before admission) and a planned move was made after successful assessment. In others, the child's birth mother had acquired a new partner and

---

11 Planning for those discharged or placed with parents (Mann–Whitney U exact tests): social work planning (p<0.01, n=68); inclusive of child (p<0.01, n=68); inclusive of family (p=0.03, n=68); expectations of change (p=0.001, n=64); clear timescales (p<0.001, n=64); expectations of support (p=0.02, n=64); risks to child (p=0.01, n=68); alternative options for child (p=0.02, n=68).

in these new circumstances it was considered safe to proceed with reunion. Overall, however, there was a sense in these cases that assessment, planning and preparation for reunion was more often undertaken carefully and to a timescale that was more suited to children's services. Plans to monitor and support the decision were also more clearly present, as the following brief illustrations suggest.

As might be expected, a greater proportion of the children discharged home (without a care order) had been voluntarily accommodated. Although many of the returns for the 'discharge' group had been well planned and executed, there was considerably more evidence of returns for this group occurring through happenstance outside the control of the authority, sometimes against the wishes of the professionals involved.

There were more examples of abrupt or unplanned returns affecting around one-third of 'discharge' group cases. In some instances, a birth parent simply took the child home or demanded their return while, in others, older children voted with their feet or failed to return from a home visit. In these circumstances, authorities sometimes proceeded with a legal challenge while in others the situation was apparently viewed more as a fait accompli. There were also examples of crises bringing about a 'quick fix' solution that was frequently viewed as a temporary measure. In these cases, placement breakdown (or the risk of it) sometimes combined with a lack of alternative placement resources to lead children to return home as a temporary solution. In other cases, pressure from parents or children led to a truncated preparation period prior to return, even where reunification had been the ultimate plan. It is the prevalence of these kinds of examples within the 'discharge' group that led to the overall finding that planning for them was generally weaker than was the case for the 'placement with parents' group.

What influenced the effective decision?

This section will point to a number of factors linking child, parent and family circumstances and local authority resources that were weighed in decisions as to whether maltreated children returned home or remained within the system. Fifteen questions were asked separately for the *home* and *care* groups, with the same question reversed for each group. For example, in relation to those who went home, we asked whether there was evidence that the child's motivation to return had 'no influence' on the decision, 'some influence' or was 'very influential'. For those who did not, we asked auditors to assess the degree to which a lack of motivation to return influenced the decision. This process was repeated for each question.

Although we consider the weighting given to child level factors, parental factors and resource issues separately, it is important to bear in mind that reunification decisions are invariably complex and multilayered and that it would be rare for a single factor to have a paramount influence.

Child factors

A number of studies have identified child and parent motivation as important factors in reunification (Cleaver 2000; Pierce and Geremia 1999), and motivation, alongside quality of parenting and school progress, has also been associated with improved well-being after return (Sinclair *et al.* 2005). In contrast, ambivalence in children or parents has been seen as a factor inhibiting return (Bullock *et al.* 1998; Harwin *et al.* 2001). Amongst those maltreated children who went home, their desire to do so was the only child-level factor that strongly influenced this decision. For the vast majority of children who returned home, their motivation had at least some influence on the decision (86%) and in almost one-half of cases (46%) it was rated as 'very influential'. Indeed, amongst older children, 10 per cent of returns occurred either because the young person had walked out of a placement or, more usually, had failed to return from a home visit.

In contrast, where children remained within the care system, a desire not to return home appeared to have less influence on the decision, having some influence for just under one-third of children (30%). This does suggest, however, that for nearly one-third of these children there was some indication on file of a reluctance to return to their parents. It is possible that rather more of those who did not go home may have also shared this reluctance, even though there was no evidence on file that it influenced the decision.

Other child-level factors appeared rather less influential on decisions to reunify children with their parents. In overall terms, less weight was given to changes in child behaviour or to whether or not children were settled in their placements. Therefore, being unsettled, unless combined with a strong desire to go home, was less likely to deliver this outcome than were a range of social work perceptions about the child's parents.

Parent factors

Amongst those who went home, the most influential parent factors were their perceived motivation to welcome the child back and to tackle the problems that led to the admission and their capacity to keep the child safe. Parent motivation and perceived willingness to address problems had some influence on the decision in three-quarters of return cases (77%) and a strong influence in more than half (56%). An assessment that risks to the safety of the child were acceptable had some influence for four-fifths of the children who went home (81%) and a strong influence for two-fifths (40%). Furthermore, where parent problems were assessed as being worse than previously thought or had deteriorated over time, this also had a strong bearing on the outcome. In two-thirds of non-return decisions, this had a strong influence (68%).

Other parent and family factors appeared to have rather less influence on the return decision. Favourable changes in household composition and circumstances appeared to carry rather less weight than parenting issues. A positive change in household composition was very influential in just over one-fifth of return cases (22%) and in household circumstances (housing, finance, employment) in just 13 per cent. However, these factors appeared considerably more influential in decisions not to return children home. Amongst those who remained in care, unfavourable or no change in household composition (58%) and in family circumstances (57%) was very influential for over one-half of children.

Resource factors

From the evidence available on files, resource factors appeared to have rather less influence on the effective decision than did those concerning children and parents. Apart from the perception that children were settled in the looked after system or, to a lesser extent, that suitable placement resources were available (some influence in 28% of cases), resource questions appeared to play very little part in decisions for children to remain within the system.

Resource factors also did not appear to influence decisions strongly for most of those who went home. However, around one-fifth of children who went home (22%) did so in circumstances where their placement was disrupted or was thought to be at threat, and for one in ten children this was a strongly influential factor in the decision (10%). The lack of suitable alternative placements also had some bearing for one in nine children (11%). In overall terms, for one-quarter of the children who went home (24%) their return was prompted by placement breakdown and/or the limited availability of a suitable alternative placement.

It was also of some concern to find that consideration of the resources that were available to support reunification did not have a stronger place in decision making. Although there was evidence that the resources that could be made available by children's services had some influence in around one-half of return decisions (49%), it only had a strong influence in 15 per cent. Even less weight was given to the potential resources of other agencies. These were assessed as having some influence in one-third of cases (34%), but were strongly influential in just one in ten (10%). Assessment of the support and services that may be required to give a child's return home the best chance of success is of obvious importance and the deployment of appropriate resources should perhaps be weighed more strongly in return decisions than appeared to be the case.

What factors predicted stay or return home?

We will now consider which factors best predicted who went home and who did not. As we have seen, the timing of this decision ranged from a period of a few days to just over three years after admission. Some children had therefore been looked after quite long-term at this point, others less so. It is also important to bear in mind that we are discussing differences in the rate at which children return home, rather than whether or not they go home in some final sense. Some of those in our *care* group will eventually have gone home, perhaps outside the timeframe of this study, while others who went home will have returned to the system once again.

We are not able to include all factors that may be important to this decision, only those that are available to us. For example, we are not able to factor in children's physical disability or mental health, as the numbers included in the survey were too small, even though disability is considered to have some impact on the rate at which children return home (Cleaver 2000; Glisson *et al.* 2000). Equally, though we know from our preceding discussion (and other findings) that parent motivation has an important influence on whether children return home, this variable did not exist in a form that could be used in the analysis that follows.

In broad terms, these findings will match those from our much larger *census* study. The *census* findings suggested that children were less likely to have returned home during the study period where they had been looked after for a longer time, they accepted the need to be in care, they were considered by social workers to have a disability and where they had come from families marked by substance misuse or domestic violence. However, none of these predicted likelihood of return as strongly as did the local authority responsible for their care.[12]

The *survey* provides greater detail than was possible from the large *census*. However, the analysis of local authority effects cannot be replicated, as the

---

12   The significance levels are for the coefficients in a logistic regression: time in care ($p<0.001$), accept need for care ($p=0.003$), considered to be disabled ($p=0.042$), families with substance misuse/domestic violence ($p=0.031$). Taken together, however, while these variables predict 99.5 per cent of those who do not go home, they constitute a weak predictor of who will return (0.5%). For this we need to know which team in which local authority is looking after the child.

survey sample was selected on the basis that broadly one-half of the children in each area went home and one-half did not.

The analysis which follows examines clusters of factors that may have had a bearing on the return decision, including child characteristics, the children's past involvement with children's services, reasons for the relevant admission, child circumstances at the time of the effective decision, social work concerns about parents at this time and social work planning.

Children's characteristics

In keeping with the *census* study findings, differences in gender (p=0.5), age at entry (p=0.5) or age at effective decision (p=0.5) had no significant bearing on decisions regarding those who went home and those who did not. Although the *census* found some differences by ethnic origin in the likelihood of return, with Asian and Chinese children being more likely to go home, this was not replicated in the much smaller *survey* sample (p=0.3).[13]

Where children were considered to have a *learning disability*, however, they were much less likely to go home within the study timeframe.[14] Only one in five (21%) children with a learning disability went home compared to one-half of those who did not have a learning disability (50%). This is consistent with broader findings on reunification, where children with learning disabilities have been found to remain considerably longer in public care than their peers (Berridge and Cleaver 1987; Cleaver 2000; Davis *et al.* 1997).

Past involvement with children's services

None of our basic measures of past involvement with children's services was associated with the likelihood of return. Irrespective of whether the problems that had led to admission were long-standing (p=0.65) or the product of a short, intensive crisis (p=0.1), whether there had been previous attempts at reunification (p=0.46) or past provision of preventive services (p=0.99), none of these factors was significantly associated with whether children went home or not on this occasion.

These findings are not without interest. Although admission through a sudden crisis where there had been little past involvement with children's services was not significantly related to return, the pattern was in this

---

13   The *census* found significant differences on likelihood of return between Chinese and Asian children and other ethnic groups. As these differences could have been an artefact of differences in local authority policies, we tested this finding by taking account of local authority and other factors. The association still held (p=0.036).

14   Fisher's exact test (p=0.01, n=135).

direction (see also Fraser *et al.* 1996; Seaberg and Tolley 1986). An admission through a sudden emergency was relevant for well over one-quarter of those who went home (29%) compared to less than one-fifth (17%) of those who remained within the system. It is equally of interest that, despite the experience of past failed attempts at reunification, this was not associated with a reduced likelihood of a further attempt being made. Concerns about the risk of children oscillating in and out of care have been raised in the literature (see Biehal 2006; Farmer *et al.* 2008) and suggest that practitioners need to assess carefully the reasons for past breakdowns and the potential for change before making further attempts.

Reasons for entry

We know from existing research – and from our *census* study findings – that maltreated children return home at a much slower rate than children looked after for other reasons (Davis *et al.* 1997; Fanshel and Shinn 1978; Landsverk *et al.* 1996). There is also evidence that neglected children tend to stay within the system longer than children who have experienced physical or sexual abuse (Courtney, Piliavin and Wright 1997; Davis *et al.* 1997; Glisson *et al.* 2000; Harris and Courtney 2003; Webster *et al.* 2005). However, where these forms of abuse are severe, this difference may reduce, suggesting that social workers are more likely to plan actively for reunion where the prospects of success appear better (Barth *et al.* 1987; Farmer and Parker 1991).

These patterns were broadly evident in our *survey* sample. The only form of maltreatment that was significantly associated with the return decision was *neglect*. Fewer than two-fifths of children (37%) returned home within the study timeframe where there was 'strong evidence' of neglect compared to almost three-quarters (71%) where there had been no evidence of neglect.[15]

With respect to parental problems that contributed to the child's admission, a number of variables were significantly associated with the return decision. These included inadequate parenting ($p<0.001$), the presence of a sexual offender in the home ($p=0.01$) and parental ill health or disability ($p=0.03$). Two others were marginally linked: substance misuse ($p=0.06$) and parental offences ($p=0.06$). However, as we will see in a moment, these problems overlap with difficulties about which social workers had serious concerns at

---

15 Fisher's exact test ($p=0.005$; $n=149$). Only a relatively small proportion of the sample did not have neglect as a contributing factor to their admission ($n=24$). We should therefore be cautious about this finding. However, its fit with the wider research on reunification gives us greater confidence in its relevance. Although the rate of return for sexually abused children was in the same direction – 20 per cent returned where there was 'strong evidence' compared to 48 per cent where there was none – it was not significant ($p=0.13$). Emotional abuse ($p=0.49$) and physical abuse ($p=0.24$) were not associated.

the time of the effective decision and, at this stage, they were much more highly correlated with the outcome of the decision. This suggests that where these problems remain unresolved and strong social work concerns persist, it is this that will be most strongly associated with a return decision.

Children's circumstances at the time of the effective decision

In Chapter 4 we looked at a list of 14 measures that took account of how children were faring in the looked after system at the time of the effective decision (see Table 4.1). The relationship between these measures and the outcome of the decision fits very well with our descriptive account in the previous section of child-level factors that appeared to influence the return decision.

In most respects, how children were getting on in care at that time was not associated with whether they went home or not. There was no association with behavioural issues, with their overall well-being, with the ties they had to adults or friends or with whether or not they were upset by contact with their families.[16]

Only four variables were associated with children being more likely to return home:

- where children wanted to go home (p<0.001, n=102)
- where they did not accept the need for care (p=0.001, n=113)
- where they were thought to be less settled in care (p=0.01, n=133)
- and, to a much lesser degree, where they were not thought to be getting on well with their carer (p=0.08, n=134).

Further analysis was undertaken using binary logistic regression to see which of these factors had the most important bearing on the decision to return children home. The model produced just one variable:

- where children wanted to go home.[17]

From the point of view of maltreated children, therefore, the decision whether or not to return them home appears to be a judgement that is rooted in how much the children want that outcome. It is made even more likely when the children appear to be relatively unsettled and do not accept the need to be separated from their parents. This appears to be much more important than how they are getting on in other spheres of life or in their

---

16 Behaviour problems (p=0.58), doing well at school (p=0.47), running away (p=0.38), offending (p=0.94), substance misuse (p=0.97), overall well-being (p=0.68), close adult tie (p=0.25), positive friendships (p=0.45), upset by family contact (p=0.22) and missed contact with siblings (p=0.25).

17 Binary logistic regression: B=2.177; SE=0.698; df=1; p=0.002; Exp(B) = 8.82.

development – provided they do not have learning disabilities and/or have not been seriously neglected. As we have seen, a proportion of older children will largely take this decision for themselves, perhaps especially where a return is not being actively planned, but in the majority of cases social workers appear to take this quite strongly into account in decision making.

A further factor associated with going home was *frequency of contact with the birth mother*.[18] Over four-fifths of those who went home (82%) were in at least weekly contact with their birth mothers, compared to half (50%) of those who did not have contact frequently. Although contact with birth fathers (p=0.14) and with other relatives (p=0.13) was in this expected direction, these findings were not significant. Having said this, it is likely that contact in itself (whilst a precondition for reunion) acts as a proxy for the quality of the mother–child relationship and for motivation and cooperation (Biehal 2007; Quinton *et al.* 1997). In these circumstances, social workers are more likely to view the prospects of return as propitious, actively plan for it to take place and support contact arrangements.

Social work concerns about parents

In Chapter 4 we also explored 12 measures of parental difficulty about which social workers might have had concerns at the time of the effective decision (see Table 4.3). Virtually all of these measures, with the exception of parental mental health (p=0.24), were associated with whether these maltreated children went home or not.[19] The greater the concerns at this time, the more likely they were to remain in the system. These measures are:

- chronic ill health or disability (p=0.03, n=147)
- substance misuse (p<0.001, n=148)
- parental offences (p=0.02, n=148)
- domestic violence (p=0.04, n=148)
- parenting (care and nurture) (p<0.001, n=148)
- parenting (approach to discipline) (p<0.001, n=148)
- parenting (supervision of child) (p<0.001, n=148)

---

18   Mann–Whitney U exact test (p<0.001, n=149).

19   Parental mental health, therefore, did not appear to present a significant barrier to the return of children, although there is some evidence in the wider literature that it may do (Rzepnicki *et al.* 1997).

- willingness to cooperate with social work and other agencies (p<0.001, n=148)
- impact of family contact on child (p<0.001, n=148)
- risks to safety of child if returned (p<0.001, n=148)
- presence of other adults in the family home (p<0.001, n=148).

Logistic regression was used to reduce these variables and the best predictive model is shown in Table 5.3.

Table 5.3 Parenting concerns predictive of return decision

	B	SE	df	Sig. (p=)	Exp(B)
Risks to the safety of child if returned	1.81	0.671	1	0.01	6.09
Presence of other adults in the home	1.03	0.401	1	0.01	2.80
Impact of family contact on child	1.43	0.409	1	0.000	4.16

Nagelkerke r^2=0.339.

In terms of social work concerns about the family at this stage, decision making seemed to revolve primarily around an assessment of the risks to the child. Although other factors listed above retained importance in decision making, greater emphasis appears to have been given to this than to the personal problems of parents or the particular limitations in their parenting styles. The presence of doubtful adults in and around the parental home clearly contributed to concerns about the child's safety should they go home, and monitoring the impact of home visits on the child – and the degree to which these were perceived as positive for the child – probably acted as a litmus test for the potential in reunification.

In addition, as we saw in Chapter 4, a return home was significantly more likely where the *parental problems that had led to the child's admission were seen as having improved* over time.[20] It is likely, therefore, that some progress (or at least lack of further deterioration) in the problems listed above contributed to the perception that the likelihood of further harm to the child had lessened and that the prospects for reunification (provided the child strongly wanted this) had improved. In overall terms, these findings are broadly consistent with those in Farmer and colleagues' (2008) reunion study. They also found that, where reasons for return home were recorded on file, the most

---

20 Mann–Whitney U exact test (p<0.001, n=149).

important primary factor was safety of the child and that this was combined (to varying degrees) with some perceived improvement in parental problems and motivation.

Assessment and planning

Our preceding discussion of planning highlighted the importance of purposeful social work activity directed towards reunion and the provision of services to address parental difficulties prior to return. It also highlighted the pressures placed on social workers arising from children, parents and broader systems within the social work environment. Table 5.1 described the findings in relation to nine measures of planning and these related to the outcome of the effective decision in differing ways.

Not all dimensions of planning were associated with the return decision. It was perhaps surprising to find that planning based around a clear expectation of the changes that were needed (p=0.85) was not associated with a return decision. This may have been influenced, as we have seen, by a small core of cases where the children's circumstances had been so severe that a return plan had never been in prospect. Rather less surprising, assessment of risks to the safety of children was a core feature of planning across all cases (p=0.69) and was therefore not associated with whether or not children returned home.

Five dimensions of planning were associated with the decision:

- involved purposeful social work planning (p=0.004, n=149)
- was inclusive of relevant birth family members (p=0.02, n=148)
- was based on clear expectations about the support that would be available to assist reunification (p=0.01, n=129)
- included consideration of alternative care options for child (p<0.001, n=149)
- was based on clarity about timescales for reunion, although this was a very marginal association (p=0.09, n=129).

In an effort to reduce these variables, they were entered into a regression equation but all retained a significant association with the return decision, as shown in Table 5.4.

Table 5.4 Social work planning variables associated with return decision

	B	SE	df	Sig. (p=)	Exp(B)
Involved purposeful social work planning	-2.82	0.691	1	0.000	0.06
Was inclusive of relevant birth family members	2.11	0.686	1	0.002	8.24
Was based on clarity about timescales for reunion	1.48	0.639	1	0.021	4.40
Was based on clear expectations about the support that would be available to assist reunification	1.66	0.600	1	0.006	5.26
Included consideration of alternative permanent placement options for child	-2.28	0.596	1	0.000	0.103

Nagelkerke r^2=0.503.

It was interesting to find that these planning measures worked in different directions (as Table 5.4 suggests).[21] Decisions for children to go home were associated with a greater involvement of birth families in planning, with a planning process that emphasized the support and services that might be needed and the need for clearer timescales within which to bring about return. Going home was also associated with less social work planning and less attention being given to alternative care arrangements for the child.

A decision for the child to remain within the system was therefore associated more strongly with a higher degree of social work planning and, not surprisingly, with a greater need to identify alternative care arrangements for the child. These findings make sense. Once a plan is agreed that looks towards long-term care, the development of a care plan, identification of a suitable placement, the assessments that may be attached and brokering these relationships involve a reasonably high level of social work activity. This is consistent with our finding that for over four-fifths of children in the *care* group (83%), there was evidence of an alternative placement having been considered with a different birth parent, other relative or family friend, compared to just over one-half (53%) of those in the *home* group.[22]

---

21   Looking at the 'B' column, a negative association is linked to staying in care and a positive association is linked to a return home.

22   Fisher's exact test (p<0.001, n=149).

In contrast, as we have seen, some children who go home do so very quickly after entering care, leaving little time for planning. Others go home suddenly, through placements ending or through their own volition, in circumstances that are relatively unplanned. However, the findings also resonate with wider research that shows the highly uneven nature of social work planning that takes place prior to reunification (Biehal 2006a; Farmer *et al.* 2008; Sinclair *et al.* 2005).

A predictive model of return

As we have seen, a total of 13 variables were associated with the outcome of the return decision. These have been highlighted in the text. Some related to the experience of children:

- neglect
- learning disability
- wanting to go home
- frequency of contact with birth mothers.

Some related to the level of social work concerns about parenting at this time:

- risks to the safety of child if returned
- presence of other adults in the home
- impact of family contact on child
- whether original problems had improved, stayed the same or deteriorated.

Finally, some related to the social work planning process:

- involved purposeful social work planning
- were inclusive of relevant birth family members
- were based on clarity about timescales for reunion
- were based on clear expectations about the support that would be available to assist reunification
- included consideration of alternative care options for child.

Further analysis was undertaken in an effort to identify, amongst these variables, which factors best predicted a return decision for this sample of maltreated children. In view of the need for parsimony, however, to avoid including measures that were assessing broadly similar things and were highly correlated together and to include only those variables that were realistically likely to predict this outcome, we ultimately reduced this list to a core set of five variables for inclusion in logistic regression.

The preceding discussion identified that risk to the safety of the child was a key component of social work concerns about parents. The presence of other adults and the impact of family contact were related features of this risk assessment. Risk to the child's safety was therefore included as a proxy measure of these overall concerns.

The planning variables were more difficult to deal with. As this phase of analysis was concerned with prediction rather than exploration of the data, it was not at all clear that the planning process in itself would predict the return outcome. It is more likely that the planning process would be coterminous with an intention to return a child or not. Once this intention was clearer in the minds of social workers, then some forms of planning would tend to take precedence over others. The planning variables were therefore excluded from this analysis.

A further problem related to levels of missing data. Although the child wanting to go home was found to be an important influence on the return decision, the number of cases where there was no evidence on file of the child's wishes meant that the sample size available for analysis would have been unacceptably reduced (n=102). This lack of case file evidence was not random. Where no evidence was recorded, these children tended to be younger (and perhaps therefore less often consulted), were rather more likely than others to have been neglected and to have accepted the need for care, and there were rather more social work concerns about the care and supervision provided by parents. As a result, they were rather less likely to have gone home than were those where there was evidence on file. We therefore decided to remove this variable from the analysis that follows.

This left five core variables to include in our final analysis, with an improved but not complete sample size (n=127):

- neglect
- learning disability
- frequency of contact with birth mothers
- risks to the safety of child if returned
- whether original problems had improved, stayed the same or deteriorated.

The regression analysis, using the forward stepwise conditional method, delivered a final model that tended to downplay the influence of child-related factors in social work decision making and emphasized a social work perspective on risks to child safety and the prospects for successful return home (see Table 5.5). This perspective is perhaps not surprising, given that the information came from social work case files. If children, carers or parents were consulted directly, a somewhat different configuration may result.

Table 5.5 Final model predicting who went home and who did not

	B	SE	df	Sig. (p=)	Exp(B)
Risks to the safety of child if returned	3.09	0.549	1	0.000	21.87
Whether problems had improved or not since child's admission	2.25	0.615	1	0.000	9.44

Nagelkerke r^2=0.658.

However, the findings offer some encouragement if, as suggested here, risks to the safety of the child form a central strand of social work thinking when decisions of this kind are being taken. Where there were no evident concerns about child safety, more than four-fifths of children (87%) returned home compared to less than two-fifths (38%) where these concerns existed. Alongside this, where there were signs of some improvement in family circumstances, this provided separate evidence about the potential that may have existed for reunification. Where there was evidence of improvement, the vast majority of children went home (88%) compared to just 4 per cent where things were considered to have got worse.

As a final check, the analysis was run again including the variable that captured whether children wanted to go home or not. This did not change the substantive findings, although wanting to go home also had some significance in the final model (p=0.013). It is likely, therefore, that for somewhat older children whose views are consulted or who are able to make the decision for themselves, a strong desire to return also contributes to the outcome.

Summary
This chapter has examined the planning and decision making process that surrounded the decision for children to return home or not. It looked at how these decisions were made and the range of factors that were taken into account when making them and identified some factors that predicted whether reunification took place.

Overall, there was evidence of quite a good degree of social work planning that was inclusive of birth families. Decision making rested heavily on social work reports and observations, but less centrally on input from external professionals.

The planning process, however, varied considerably between local authorities. For most of the authorities, this pattern of variation was not consistent. In one area where planning was weaker overall, there was more evidence of parents removing children, of planning drift and of returns occurring through default. At this micro-level, differences in case management, assessment and planning shed further light on our *census* study finding that the care pathways of maltreated children tend to be shaped more by the policies and procedures of local authorities than by the characteristics of children.

At the level of the child, children's desire to go home was the only factor that strongly influenced a return decision. Amongst older children, one in ten returned of their own accord. With respect to parent-level factors, the most influential in return decisions were parents' motivation to have the child home, to tackle the problems that had led to admission and their capacity to keep the child safe.

Resource factors generally appeared to have little influence on decisions either way. However, for one-quarter of children (24%) who went home, their return was prompted by an imminent placement breakdown or the lack of a suitable alternative placement.

Children were less likely to go home within the timeframe of this study where:

- they had a learning disability
- they had been neglected
- they did not want to go home
- contact with the birth family was not frequent
- there were greater concerns about parents (especially about risks to child safety, the presence of other adults at home and the impact of contact on the child)
- parental problems were perceived not to have improved.

Further analysis identified two factors that best predicted whether children went home. This was most likely where:

- the risks to the safety of the child were assessed as acceptable
- there was some evidence that the problems that had led to the child's admission had improved.

From a social work perspective, therefore, risks to child safety are an important strand of social workers' thinking when decisions of this kind are being taken. Where there were signs of improvement in family circumstances, this also provided separate evidence about the positive potential for reunification.

6

How the Effective Decision Was Made: Experiences of Parents and Children

The last two chapters have presented mainly quantitative findings from case files on how the decision to return children home or not was made, the circumstances of children and parents at that time and the range of factors that were taken into account when reaching that decision. We also identified some of the factors that appeared most important in predicting reunification for this sample of children.

Inevitably, the patterns that we have presented have tended to flatten out the complexity in the lives of these children and their families. This chapter will attempt to redress this balance somewhat by using qualitative information from case files, parents and children to provide a number of illustrative case studies. These case illustrations will rehearse some of the main themes identified in the earlier chapters but present them in a more rounded way, taking greater account of the views and experiences of the parents and children concerned.

Decisions for children to remain in care (*care* group)
We will begin by briefly describing three cases where the effective decision was for the children concerned to remain looked after.

Helen

Helen, whose story was first introduced in Chapter 3, had entered care aged ten with her sister and was placed (temporarily at first) with foster carers under an emergency protection order. As we have seen, Helen had expected to return home after a few days and became frustrated when this did not turn out to be the case. Her mother, Carol, had been the subject of quite long-standing concerns in relation to her history of relationships with violent and abusive partners, her misuse of drugs and her perceived inability to protect her children from violence. Carol herself had called the police during one violent episode and this had precipitated the children's removal. Carol had not accepted the legitimacy of this response and had wanted her children returned. The consequences of separation had been devastating for Carol:

> As soon as I had my kids taken off me, all my family stopped talking to me, so I were left totally on my own and, to be honest with you, I'm surprised I'm still here. Because my kids were my life, and to take that away from me, they might as well have taken everything.

Approximately three months after being removed, the decision was made that the children should remain looked after. At the time this decision was made, Helen was doing well at school and was fairly settled in her foster placement, although she did express a desire to return home to her mother. Carol, on the other hand, was not doing so well. At this time there were serious social work concerns with regards to her mental health and continued drug use. Arrangements were made for Helen to see her mother twice weekly during this period for supervised contact, although Carol did not always show up and contact between them was irregular. These factors were likely to have been taken as signs that the prospects for reunification were not propitious. Having said this, Carol had not only lost her informal support network, but there was little evidence on file to suggest that she had received professional help during this period to address her difficulties.

The decision resulted from a core assessment, during which both Helen and Carol were consulted. Reports were considered from a psychologist (for family court proceedings), police interviews, school teachers, from Helen's children's guardian and from social work assessments. These concluded that, although Carol's violent partner had been imprisoned, there was little prospect that this cycle of domestic violence would not continue with future partners, that Carol's ability to protect her children would improve or that she would make the lifestyle changes required to meet her children's needs adequately. The problems that had led to Helen's admission were therefore not considered to have improved. As we will see in later chapters, however, this decision did not extinguish their desire to be reunited.

Nadine

Nadine entered care when aged seven. She had lived with her father and stepmother. Her stepmother suffered from severe mental health problems. Her father was apparently unable to manage Nadine's behaviour without recourse to serious physical chastisement. Both parents were misusing drugs and alcohol and had left Nadine in the care of unsuitable adults. These problems had been long-standing (certainly for more than two years). Her parents had previously requested help from children's services and there was evidence on file of two periods where family support services had been provided, though not consistently.

The decision for Nadine to remain looked after was ratified some 12 months after her admission, although the prospects for return had seemed unlikely for some time previously. At this time no work was being done with the family to address their difficulties. Nadine did not want to return; she seemed to be relatively settled in placement and accepting of care. However, her behaviour was very challenging and her overall mental and emotional well-being was poor, although she was faring reasonably well at school. Her foster carers were receiving support from the Child Psychology Service, to help them manage her behaviour, and Nadine was on a waiting list to receive therapeutic support in relation to her past experiences. Nadine continued to have weekly supervised contact with her father.

Serious social work concerns persisted in relation to the mental health of her stepmother, who was receiving mental health services, the capacity of both parents to provide appropriate care, discipline and supervision of Nadine and their willingness to cooperate with service providers. Psychological assessments undertaken reinforced the need for a long-term alternative permanent placement.

Joe

In Chapter 3 we saw that Joe was placed with foster carers at the age of eight after long-standing concerns about his serious neglect by his mother, who was heavily drug-dependent and involved in a violent relationship with her partner. Joe and his two siblings had previously been on the child protection register for neglect and family support services had been provided for at least two years but had brought no significant change to the quality of care the children received.

The decision for Joe to remain looked after was made seven months after he had entered care. Joe had settled well in care, had a good relationship with his foster carer and wanted to stay. However, the effects of his experiences had also stayed with him. His emotional well-being was considered to be poor; he was not doing very well at school and had very few (if any) existing friendships. Attempts had been made to place Joe with his father, but he felt unable to care for him as he already had several children of his own from his current relationship. Concerns about his mother's mental health and drug use were (if anything) heightened at this time; her life had spiralled downwards, she was unable to engage with any agencies and the prospect of a future reunion had been largely discounted. This was the conclusion drawn from assessments undertaken by a psychiatrist, a specialist assessment team and Joe's social worker.

Themes and issues

The case illustrations highlight some of the themes presented in previous chapters.

First, they point to the co-occurrence of quite deep-seated and persistent difficulties that exist in many families where the serious maltreatment of children is present.

Second, they highlight the challenges presented to social workers in trying to engage with and obtain cooperation from parents whose own lives may be out of control and who may not recognize the impact of their behaviour patterns on their children. In scenarios such as Nadine's, it also makes one wonder why it took as long as it did before a decision to remove her from her parents' care was made.

Third, they also hint at the dramatic psychological consequences that removal of a child may have for parents. Even where homes have been violent places and parents neglectful, as Carol's experiences suggest, the intervention of children's services may result in loss of informal support networks and potential for a further downward spiral in mental health and in use of drugs and alcohol. These risks need to be addressed if reunification is to be considered as an option.

Fourth, where parents persistently appear uncooperative or where their lives are too chaotic to maintain appointments, these are highly likely to be read as signs that parents are unwilling to change and/or that the prospects for return are not realistic.

Fifth, they highlight the need for a focused period of assessment to gauge whether return is feasible. This should be based on transparent written agreement with parents, clear expectations of what needs to change and a timescale for doing so. In these illustrations, the key decision may have actually been taken some time before it was formally ratified, as none of these parents was in receipt of services during this period and not all were clear about what further changes they needed to make.

Sixth, timeliness for the child is an important issue here, if an alternative pathway to permanence is needed. In Andrew's case (discussed in Chapter 3), it took two years after his admission before a final decision was made. By this time, he was aged nine. In the interim he had experienced several failed attempts to reunify him with his mother and to place him with other family members. By this age, his options for permanence had been significantly reduced.

Finally, the case studies do point to the central place in decision making of an assessment of future risks to child safety and of whether parental problems had improved or not as being highly influential in decisions for children to return home. These were the key factors predicting return that were identified in our previous chapter.

Decisions to return children home (*home* group)

The case studies provided five stories of return home. Three will be presented in some detail. Each story is inevitably different but, as we will see further below, some common themes and issues will be identified that connect with the broader quantitative findings presented in our earlier chapters.

Marcus

Marcus came into care at the age of seven. He had a diagnosis of attention-deficit hyperactivity disorder (ADHD) and, for a considerable time, had experienced bullying at school in large part due to his unkempt appearance. His mother, Amanda, had recently separated from Marcus's father. She had a moderate learning disability and had been struggling to manage Marcus's behaviour and the upkeep of the home for some time. The family had also been targeted by others in the neighbourhood and this had prompted the father to leave. Amanda did not accept that she had received sufficient support from children's services or the need for Marcus and his brother to be separated from her. However, the social work record suggested that insufficient changes had been brought about in her parenting despite provision of family support services for almost two years.

The plan for Marcus to return home was formulated at the point of admission and was completed within seven months. He had settled well in his foster placement, although his behaviour was difficult and he was struggling at school. Work was being done with him through a family centre to help him to manage his behaviour and accept reasonable boundaries and he had a personal mentor at school. Alongside the work with Marcus, Amanda accessed parenting skills training through the same family centre. She was also reunited with her partner (both had received counselling) and they were rehoused in a different neighbourhood and given financial advice and assistance to help them settle. Amanda had developed a close relationship with Marcus's foster carer and she felt that this, together with improvements in the home environment and in her perceived ability to cope, had been pivotal in getting both her sons returned:

> It was me and the foster carer that built up this friendship between us for me to get (Marcus) back... When the (foster carer) piped up and said, 'It's time for them to go home', well, I nearly fell off my chair 'cause it was such a shock and it's the last thing you expect to hear from a foster carer.

In practice, her willingness to cooperate and make the changes that were considered necessary had led the foster carer, social worker and the external professionals involved (health and education) to recognize that the proposed reunion could go ahead. This delighted Marcus, who thought that this was the right decision for him, although he missed his foster carer, to whom he had also grown close:

> I do miss [my foster carer] as well and when you get to know people for six months and that, it's a long time... I do miss my foster mum but if I was with her I'd miss my mother.

Jonathan

As we saw in Chapter 3, Jonathan came into care aged seven very much against the wishes of his mother, Josie. She felt that an isolated incident of domestic violence by Jonathan's father had prompted his entry to care and that the presence of his father (subsequently imprisoned) was the key issue. In contrast, the social work record suggested that this had been anything but an isolated incident; that Jonathan had witnessed serious violence and suffered physical injury on numerous occasions and that he had been left with unsuitable adults, about whom a sexual assault against Jonathan was suspected but not proven. Intermittent family support had been provided over a lengthy period, including offers of parenting classes and play therapy for Jonathan and his two siblings, although these were unlikely to have been anywhere near sufficient for the extensive needs of this family.

Four months after entry, a decision was made that Jonathan should return home. Although he had settled well in care, had a positive relationship with his foster carer and had resumed regular schooling, this was what Jonathan very much wanted. In the meantime, he had also been statemented for his educational needs and was receiving additional classroom support and out-of-school support from workers at a family centre. Despite her continuing resentment, Josie had also cooperated fully with the reunification plan. She attended counselling for herself, a Sure Start parenting course and additional groups looking at the implications of domestic violence for herself and her children and had received additional support through the family centre. Although there were still some concerns about how Josie would cope when Jonathan and his siblings returned, the final decision was aided by a psychologist's report that suggested that Josie had made sufficient positive progress for reunion to take place.

Josie remained suspicious. She felt that she had been under close surveillance and was being continuously tested, but with the rules not always clearly spelt out: 'They freak you out... I think they do it intentionally. I think they're testing you.' Although she had passed these tests successfully, Josie also harboured concerns about how she would manage once Jonathan was returned to her.

Laura

Laura came into care when aged eight. She lived with her mother, stepfather and her three siblings. There had been long-standing social work concerns about parental drug misuse, domestic violence and physical chastisement and neglect of the children. Intermittent family support services had been offered in the past, culminating in the children being placed on the child protection register for six months preceding entry. Although there had been a written agreement that the parents would separate to enable work to be done on these issues, the agreement was not adhered to and the children were removed from their care.

Laura was placed in foster care separately from her sisters. Although she recognized a need for temporary care, she desperately wanted to return home. Her mother, Paula, was also highly motivated. She agreed to continue working with the social worker and family support team and, after four months, a decision for reunification was taken. Work was undertaken to improve her parenting skills, she attended treatment for substance misuse and her partner (about whom there were continuing concerns) moved out of the home. Although a clear reunification plan was developed (returning one child at a time to allow Paula to adjust), Laura pre-empted her return home once her foster placement began to break down. The final decision to support this return was taken on the basis of evidence from all professionals involved, including social workers, teachers, health visitors and the substance misuse team.

Paula appreciated that the changes she had to make were very clearly laid out. The intervention also came at a time when she realized that she needed to make them; that things could not continue as they were:

> We had case conferences and everything was put out, like: 'This is what is going to happen. This is what needed to be achieved.' It was like a goal target of what you needed to do... The key worker never beat around the bush, she told me as I needed to be told, and for me as a person, I needed to be told... It helped me, whereas two years ago I'd have said: 'No way.' But it was something that needed to be looked at and it needed to be done and I achieved it.

In contrast to these stories, the returns of Gareth (aged ten) and Stephen (aged 12) were unplanned. Both boys took events into their own hands in different ways. Stephen was only in care for three weeks and, during this time, he had absconded from two foster placements. Although a placement was arranged with his father, he quickly left it and returned to his mother. He was still living there some three years later, despite ongoing concerns about his mother's substance misuse and its effects on her parenting. Gareth, looked after for five months, failed to return from a home visit to his parents. This placement eventually broke down and, at interview some five years later on, Gareth had been living with his older sister for a year on a residence order. Although this arrangement had been negotiated with and supported by his social worker, it is evident from these brief scenarios (and from our earlier evidence) that the timing and nature of children's returns are frequently not fully within the control of children's services.

Themes and issues

Although each of these stories has distinct features, a number of issues emerge from these illustrations that tend to reinforce the findings on reunification from previous chapters.

First, the motivation of child and parent to make reunion happen is an important ingredient. However, as we have seen, it is generally not sufficient unless (like Gareth and Stephen) older children take events into their own hands.

Second, of greater influence in these cases was the perceived willingness of parents to recognize the need for change and to cooperate with agencies to bring about those changes within an agreed timeframe. The engagement of parents and children meant that social workers were able to plan proactively, retain greater control over the timing of events and work in a more inclusive way with parents, children and other professionals. Of course, events may always unsettle planning, as can occur when placements end unexpectedly or when parents are unable to meet expectations.

Third, while relationships with parents will differ greatly, there was some evidence that parents often appreciate honesty, clarity of expectations, direct support to make the changes required and transparency about the consequences should these interventions fail.

Finally, however, it is also necessary to be mindful of the continuing feelings of ambivalence, suspicion or resentment that are likely to be felt by parents. It is probable that many parents would share Josie's feeling of having been continuously tested and placed under surveillance. In many respects, she is right. The challenge for practitioners working to safeguard children is to carry out this regime of surveillance and testing whilst at the same time having a menu of creative strategies that help to keep parents engaged in a process of change.

Summary

This chapter has presented a number of case studies using qualitative information drawn from case files and interviews with parents and children to explore how the decision for children to remain looked after or return home was reached. In doing this, the aim has been to add texture to the mainly quantitative findings presented in our preceding two chapters on decision making.

The case studies highlight some of the challenges confronting social workers and other professionals working with maltreated children and their families, including the complex multilayered family difficulties that often underpin maltreatment, the challenges of engaging parents whose own lives are frequently chaotic and the difficulties inherent in maintaining control over assessment, planning and the timescales for change.

Reunification was aided where parents and children were motivated for it to happen, where parents recognized the need for change and were prepared to cooperate with agencies in bringing this about within an agreed timescale and where sufficient support was available to help them do so with some degree of success. In these circumstances, it was made somewhat easier for social workers to retain control of the planning process and the timing of events. Even where parents remain resentful or suspicious about social work involvement, it is likely that they will need some help to allay their fears and adjust to the return of their children, provided this is delivered in the right way for them.

Where reunification is not a realistic prospect, timeliness in decision making is important if other pathways to permanence for children, including adoption, are not to be foreclosed. In some of these cases, it appeared that an informal decision not to return the child had been taken and parent services had largely ceased some time before its formal ratification. In another case, failed attempts to reunify a child continued beyond what appeared to be a reasonable period of time. Delays of this kind are unlikely to help children find a settled home.

7

Children's Experiences at Home and in Care: The First Six Months

This chapter will compare the initial progress of children after the effective decision was made for them to return home or remain within the system. It will also look within the reunification group to explore which maltreated children appeared to be faring better or worse at home during a period of six months after their return. Given the small numbers in this group (n=68), findings should be viewed as exploratory rather than conclusive.

The broad focus of this chapter is on the first six months after the effective decision. This is the case for children who remained within the looked after system. However, for those who went home there was inevitably some delay between the effective decision and their actual return. Just over one-half of this group (52%) returned within one month, almost three-quarters (71%) within two months and virtually all (93%) within six months of the decision being taken. Only five children remained longer within the system, the longest being just under one year. The period of analysis for the *home* group will be the first six months after this return. The information for this analysis derives from our audit of social work case files.

Where did the children go?

In most cases, the outcome of the effective decision did not disturb the placements of children in the *care* group (n=81). Most children were placed in foster care with strangers (61) or with family and friends (16). Only a small minority were placed in children's homes (2), for adoption

(1) or in 'other' circumstances (1).[1] However, as we will see further below, some children subsequently made planned moves from short- to long-term placements during the six-month period and others changed placement because of difficulties that had arisen.

Inevitably, the scenarios for children who went home were more complex. Table 7.1 shows the different family forms to which children returned through discharge or 'placement with parents'. The majority returned to a lone birth parent and only around one in eight to a family comprising both birth parents. Around one-fifth returned to a birth parent who was living with another adult, sometimes described as a step-parent and sometimes not.

Table 7.1 Composition of families to which children returned

	Per cent (n)
Lone birth parent	60 (41)
Two birth parents	12 (8)
Birth parent and other adult	19 (13)
With parental figure	3 (2)[2]
Birth parent and relative	6 (4)
Total	100 (68)

However, this static picture tells us nothing about patterns of continuity and change for reunified children. Studies have reported a high degree of change in family structures while children are looked after away from home (Bullock *et al.* 1998; Farmer and Parker 1991; Fisher *et al.* 1986). There is some evidence that the rate of reunification to lone-parent families may be slower than that to two-'parent'-family forms, even if one is not a biological parent (Landsverk *et al.* 1996), and also that the stresses associated with lone parenting may be associated with a higher risk of breakdown (Schuerman, Rzepnicki and Littell 1994).

Although we found no clear associations between changes in family form and children's progress at six months, perhaps due to the sample size, Table 7.2 does highlight the degree of change in the structure of children's

---

1   This was an unaccompanied asylum-seeking child living with strangers who were later approved as family and friends carers.

2   These two children had lived with their grandparents prior to the relevant admission and returned to the same household. In this respect, this was their family home and they were included in the *home* group for this reason.

families while they were away from home. Just over one-half of the children (54%) had experienced some change in family composition during their time in care.

Table 7.2 Changes in family composition on return (n=68)

	Per cent (n)
Returned to same birth parent(s)	49 (33)
Returned to a different parent	21 (14)
Returned to lone parent (father figure had left)	19 (13)
Returned to two parents (father figure had joined)	7 (5)
Other	4 (3)[3]
Total	100 (68)

Around one-half of the children had returned to the same birth parent(s) who had been caring for them before they entered care, although other members of these households (including siblings and other relatives) had sometimes changed in the interim. One-fifth had gone to live with a different parent. In all but one of these cases, the children had moved to live with their birth fathers and they were generally joining their existing families.

In other cases, children were returning to scenarios in which important father figures had either left or were newly arrived. One-fifth had returned to birth mothers who were living alone (or with other children) in circumstances where birth fathers or stepfathers had left the scene. A further five children had been living with their lone mother before entering care but returned to a situation where their birth father had returned (two) or a new partner had joined (three).

The adjustments that were likely to be needed for children to settle in once again were also mirrored in the shifting nature of sibling relationships (n=66).[4] While just over one-third of children (35%, n=23) who went home did so alone, more than half of these were reunited with siblings who had not been looked after (13). Most children, however, returned home together with

---

3   'Other' includes the two children who had returned to the same grandmother who had cared for them previously and one girl who had been living with her aunt before care but returned to her birth mother.

4   Only two children in the *home* group had no siblings.

siblings who had also been looked after (n=43), the majority (30) having lived together in the same placement and returned at the same time.

We were interested to see whether these sibling relationships were associated with children's early progress at home over the first six months. Although the findings must be considered tentative, there was some association with documented social work concerns about the overall progress of children.[5] Going home alone rather than returning with other looked after siblings was associated with a greater degree of social work concern at this stage and this was also the case where children had been reunited with siblings who had not been looked after.[6] At this early stage, therefore, returning with other looked after siblings appeared to offer some protection, while going home alone or reunion with siblings already *in situ* appeared to be more troublesome and gave rise to greater concerns.

Comparing the progress of children

The case file audit provided three ways of comparing patterns of early child progress during this six-month period:

- First, a cluster of questions identified the degree to which there was evidence of social work concerns about children's overall progress in relation to their safety, whether they appeared to be thriving, whether they had problems at school or in their behaviour and about the quality of care being provided by parent or carer.

- Second, we assessed the placement stability of children at six months. On the basis of the evidence on file, auditors were asked to rate whether a) placements had lasted and were considered reasonably successful, b) whether they were continuing despite quite serious concerns or c) whether they had disrupted and the child had moved to live elsewhere.

- Finally, we asked auditors to rate whether, in light of all information available, the effective decision appeared to have been justified by outcomes for the child at the six-month stage.

---

5   Concern about overall progress was measured through a count of social work concerns in relation to child safety, problems at school, behaviour problems and quality of parent care. These variables are described more fully in the next section. There were no significant associations between sibling composition and placement stability at six months.

6   Mann–Whitney U exact tests: going home alone (p=0.03, 0.26, n=66); reunification with siblings not looked after (p=0.007, 0.33, n=66).

Obviously, there is a sense in which these measures tend to be overlapping. Whether or not the decision appeared justified is likely to be a reflection of the extent to which children had settled at home or in care and the degree to which practitioners worried about their progress.[7] Descriptively, however, they provide slightly different angles from which to view a broadly common set of issues.

Overall concerns about the child's progress at six months

Evidence from the case files suggests that there were no recorded concerns during this designated six-month period for just over one-fifth (22%) of children who went home and for just over one-third (35%) of children who were looked after. Table 7.3 shows that documented concerns about children who had returned home were significantly higher in relation to child safety (52%), failure to thrive (12%), although numbers were very small, and the quality of care provided by parents (63%).

Table 7.3 Social work concerns about progress of children at home and in care at six months (n=149) – per cent (n)[8]

Concerns about	Home group	Care group	Sig. (df=1)
Child safety	52 (35)	16 (13)	<0.001
Failure to thrive	12 (8)	(0)	0.01
School problems	44 (30)	41 (33)	0.8
Child behaviour problems	46 (31)	48 (39)	0.9
Care provided by parent/carer	63 (43)	19 (15)	<0.001

7   The measures were indeed quite highly correlated. For example, whether the decision was justified correlated quite closely with overall progress concerns (p<0.001, 0.517, n=143) and especially with whether children were assessed as being settled (p<0.001, 0.793, n=143).

8   Significance assessed using Fisher's exact tests. Factor analysis on the four main items (using varimax rotation and a cut-off of 1 for eigenvalue) produced a single factor solution with the following loadings: child safety 0.779, child behaviour 0.782, school problems .815 and parent care .653. Scale reliability was adequate (Cronbach's alpha 0.752) and, overall, this component explained around 58 per cent of variance. The four items were therefore included in a scale as a proxy measure for 'overall child progress' at six months and will be included in later analyses. 'Failure to thrive' had been excluded due to its very low numbers.

These findings should not be particularly surprising. Decisions to return previously maltreated children to their families are likely to carry greater risks than decisions for them to remain within the looked after system, although our awareness of the risk of children being abused in residential and foster settings is growing (Biehal *et al.* 2010; Sinclair and Gibbs 1998). The findings are also consistent with the literature on reunified children which has highlighted a heightened risk of re-abuse or neglect amongst those who return home (Biehal 2006; King and Taitz 1985; Sinclair *et al.* 2005). This literature also suggests that children returning home tend to fare worse at school and display more emotional and behavioural problems than do those who are fostered or adopted (Lahti 1982; Sinclair *et al.* 2005; Taussig *et al.* 2001). As Table 7.3 suggests, however, these differences were not evident in the early stages of follow-up. Subsequent chapters will consider how these factors played out over three to six years.

Amongst those looked after, Table 7.3 shows evidence of concern about safety for 13 children. Notes provided by auditors indicated a range of concerns. These included scenarios where birth parents had removed children from placements or where concerns arose during children's contact with their birth families. In other instances, concerns centred on the risky behaviours of children, including risks associated with running away, truancy and exclusion at school and self-harming or aggressive behaviour that posed a risk to their safety or to that of others. In one instance, a girl aged 12 who had sustained severe and chronic neglect and sexual and emotional abuse in the past continued to place herself in situations that made her vulnerable to further re-abuse by adults.

Within the *care* group, concerns about the quality of care provided by caregivers was also evident for 15 children. These included concerns arising from marital problems experienced by foster carers or from the perceived capacity of grandparent carers to protect children from the risks of harm associated with birth-parent contact. Other scenarios centred on the relationship between foster carers and children, including their perceived ability to manage challenging behaviour, to provide firm boundaries or to negotiate conflicts between foster children successfully. In one or two cases, these misgivings had been amplified by complaints received from birth parents or children.

For more than one-half of the *home* group, there were evident concerns about safety and parenting over this period and these concerns were mostly overlapping. Looking at the 35 children where safety concerns were documented, around one-fifth related to the reoccurrence of neglectful behaviour and around one in seven to the re-emergence of physical, emotional or sexual abuse. These often coexisted with other child and parent difficulties as the following brief illustrations suggest.

Box 7.1 Case Studies

There was concern that the mother's mental health appeared to be deteriorating. She was also refusing medication. There was concern about the abusive relationships in her life. The social worker comments on the lack of basic provisions in the home and queries who is actually living there. Children's services did not believe she was able to provide for the emotional and physical needs of her child. (Child aged three; re-entered care.)

Home conditions remained very poor. The home was dirty and lacked amenities. Child and sibling had dirty clothes and were unable to have baths. (Child aged nine; placement at home continued despite these concerns.)

Mother did not adhere to agreement regarding required strategies to protect the child from her older sibling or from visitors to the home. The child was placed on the CPR [child protection register] for 'actual emotional harm' prior to being accommodated and, subsequently, 'likelihood of sexual harm' was added to the reasons for remaining on the register. (Child aged four; placement at home continued despite these concerns.)

As the last illustration suggests, concerns were accentuated where parents were unwilling to keep to agreements that had been made prior to reunion. In some instances, this related to the continuance or re-emergence of drug and/or alcohol use or a refusal to comply with treatment programmes. These difficulties were evident in at least one in six cases. For around one in nine, concerns arose from domestic violence, including the reintroduction of violent partners who had left or new relationships that gave cause for concern.

Box 7.2 Case Studies

The mother had got involved in a violent relationship after the children were returned to her care. Her health and emotional well-being deteriorated rapidly and she was unable to cope with all four children. Children's services decided to remove this child and one other sibling to relieve strain and prevent all the family being separated.

The mother's drug use led to a chaotic lifestyle. Her lack of cooperation with children's social care and failure to make appointments meant that the social worker was not able to see the child. (Child aged two; placement at home continued despite concerns.)

In around one in five cases, however, concerns tended to focus on the behaviour of children, sometimes manifested in response to abusive or neglectful parenting. In these circumstances, parents had difficulty managing aggressive behaviour or in imposing boundaries to prevent children truanting from school, running away or staying out without permission.

Box 7.3 Case Studies

Concerns expressed at the end of the six-month period when there were several calls to the police from the mother that were referred to children's services. Child was alleged to be out of control, smashing up the home, fire-setting and being verbally abusive to mother. Children's services and the police believed he was being neglected. (Child aged 11; re-entered care.)

Child returned to a pattern of threatening aggressive behaviour in the home, including assaults to her mother. She started staying out overnight with inappropriate people, placing herself at risk of harm. (Child aged 12; re-entered care at mother's request.)

With respect to social work concerns about the progress of children in the *home* group, documented concerns about child safety and quality of parenting were less likely to be evident where children had returned to a different parent.[9] This was not surprising, given that these parents had generally not been responsible for the child's maltreatment and their capacity to provide care was likely to have been assessed prior to the return being made. Differences were quite marked. In the majority of cases where children had returned to the same parent they had been living with prior to entering care, there were concerns about safety (61%) and parenting (71%). In contrast, return to a different parent had resulted in fewer concerns (21% and 29% of cases respectively).

Looking across the sample as a whole, concerns raised at this stage were frequently accompanied by interventions to ameliorate these difficulties. Most cases were still open at this stage, so only four children were re-referred to children's services. In two-fifths of cases (37%) plans were made to renew or increase support and services. Use of short breaks was rare, however, and only two children accessed this service. Nine children were made subject to new child protection investigations and, as we will see below, over one-third of those who went home (35%) had re-entered care within six months of their return.

Were the children settled at six months?

Using the evidence recorded on file, auditors were asked to assess whether each child's placement was:

- continuing and considered reasonably successful

- continuing, despite quite serious concerns

- or whether the placement had changed and the child had moved to live elsewhere.

Table 7.4 shows that most children had made no moves during the relevant six-month period. While broadly similar proportions of children in both the *home* and *care* groups were likely to have experienced a change of placement, the placements of children at home were significantly less likely to have been assessed as successful and more likely to have been the subject of serious concerns.[10]

---

9   Fisher's exact tests: child safety (p=0.014, n=65); parent care (p=0.01, n=65). Returning to a different parent was not associated with school problems (p=0.76) or child behaviour difficulties (p=0.55) nor with children being more settled in placement at six months; home breakdowns were just as likely for either group (p=0.98).

10   Chi-square, Fisher's exact test: p=0.03, n=149.

Table 7.4 Placement stability of *home* and *care* groups during six-month period – per cent (n)

	Home group	Care group
Placement continued, reasonably successful	47 (32)	64 (52)
Placement continued, quite serious concerns	16 (11)	5 (4)
Placement changed	37 (25)	31 (25)
Total	100 (68)	100 (81)

Amongst those who had changed placements, different patterns were evident for the *home* and *care* groups. Within the *home* group, all but one of those who had changed placements had re-entered the looked after system because arrangements at home had disrupted.[11] To a large degree, the reasons for readmission reflected the wide-ranging safety and parenting concerns discussed above. In some instances, a return to care was viewed as a temporary measure, allowing time to work with parents with a view to a further attempt at reunification. In other cases, there appeared to be an acceptance that further attempts were neither safe nor feasible and that other long-term permanence plans were needed, either in stranger care or with relatives. For around one in five of this group, there was evidence that they had never really settled. Either they had moved between relatives or family friends or they had been left with a relative by a birth parent who had felt unable to cope. These relatives had then, in turn, approached children's services with a request to take the children.

Within the *care* group, patterns of placement change were often different (n=25). Although any placement change for a child is likely to have disruptive effects, almost three-quarters of these children (18) were assessed by auditors as being settled once again at six months. Most of these children had made planned moves from short- to long-term foster placements or had moved on to kinship foster care after assessments had been completed on their relatives.[12] In this respect, they represented planned moves for broadly positive reasons. A further group of children had made a single enforced placement change

---

11   This amounts to 35 per cent of all those who had returned home. In addition, one child moved straight from her birth mother after allegations of physical assault to her birth father.

12   This group accounted for around three in five (11) of the 18 children assessed as settled at six months.

but were assessed as having settled into their new placement at this stage. Reasons for these moves varied and included retirement or marital problems amongst foster carers and conflicts with particular carers or between siblings in placement. However, only two children who were rated as being settled at six months had care careers that had involved two or more placement moves.

If the terms of Table 7.4 were therefore recast to assess the degree to which children were thought to be 'settled' at six months, the differences between the *home* and *care* groups would inevitably be stronger.[13] More than four-fifths (86%) of children in the *care* group were considered to have a settled placement at this stage compared to less than one-half of those who had returned home (47%).

Did the effective decision appear justified at this stage?

Auditors were also asked to assess the evidence on file and judge, in light of the progress that had been made during the six-month period, whether the decision to return a child home or not appeared to be justified by the outcome at this stage.[14] It was not surprising to find, given its overall correlation with placement stability and social work concerns about child progress, that the differences between the *home* and *care* groups were highly significant, as shown in Table 7.5.[15]

Table 7.5 Whether the effective decision appeared justified at six months by *home* and *care* group – per cent (n)

	Home group	Care group
Yes, definitely	35 (24)	89 (72)
Yes, to some extent	12 (8)	10 (8)
Probably not	26.5 (18)	1 (1)
Definitely not	26.5 (18)	(0)
Total	100 (68)	100 (81)

13   Chi-square, Fisher's exact test: p<0.001, n=149.

14   It is worth reiterating at this point that the case file audits were undertaken by highly experienced social work managers and practitioners within the participating councils; practitioners who were well versed in reviewing files and in key aspects of social work decision making.

15   Mann–Whitney U exact test: p<0.001, 0.595, n=149.

Where decisions had been made for the child to remain looked after, there was almost universal agreement amongst auditors that this had been the right decision for them in the context of the circumstances at the time and the progress that had been subsequently made. This was the case, however, for less than one-half of the children who went home (47%), and for more than one-quarter subsequent experience suggested that the decision had definitely not been in their best interests.

Overall, therefore, the findings highlight the risks attached to decisions to reunify maltreated children. During the early months of return, those who went home were much more likely to be exposed to the risk of further maltreatment and experience relatively poor-quality parenting and were also more likely to be unsettled, with more than one-third (35%) re-entering the looked after system. This is not to say, of course, that return should not happen. In any event, as we have seen, this is often not fully within the control of children's services. However, it does reinforce the importance of careful assessment and planning, of weighing carefully factors that may be indicative or counter-indicative of the likelihood of success and of delivering a range of services that may give reunion the best chance of success. It is to the provision of these services that we now turn.

Support and services

Information was collected on frequency of contact with social workers and on a range of services that may have been accessed by children and birth parents during this six-month period.

Social work contact and activity

There was no evidence of any cases having been formally closed during this period. However, some files lacked evidence of contact patterns with children (5%) and birth families (9%). There was only one instance where there had definitely been no contact with a birth parent and this was due to their unavailability and lack of cooperation. Table 7.6 shows patterns of contact with social workers for the *home* and *care* groups.

Table 7.6 Child and birth family contact with social workers during six-month period by *home* and *care* group – per cent (n=149)

	No evidence	At least weekly		At least monthly		Less often		Sig. (p=)
		Home	Care	Home	Care	Home	Care	
Child	5	28	9	57	72	9	15	0.007
Family	9	29	6	54	51	10	31	0.004

Across the sample as a whole, frequency of contact with children and birth families was relatively high. The majority of children (83%) and of birth families (69%) were in at least monthly contact with a social worker. However, frequency of contact was significantly higher for children placed at home. More than one-quarter of these children and parents were in at least weekly contact with a social worker compared to fewer than one in ten of those in the *care* group. With respect to the latter, contact was more in line with statutory visiting requirements.

Monitoring and supervision was a central strand of social work activity for both the *home* (90%) and *care* (89%) groups. Social work assessment was also common to both groups (72% and 79%, respectively). Across the sample as a whole, other areas of social work activity were less common – counselling and mediation (26%), family therapy (6%), parenting skills guidance (50%), child behaviour guidance (41%), practical assistance with housing or equipment (33%) and help with finances or debts (29%). Only in relation to parenting skills guidance and practical assistance were there significant differences between the *home* and *care* groups.[16]

These eight dimensions of social work activity were explored further to see if it would be possible to create a meaningful score measuring the intensity of social work interventions. This could then be used in later analyses to see if it was associated with whether placements lasted or not. Factor analysis identified two components to social work activity.[17] The first component, which we will call 'social work interventions', loaded on to parenting skills guidance (0.737), financial help (0.677), practical help (0.668),

16   Chi-square, continuity correction: parenting skills (p<0.001, df=1, n=149); practical assistance (p=0.01, df=1, n=149). Three-quarters of parents with children at home received parenting advice (74%) compared to just 30 per cent of parents whose children were looked after.

17   Factor analysis was undertaken using varimax rotation, specifying an eigenvalue cut-off of one and a two-factor solution. Cronbach's alpha for 'social work interventions' (0.675) and for 'supervision' (0.490).

child guidance (0.590), family therapy (0.506) and counselling/mediation (0.458). The second component, 'supervision', loaded on to monitoring and supervision (0.722) and assessment (0.674). As as we have seen, monitoring and assessment cut across both the *home* and *care* groups equally (and its reliability was low), we have not used this in analysis. However, the six variables in 'social work interventions' were used to create an 'intervention score' (0–6 scale).

Across the sample as a whole, this analysis showed two things. First, there was a weak correlation between more interventions during this six-month period and greater social work concerns about the overall progress of children. Second, as these concerns were significantly higher for children in the *home* group, these children and families tended to receive higher-intensity interventions and, as we have seen, more frequent social work contact.[18] In this respect (and in common with other research findings on social work contact), social workers were broadly responding to difficulties in the relationships between children and their families through the provision of additional family-focused services (Dixon *et al.* 2006; Sinclair *et al.* 2005).

However, if we focus only on the *home* group for a moment, the evidence may also provide a subtly different story about the relationship between planning and interventions for children who went home. Where social work planning for reunion had been more comprehensive, this tended to be associated with a higher social work intervention score and reduced concerns about child safety and parenting over the six-month period. Furthermore, these children who had received relatively 'good' planning were more likely to have been rated by auditors as being settled at home at six months than were those who had gone home after a 'poor' or truncated planning process.

This may therefore suggest that, while overall concerns may have been higher for those children who had returned home, there may be some follow-through from 'good' planning and the delivery of social work services that support reunion to improved initial outcomes, at least at six months.[19] Although, as we have seen, a comprehensive and well-organized planning process cannot

---

18   Interventions and social work concerns about overall child progress (Kendall's Tau-b: $p=0.02$, t 0.147, $n=149$). Interventions and *home* group (Mann–Whitney U exact test: $p=0.002$, 0.258, $n=149$).

19   The planning variables were presented in Chapter 5 (see Table 5.1). These were summed to provide a planning score. The planning score was positively correlated with a higher social work intervention score (Kendall's Tau-b: $p=0.007$, t 0.262, $n=64$), with children being more settled at six months (Mann–Whitney U exact test: $p=0.01$, $n=64$) and with reduced social work concerns over the six months (Kendall's Tau-b: $p=0.02$, t -0.222, $n=64$).

always be achieved, these findings add further weight to the evidence for doing so whenever it is possible (see also Biehal 2006; Farmer *et al.* 2008).

Services provided to children

Information was also collected on children's access to a range of different services during this six-month period. Table 7.7 shows the services accessed by the sample as a whole and separately by the *home* and *care* groups. No children had accessed a substance misuse service during this period.

Looking at the sample as a whole, the most common services utilized were health services and family centres. The marginal difference between those at *home* and in *care* in use of health services (p=0.07) is likely to reflect the statutory responsibility of councils to assess and monitor the health of looked after children. The greater use of family centres by looked after children tends to reflect their use as venues for supervised contact between children and their families. Only a minority of children accessed therapeutic services during this period, although one-quarter had contact with a mental health professional. However, children in the *care* group were significantly more likely than those at home to have accessed mental health and counselling services.

Table 7.7 Child service use during six months by *home* and *care* group – per cent (n=149)

Child service	All % yes	Home group % yes	Care group % yes	Sig. (df=1)
Education welfare officer	10	12	9	0.59
Education psychologist	17	13	21	0.28
Mental health professional	24	15	31	0.03
Counsellor	11	2	19	0.001
Youth offending service	4	6	3	0.41
Adolescent support service	5	6	4	0.7
Health service	56	47	63	0.07
Family centre	30	19	40	0.01

A count of these services showed that children in the care group were more likely than those at home to have accessed a greater range of services.[20] While just over one-quarter of children (26%) accessed no services at all, this accounted for two-fifths (41%) of the *home* group and just one in seven (14%) of those looked after.[21]

Although child service use was not associated with whether children were assessed as being settled or not at six months (p=0.71), there was an association with social work concerns about overall child progress at this time. A greater range of services were accessed where these concerns were higher.[22]

These findings presented us with a conundrum. We know that overall concerns were greater for children who had gone home and that they were faring less well. We also now know that looked after children accessed more of these services and that accessing these services was associated with greater concerns about child progress.

Further investigation provided an interesting solution. The association between greater child service use and social work concerns about child progress was significant for both the *home* and *care* groups, although it was more strongly significant for the *care* group.[23] This suggested the presence of two sub-groupings within the *care* group: those who were assessed as being 'settled' or 'unsettled' at six months. Where children were rated as 'unsettled', social work concerns about their progress were significantly higher and their use of child services was also higher when compared to those who were rated as 'settled'.[24]

In summary, therefore, children who had returned home were likely to be faring less well at the six-month stage and were subject to greater social work concerns about their progress. This was reflected in more frequent social work contact and more family-focused interventions. Yet these children were accessing fewer child-focused services than were those looked after and two-fifths had accessed no services at all. This inevitably raises

---

20 The count included the first eight services. Family centre was excluded as its use was likely to have been primarily as a venue for contact. Mann–Whitney U exact test: p=0.001, 0.276, n=149.

21 The maximum number of services accessed by children was four (mean service use 1.26).

22 Kendall's tau-b: p=0.001, t 0.228, n=149).

23 Mann–Whitney U exact tests: significance for *care* group (p=0.000, 0.435, n=81); for *home* group (p=0.003, 0.358, n=68).

24 Mann–Whitney U exact tests: social work concerns (p=0.000, 0.48, n=81); use of child services (p=0.01, 0.28, n=81).

the question of whether children at home were failing to access a range of services from which they might have benefited and whether the attention of social workers had been drawn away (in many cases) from the children's needs in favour of managing difficulties within the family as a whole.

Within the *care* group, in contrast, although these children were generally faring better and were subject to fewer concerns overall, higher use of child services was associated most strongly with the greater concerns social workers carried about those who were considered to be relatively unsettled.

Having summarized the findings in this way, we also need to be mindful of subtle differences within the *home* group. Some of these children appeared to be quite settled at home, and being settled was associated with children and parents having received more comprehensive preparation and planning for reunion and a higher level of social work services to support the reunification process.

Services accessed by parents

Table 7.8 shows the services accessed by birth parents during this six-month period. There was evidence on file that sizeable minorities of parents had accessed housing (36%), substance misuse (24%), parenting (24%) and health services. Very few parents appeared to have accessed financial or counselling services or services related to parental offending.

Table 7.8 Parent service use during six months by *home* and *care* group – per cent (n=149)

Parent service	All % yes	Home group % yes	Care group % yes	Sig. (df=1)
Housing	36	46	28	0.04
Financial assistance	11	18	5	0.02
Mental health service	20	15	24	0.22
Counselling	11	15	9	0.30
Health service	21	21	21	1.0
Drug/alcohol service	24	22	25	0.85
Services linked to offending	11	15	9	0.3
Parenting skills training	24	43	9	0.000

Across the sample as a whole, just over one-fifth of parents (22%) did not access services. It was not surprising to find that the birth parents and primary carers of children in the *home* group tended to access more services than was the case for parents of looked after children.[25] As Table 7.8 shows, this was significantly the case in relation to housing (46%), financial services (18%) and parenting skills training (43%). Whether the provision of these services to parents had a bearing on the stability of children at home will be considered in the final section of this chapter.

What factors were associated with children who went home still being there at six months?

We have seen in this chapter that well over one-third of children who went home (37%) had experienced a breakdown within six months of reunion. This section will examine factors that were associated with breakdown. It is important to bear in mind that this is a very small sample of maltreated children for this type of analysis (n=68). We will therefore confine ourselves to descriptive statistics and (wherever we can) situate our findings in the context of wider research findings on reunification. Although our findings should therefore be read with caution, they are nonetheless potentially important with respect to the messages they convey for policy and practice.

Relatively few factors were associated with breakdown or, conversely, with placements continuing 'successfully' at this stage. We considered all the data that were available to us in relation to children's characteristics (including age), the forms of maltreatment they had experienced, their involvement with children's services prior to admission and the family difficulties associated with their entry to care. None of these appeared to have a bearing on how things worked out subsequently. We also looked at how children were faring in the looked after system at the time the effective decision was made and at the degree of social work concerns about their parents' difficulties. Once again, none of these factors was associated with later breakdown.

The only care career factor that was associated with stability at home after six months was the length of time children had been looked after. Where children had returned home quickly, the risk of breakdown was higher.[26] This is consistent with findings from some large-scale US studies on reunification which found that children who returned home within 90 days of admission had the highest rates of re-entry (Courtney *et al.* 1997; Courtney 1995; Wulczyn 1991).

---

25   Count of eight parent services, Mann–Whitney U exact test: p=0.03, 0.177, n=149.

26   Mann–Whitney U exact test: p=0.000, 0.420, n=68.

Going home more slowly gives more time for planning. It was not surprising to find, therefore, that aspects of the assessment and planning that surrounded the effective decision were associated with placement outcome at six months. Children who went home were more likely to be stable at six months where social work planning for the reunion had been proactive and purposeful and where the planning process had been fully inclusive of children and birth parents.[27] The importance of purposeful and inclusive social work planning has been highlighted in the UK literature on reunion, alongside the need for return decisions to be based on clear evidence that positive change in the presenting problems that led to admission has taken place (Aldgate 1980; Biehal 2006; Cleaver 2000; Farmer *et al.* 2008). Consistent with this, reunified children were also much more likely to be stable at six months where there was evidence that the problems that had led to the child's admission had improved by the time the decision to reunify was made.[28] Where there had been no evidence of improvement, over one-half (54%) of placements had broken down within six months compared to just over one-quarter (27%) where there had been signs of improvement.

The support and services provided to children and their families once reunification has taken place have been found to be inconsistent (Biehal 2006; Farmer *et al.* 2008; Sinclair *et al.* 2005). Although the services provided to children over this six-month period were not associated with whether their reunions had endured, this was the case for family-focused social work interventions and parent services. Where families had received more post-reunion services, it was significantly more likely that these placements would be continuing with some degree of success.[29]

In summary, therefore, a number of factors were found to be associated with whether or not children's reunions had remained stable at the six-month stage. They were more likely to continue where:

- children went home more slowly

- planning for reunion was purposeful and inclusive

- the presenting problems that had led to admission had improved

- more family-focused social work interventions were provided

- parents were able to access more services.

---

27   Mann–Whitney U exact tests: purposeful social work planning (p=0.003, 0.350, n=68); inclusive of child (p=0.014, 0.301, n=68); inclusive of birth family (p=0.04, 0.253, n=68).

28   Mann–Whitney U exact test: p=0.006, 0.327, n=68.

29   Mann–Whitney U exact tests: social work intervention score (p=0.001, 0.390, n=68); count of parent services (p=0.007, 0.326, n=68).

Although we need to be cautious about these findings, given the small sample size, their fit with broader findings in the reunification literature should provide greater confidence in their relevance. These findings also convey important messages for reunification practice with maltreated children in relation to the timing, planning and support of the reunion process. How children got on subsequently and the degree to which factors such as these continued to have an influence at final follow-up will be considered in subsequent chapters.

Summary

This chapter compared the progress of children during the first six months after the effective decision (*care* group) or after their return home (*home* group). It considered how the children were getting on and the support and services provided to help them and their families and, within the *home* group, identified factors associated with breakdown and re-entry to the looked after system.

While there were no differences between the *home* and *care* groups in documented concerns about child behaviour or difficulties at school, there were significantly more concerns about child safety and quality of parent care for those who had gone home. Amongst those who went home, however, these concerns were less evident for children who had returned to a different parent.

Within the *care* group, concerns about safety centred on the removal of children from placements by parents, worries about safety of children during family contact or on the risk behaviours of children themselves through, for example, truancy or running away. Concerns about quality of care were varied and included marital difficulties between carers and the ability of relative carers to protect children or arose from conflicts between children and carers.

Within the *home* group, concerns about child safety (52%) and parenting (63%) were generally overlapping. Around one-fifth related to the reoccurrence of neglect and one-seventh to the re-emergence of physical, emotional or sexual abuse. These often coexisted with other parental difficulties, including drug or alcohol use or domestic violence. In around one-fifth of cases, concerns were connected to the behaviour of children, sometimes linked to abusive or neglectful parenting.

Placements of children at home were significantly less likely to have been considered successful at six months. Twenty-five children had moved (37%) and all but one had re-entered the looked after system.

Although there were fewer concerns about the placements of looked after children, 25 children had moved (31%). However, almost three-quarters of these children were rated as settled at six months. In most cases, children had made a single move from a short- to long-term placement or to a placement with relatives mostly for 'positive' reasons. Over four-fifths of the *care* group (86%) were therefore rated as 'settled' at six months compared to less than one-half (47%) of the *home* group.

Across the sample as a whole, frequency of contact with social workers was significantly higher for children living at home. Family-focused social work interventions were higher where concerns about the progress of children were greater and, consequently, these were also significantly higher for children and parents in the *home* group as efforts were made to shore up children's placements at home.

Within the *home* group, however, some children appeared to be quite settled at six months. This appeared more likely where parents and children had received more comprehensive preparation and planning for reunion and more intensive post-reunion social work services.

Children in the *care* group accessed rather more child-focused therapeutic services over this period than did children at home. This was particularly the case for children within the *care* group who were assessed as being 'unsettled'. Two-fifths of children in the *home* group (41%) accessed no services at all.

Birth parents with children at home also accessed more services than did parents of looked after children, especially in relation to housing, financial assistance and parenting skills training.

What factors were associated with breakdown at home? Although we should be cautious about these findings, children who went home were more likely still to be living there at six months where:

- they had been looked after for longer prior to return

- planning for reunion was purposeful and inclusive of children and birth family

- there was evidence that the problems that had led to the child's admission had improved

- after return, more family-focused social work interventions had been provided

- parents had been able to access more services to help them manage.

These findings fit with broader research on reunification and convey some important messages related to the timing, assessment, planning and support of reunion for maltreated children.

8

Placements and Stability at Follow-Up

In the last chapter we described the children's circumstances at six-month follow-up. In this chapter and the next we examine the children's circumstances two to six years later. On average, this was around five years after the relevant admission and four years after their initial return home (for the *home* group) or the date of the effective decision (for the *care* group).[1] This chapter considers where these children were living and whether they appeared to be settled, while the next discusses their well-being at follow-up.

Information on the children's circumstances and progress was available for virtually the whole sample (146, 99%) and was provided through questionnaires completed by their social workers (for 135, 91% of the sample) and/or teachers (for 90, 60% of the sample).

Status at follow-up

Two-thirds of the children (66%) were still looked after at follow-up, the majority of them in the *care* group. However, it was also the case that 41 per cent of the *home* group had either returned to care by this point or had remained on a care order throughout our follow-up period. Table 8.1 provides a picture of the legal status of children at follow-up.

---

1   Time *from the effective decision* to follow-up (n=146): two years (7%), three years (19%), four years (41%), five years (25%), six years (8%). The mean and the mode were both four years. Time *from admission* to follow-up ranged from 42 to 75 months (standard deviation 8.245) for the home group and from 39 to 73 months (standard deviation 8.345) for the care group (39 to 75 months overall). Mean time from admission to follow-up was 57 months for the *home* group and 56 months for the *care* group.

Table 8.1 Legal status at follow-up (n=149)

	Home group n=68 per cent (n)	Care group n=81 per cent (n)
Accommodated	12 (8)	7 (6)
Care order – in care placement	18 (12)	75 (61)
Care order – placed with parent	10 (7)	4 (3)
Interim care order	1 (1)	0
Adopted	0	4 (3)
Freed for adoption	1 (1)	0
Residence/Special Guardianship Order	6 (4)	3 (2)
No legal order/not accommodated	40 (27)	0
Not known	12 (8)	7 (6)

A small number of children in both groups who were still in care were placed with parents on care orders. Other children had moved to permanent placements outside the care system, via adoption, residence or special guardianship orders, and so were unlikely to be reunited with their parents. In one case, however, the residence order was held by the child's father, who had come forward when an adoptive placement was being sought. Amongst those at home, a substantial minority were no longer subject to an order (40%). As might be expected, a much higher proportion of those in the *care* group (79%) were still subject to care orders when compared to those in the *home* group (29%).

Placements at follow-up

Our *census study* identified 589 children who had either been discharged home or placed with parents while remaining on a care order. Of these, 78 per cent were living at home at the end of the study period and most of the remaining children had re-entered care. Among our *survey sample*, just over half of the *home* group (53%) were living with their parents by follow-up, as shown in Table 8.2, although it is likely that at least some of the small group on whom data were missing at this point might have been living with their parents.[2] All of those in the *home* group who were no longer living with parents (n=24) had returned to care at some point (no information was available on the remaining 12%). All three of the children in the *care* group who were known to be living with parents by follow-up were still on care orders.

Table 8.2 Placements at follow-up (n=149)

	Home group n=68 per cent (n)	Care group n=81 per cent (n)
With birth parents	53 (36)	4 (3)
In foster/residential care or semi-independent accommodation	28 (19)	83 (67)
With relatives holding Residence or Special Guardianship Orders	6 (4)	2 (2)
With adoptive parents/ prospective adopters	1 (1)	4 (3)
Lost to follow-up	12 (8)	7 (6)

Very few children were living in residential placements: just five in the *care* group and one child in the *home* group. One-quarter of the fostered children in each group were placed with relatives, as were all of those on residence or special guardianship orders. In total, 13 per cent of the *home* group and 21 per cent of the *care* group were living with members of their extended family.

Among the children who were still looked after, 23 per cent (20) were fostered by relatives. This is double the proportion in kinship care placements (11%) in England as a whole (Department for Children, Schools and Families 2009a). The higher proportion in kinship placements in this study may be due to the fact that, by follow-up, all of the children still in care had been looked after long term (that is, for five years, on average), and kinship foster placements are often intended to be long-term (Sinclair *et al.* 2007) or to provide an alternative to adoption (Sinclair *et al.* 2005). Evidence from the

---

2   If all of those in the *home* group for which these data were missing had been with birth parents, the total proportion of the *home* group living with birth parents at follow-up would be 63 per cent. However, some of these might have since re-entered care in another authority.

US also suggests that children placed in kinship care tend to return home to parents more slowly (e.g. Courtney and Wong 1996; Davis *et al.* 1997; Wells and Guo 1999).

It is therefore possible that reunification is viewed as less urgent by agencies because children are placed with kin and the family adapts to this modus vivendi. Alternatively, it may be the case that there is something different about the circumstances of children in kin and non-kin placements. For example, two studies in the US found that a higher proportion of children in kinship placements had been removed for neglect and, as we saw earlier, children placed due to neglect typically remain longer in care (Grogan-Kaylor 2001; Landsverk *et al.* 1996). However, in our study the children in kinship placements were no more likely to have experienced neglect than those in other types of care placements, possibly because the majority of our maltreated sample had experienced neglect in the past.

Stability

We saw in Chapter 7 that roughly one-third of the children in each group had moved within six months of reunification or the effective decision. For the majority of those in the *care* group, this had been a planned move to a long-term placement, whereas all moves for the *home* group had been placement disruptions. By the time of our second follow-up, three to four years later on average, 65 per cent of the *care* group had been settled in their current placement for two years or more, compared to only 41 per cent of those in the *home* group.

Six months after their initial return home, just under two-thirds (43) of the *home* group were still living with their birth parents. As we saw in the previous chapter, in some cases a return to care had been planned as a temporary measure to allow time for further work before a subsequent attempt at reunification. In other cases, it had become clear that the return was unsafe or unfeasible and that alternative permanency plans were needed. Between this six-month point and the time of our subsequent follow-up, an average of four years after the index reunion, the proportion living with parents had halved. At this point, 25 of the *home* group were living with birth parents, but only one-third (22) had remained with their parents continuously since their index return. Table 8.3 shows the movement in and out of care experienced by many of the *home* group between our six-month and our subsequent follow-up.

Table 8.3 *Home* group: developments over time (n=68) – per cent (n)

Placement status at follow-up				
Placement status six months after reunification	With birth parents	Returned to care	Lost to follow-up	Total at six months
With parents	37 (25)	18 (12)	9 (6)	64 (43)
Returned to care	16 (11)	18 (12)	3 (2)	37 (25)
Total at follow-up	53 (36)	36 (24)	12 (8)	100 (68)

Over half of the *home* group had moved at some point following the index return. Many (25) had moved within six months of reunion and a further 15 had done so by the time of our final follow-up (including three with parents at both follow-up points, who had not been at home continuously).

The *home* group: time to return home

For the *home* group, the time from the relevant admission to the children's (initial) return home during the study period ranged from three days to just over three years.[3] Our *census* study found that children who had been looked after longer by the start of the study were generally less likely to return home during the course of it. As we saw in Chapter 5, length of time in care was one of a range of factors which, cumulatively, contributed to the chance that a child would return home. Consistent with both our *census* study and national statistics, we found that most children in our *survey sample* who returned home did so quite quickly. Half of the children had returned home within six months of admission and 70 per cent had done so within one year, as shown in Table 8.4.

---

3   Time from admission to first return home ranged from three to 1214 days, mean 322.93 days (standard deviation 329.579).

Table 8.4 Time from admission to first return
home for *home* group (n=68)*

Time in months	Per cent (n)
0–3	34 (23)
>3–6	15 (10)
>6–12	21 (14)
>12–24	16 (11)
24–39	15 (10)

*The column does not total 100% due to rounding.

Many other studies have found that the probability of reunification is greatest immediately following placement and that the likelihood of discharge appears to decrease as time in care increases (Bullock *et al.* 1993; Courtney and Wong 1996; Courtney 1994; George 1990; Millham *et al.* 1986). The most recent British data on this issue come from a survey of 7399 looked after children. This study reported that the care system rapidly winnows out short-stay children, so there is a high rate of discharge during the first 50 days of placement but a decline in the likelihood of leaving thereafter (Sinclair *et al.* 2007). As we shall see later, in our discussion of re-entry to care, the rapidity with which return home took place was associated with the subsequent stability of the reunification.

Where strong evidence of neglect was available to decision makers, they were less likely to plan for children to return home quickly. Previous research has found that children who are placed for reasons of physical or sexual abuse tend to return home more quickly than those placed for neglect (Courtney and Wong 1996; Davis *et al.* 1997; Grogan-Kaylor 2001; Landsverk *et al.* 1996; Wells and Guo 1999). This was also true for our sample. We found that children were less likely to return home within two years of the effective decision if there was substantiated evidence of neglect. The experience of neglect was significantly more common for our *care* group (82%) than for our *home* group (57%).[4]

---

4   Chi-square test significant at p=0.004. There was 'some' evidence of neglect in relation to 10 per cent of the *care* group and 18 per cent of the *home* group, but this had not been substantiated.

Re-entry to care

Among the 589 maltreated children in our *census sample* who returned home, 22 per cent were known to have returned to care within the *census* follow-up period. However, we do not know whether all of those at home at the end of the study period had been reunified only once. Among the children in our *survey sample*, 59 per cent (40) were known to have re-entered care at some point between their index reunification and our final follow-up, as shown in Table 8.5.

Table 8.5 Re-entry to care by the *home* group (n=68)

Placement status at follow-up	Per cent (n)
Continuously with birth parents (discharged/placed with parents)	32 (22)
Returned to care at some point	59 (40)
Not known	9 (6)

Due to the considerable variation in the stability experienced by children in the *home* group, for some of our analyses we divided this group into those whose reunification had been stable and those whose reunification had disrupted. The *stable reunion* group comprised the 22 children in the *home* group who had returned to parents and remained there continuously throughout the research period. In contrast, the 38 children in the *unstable reunion* group had been reunified but had returned to care at some point (although 14 of them were back at home again by follow-up). As we saw earlier, the vast majority of the children in the *care* group had remained in care throughout, although three of them had been placed with parents by follow-up.[5]

Both our *census study* and a number of previous studies have found that older children may be more likely to re-enter care (see Biehal 2006).[6] However, this was not the case among children in our *survey sample*, possibly due to the much smaller sample size. Neither the age at which children had

---

5   Two children whose placements had disrupted within six months of return were lost to follow-up. For the sake of clarity, the three children in the *care* group placed with parents at follow-up were excluded from our analyses of stability and well-being at follow-up.

6   Mann–Whitney U test comparing age at index return for reunified (stable) and reunified (unstable) groups non-significant (p=0.997). Mann–Whitney U test comparing age at follow-up for reunified (stable) and reunified (unstable) groups non-significant (p=0.644). In the *census* study, amongst a range of predictors of who would remain at home, older age proved to be significant (p<0.001).

returned home nor their age at follow-up had any bearing on whether or not the reunification had been stable. The mean ages of the children in each group at follow-up are shown in Table 8.6.

Table 8.6 Age at follow-up by outcome group (n=135)

Age in years	Stable reunion (n=22)	Unstable reunion (n=38)	Care group (n=72)
Mean age	11.5	11.79	11.58
Range	4–16	5–17	4–16
(Standard deviation)	(2.94)	(3.57)	(3.24)

In relation to other child-level factors, studies on larger samples of reunified children have indicated that those with more serious behavioural difficulties may be more likely to re-enter care (Barth *et al.* 2007; Farmer *et al.* 2008). However, among the reunified children in our *survey sample*, neither the type of maltreatment experienced prior to admission, the number of forms of maltreatment nor the seriousness of children's behavioural difficulties was associated with the subsequent stability of reunion.

We also examined whether any factors present at the time of the decision to reunify the child were associated with the subsequent stability of the return. Previous research has identified a number of parent-related factors associated with re-entry to care, including mental health problems, social isolation and the number and severity of parental problems. For the children in our *census sample*, re-entry to care was associated with parental substance misuse and domestic violence.[7] In the *survey sample*, the only parent-level factor associated with re-entry to care was substance misuse. Where concerns about parental substance misuse had existed at the time of the decision, 81 per cent of the children subsequently re-entered care.[8] Research in the US has similarly found that where drug or alcohol misuse contributed to the decision to admit the child to care, there is a higher risk of re-entry to care following reunification (Brook and McDonald 2009; Frame, Berrick

---

7   This was one predictor identified through logistic regression (p<0.001). Other predictors were being placed with parents (p<0.001), older age (p<0.001) and period at risk (p=0.005) and whether the child appeared to be 'doing well' (p=0.003).

8   Chi-square test, exact significance p=0.017. Among children whose parents had problems of substance misuse at admission, three-quarters had re-entered care by follow-up, but this association was not statistically significant.

and Brodowski 2000; Hess, Folaron and Jefferson 1992; Jones 1998; Shaw 2006; Terling 1999).

We saw in Chapter 5 that one factor associated with a decision to return children home was the frequency of children's contact with their mothers. On the basis of research findings showing that children who remain in care long-term have less parental contact than those who return home more quickly, it has become widely accepted that parental contact during placement increases the likelihood of reunion. However, this view has been challenged on the grounds that it is not legitimate to view the bivariate relationship between contact and return, which is true at a *descriptive* level, as if it were explanatory (Quinton *et al.* 1997). No compelling evidence exists that it is contact per se that brings about reunification. However, regular contact may indicate the presence of a number of other factors, including a positive relationship and strong attachment between parent and child, parental motivation and social work activity to support reunion (Biehal 2007; Cleaver 2000).

Our findings at follow-up add a further dimension to this debate. Children who had (at least) weekly contact with their mothers prior to returning home were no less likely to subsequently re-enter care than those who had less frequent contact. Just under half (47%) of those who had had at least weekly contact with their mothers prior to reunification remained settled at home, but just over half (53%) subsequently re-entered care. Although frequency of contact while in care may be associated with the likelihood of reunification, it is not related to the likelihood that the reunification will endure.

We also saw earlier that children who re-entered care within six months of returning home were likely to have returned to parents more quickly than those who did not re-enter. By follow-up, an average of four years later, it remained the case that the children who had re-entered care by this point tended to be those who had returned home more quickly. Children who subsequently re-entered care had returned home after a mean of 285 days, whereas those who had remained continuously with their birth parents following the return home had spent a mean of 407 days in care prior to reunification. Analysis of data on large samples of children in the US has similarly found that the likelihood of re-entry to care is higher for those children who had shorter stays in care (Courtney *et al.* 1997; McDonald, Bryson and Poertner 2006; Shaw 2006; Wells and Guo 1999; Wulczyn 2004). However, one study found that children with the shortest stays in care (under 30 days) were no more likely to re-enter following reunion and suggested that this might be related to the reasons for such short admissions (McDonald *et al.* 2006).

The proportion of reunified children in our study who re-entered care was somewhat higher than in other English studies of children in care (Bullock *et al.* 1993; Dickens *et al.* 2007; Farmer and Parker 1991; Packman and Hall 1998). One recent study, for example, which followed up 180 children for two years after they had been reunified with parents, found that 47 per cent of the returns had ended prematurely and that most of these children had returned to care (Farmer *et al.* 2008). These figures are broadly compatible with the 37 per cent return rate found among a sample of foster children tried at home over a period of three years (Sinclair *et al.* 2005) and the slightly higher rate of 'returnees' found among those looked after over the course of a year (Sinclair *et al.* 2007).

Variation in the types of children included in – and the follow-up periods of – different studies makes comparison difficult. The higher rate for our sample may partly be due to the fact that our follow-up period was substantially longer than in these studies – an average of four years from the initial return home – so there was more opportunity for reunifications to disrupt. It is also possible that the high rate of re-entry for our sample is due to the fact that all of these children had entered care as a result of abuse or neglect, whereas this was not the case for the other samples. However, the aforementioned study by Farmer and colleagues found that reunified children whose primary reason for entry to care had been maltreatment were *less* likely than others to re-enter care, possibly because of greater selectivity in determining which children may be returned in these situations and the potentially greater support provided to them. Nevertheless, in that study past experience of physical abuse was one of a number of factors associated with re-entry to care.

It is also possible that our recruitment difficulties led to a degree of sampling bias, as some parents of children who had not returned to care were unwilling to be included in the study. As a result, our *home* group may include a disproportionate number of re-entrants to care. This sampling issue is discussed in Chapter 2. It is likely that the somewhat higher re-entry rate that we found relative to other studies is due to a combination of factors, including not only sampling bias but variation in length of follow-up between studies, the high proportion of substance-misusing parents in our sample and our focus solely on children who had been admitted as a result of maltreatment, rather than on all reunified children.

Children placed with parents

Eight per cent of all children who are looked after in England at any one time are placed with parents while subject to a care order (Department for Children, Schools and Families 2009a). Our *census study* found that maltreated children were less likely to return home, but where they did, they were more likely than other looked after children to do so through placement with parents. Nearly half (44%) of the maltreated children in our *census sample* who had returned home within the two-to-three-year follow-up had been placed with parents, compared to only 14 per cent of those who were not admitted for reasons of maltreatment.[9] Furthermore, the children in our *census sample* who were placed with parents had been in care longer at the time of the return (for 35 months, on average) than those who were discharged home (an average of 21.5 months). The *census study* found little evidence that the profile of children placed with parents was very different from that of children discharged home, in terms of child characteristics or the nature of their difficulties. The main difference was that the families of children placed with parents were more likely to be seen by the social workers as needing 'intensive support' (52% as against 38%).[10]

Our *survey sample* included 27 children who had been placed with parents at some point during our follow-up period. At the point of follow-up, ten of these children were placed with parents, seven of them in the *home* group and three in the *care* group. In total, 35 per cent of the *home* group in our *survey sample* had been placed with parents. Like the children in our *census sample*, those who were placed with parents had been in care longer than those who did not return home on an order. The average time to reunification was 15.4 months for children placed with parents, compared to eight months for those discharged from care.[11] Three-quarters of the children placed with parents had been in care for over six months before they returned home, as shown in Table 8.7.

Table 8.7 Time to return for children placed with parents (n=68) – per cent (n)

	Placed with parents n=24	Not placed with parents n=44
0–3 months	8 (2)	52 (23)
>3–6 months	17 (4)	9 (3)
>6–12 months	25 (6)	21 (9)
1–2 years	29 (7)	9 (4)
2 years or more	21 (5)	11 (5)

9   Chi-square test significant at p<0.001.

10   Social workers answered this question on a four-point scale from 'strongly agree' to 'strongly disagree'. We used all the information in testing the difference (Chi-square for linear association 7.51, df =1, p=0.006).

11   Mann–Whitney U test exact significance p=0.001.

Where a parent's illness or disability had contributed to the index admission, children were less likely to have been placed with parents and more likely to have been discharged home. Parental difficulties prior to the admission, the children's ages at admission and the type of maltreatment experienced were not associated with the likelihood of returning home on an order. However, our *census* study identified considerable local variation in the use of placement with parents, which ranged from 1 to 17 per cent across authorities.

As we saw in Chapter 5, assessment and planning for reunion had been particularly strong for children who had been placed with parents. Nevertheless, 44 per cent (11) of the children placed with parents re-entered a care placement at some point during our follow-up period. A few of these children had subsequently returned home yet again. At the point of follow-up, care orders had been discharged for nearly one-third of the children who had been placed with parents, but just over one-quarter had returned to care, as shown in Table 8.8.

Table 8.8 Status at follow-up for children ever placed with parents during the research period (n=26)[12] – per cent (n)

Placed with parents	Discharged to parent	In a care placement	Lost to follow-up
37 (10)	30 (8)	26 (7)	4 (1)

At this point, an average of four years after the index return, those who had been placed with parents were nearly twice as likely to be in a care placement (65%) than were those who had not returned home on an order (35%) This was also the case for our much larger *census sample*, as 31 per cent of children placed with parents subsequently re-entered care compared to 15 per cent those discharged home.[13] This suggests that in many cases, reunification using the placement-with-parents route may have been attempted in unpropitious circumstances, where local authorities had continuing concerns about the care that the children would be likely to receive at home and wished to monitor their well-being. It is also likely that children placed with parents might be more likely to re-enter care because they were under a greater surveillance than those who were no longer on care orders or accommodated. For children placed with parents, there

---

12 One child previously placed with parents had moved to permanence outside the care system.

13 Chi-square tests, exact significance p=0.034 for *survey sample*; p<0.001 for *census sample*.

was therefore a greater chance that any subsequent maltreatment would be detected and this might trigger a return to care. This does, of course, raise questions about the level of maltreatment that may remain undetected in circumstances where children had been discharged home and the case subsequently closed.

Planning and the stability of reunions

In Chapter 7 we investigated the association between the nature of planning and support for reunification and the stability of reunion during the first six months after reunification. These factors continued to have some resonance over the entire follow-up period, although not all of them continued to meet the threshold for significance. Children in our *home* group were more likely to have remained continuously with their parents by our final follow-up where:

- planning for reunion had involved purposeful social work activity (p=0.02) and was inclusive of the child (p=0.003)
- the presenting problems that had led to the child's admission appeared to have improved prior to reunion (p=0.055)
- more family-focused social work interventions had been provided over the first six months after reunion (p=0.002)
- parents had received more services to assist them at that stage (p=0.057).

These findings suggest that this early period may be important and that getting things right at that stage may make some difference to stability in the longer term. The findings also reinforce some of the key messages that have arisen from reunification research, including the need for purposeful and inclusive planning, evidence that problems have changed for the better and for the provision of services of sufficient intensity to enhance the prospects of success.

In general terms, as we will see below, use of specialist services was associated with children and families being in greater difficulty. We also need to bear in mind, therefore, that provision of these services may flow from the determination of some social workers to keep children in the community (perhaps at all costs), even where they are not apparently doing very well in other respects. Although stability is one measure of a 'good' outcome, being stable at home is not necessarily the same thing as being happy or doing well at home. The well-being of these children will be considered in our next chapter.

Support services and stability

We asked social workers to indicate whether or not any support services had been provided to children or parents at any point over the past three years. Given the length of time involved, the information they provided on this issue is likely to be approximate.

In Chapter 7, we reported that children in our *care* group had accessed more in the way of child-focused services during the first six months after the effective decision than those in our *home* group. By the time of our final follow-up, the children in our *home* group were more likely to have used services intended to address problems of offending or substance misuse services than those in our *care* group, suggesting that children in the *home* group were more likely to have been involved in these activities than those who remained in care.[14] Although a higher proportion of those in the *unstable reunion* group used these services compared to those in the *stable reunion* group, this difference was not significant.

Children in the *home* group were also more likely than those in the *care* group to have received counselling, education welfare and family support services during the three years prior to follow-up in an attempt to maintain children's placements with their families.[15] Again, this suggests that the children who returned home were more likely to have experienced difficulties than those who remained in care. Children in the *stable reunion* group had been significantly more likely to receive counselling than those in the *unstable reunion* group.[16] Perhaps surprisingly, children who had been placed with parents were no more likely to receive any of the above services than those who had been discharged when they returned home.

Parents had also received a range of support services in the three years prior to our final follow-up. Nearly half of them (47%) had received support with housing and a smaller number had accessed a range of other services at some stage, including counselling (30%), mental health services (27%), parent training (29%) and drug or alcohol services (23%). Although there were few significant differences in the nature of services accessed by parents in our three outcome groups, parents in the *stable reunion* group were rather more likely to have accessed housing services and parenting skills training

---

14   Chi-square exact significance for substance misuse services (p=0.003, n=126); for youth offending service (p=0.006; n=126).

15   Chi-square exact significance for counselling (p=0.059; n=119); education welfare (p=0.005, n=118) and family support services (p=0.002, n=125).

16   Mann–Whitney U exact test used to compare service use for *stable* and *unstable reunion* groups. The only significant difference lay in relation to counselling services, significant at p=0.023.

than were parents in the *care* group.[17] Again this is likely to reflect efforts to maintain the stability of home placements.

Conclusion

Reunification is generally viewed as a desirable outcome for children. In some cases, family courts may insist on an attempt at reunification before alternative plans for permanence are agreed, while in others social workers may be over-optimistic about the presumed benefits of reunification for the child (Biehal *et al.* 2010). However, by the time of our follow-up, an average of four years after reunification, 59 per cent of the children who were reunified had returned to care at some point, although a few were subsequently reunified yet again. Only one-third of those who returned home had remained there continuously throughout. Reunification had not, therefore, provided stability for over half of the children who returned home. Why should this be so?

One possible explanation may lie in the apparently high thresholds for entry to care in the authorities in which many of the children in this study lived. The vast majority of the children in this study were on care orders and, as other research has shown, care proceedings are often undertaken as a last resort. It is extremely rare for care proceedings to be taken unnecessarily (Hunt *et al.* 1999; Masson *et al.* 2008). High thresholds for admission may be influenced not only by concern about resources but by the bleak view of the care system evident in much public and professional debate.

Furthermore, thresholds for admission may vary across local authorities, just as thresholds for the investigation of maltreatment may do (Gibbons, Conroy and Bell 1995). This suggests that decisions about the interventions necessary to safeguard children are not determined solely by considerations of need and risk of harm. These individual decisions are also shaped by local policy and by authority-level or team-level practice, and local policy and practice are inevitably underpinned by concerns about the management of resources as well as by professional considerations. Decisions about the best way to safeguard individual children are thus to some degree shaped by concerns about gatekeeping resources as well as by assessments of risk. This local variation may have implications for the stability of reunification. Studies of large administrative datasets in both England and the US have found that,

---

17 Chi-square exact significance for *stable reunion* and *care* groups: housing services (p=0.04, n=104); parent skills training (p=0.005, n=98). Although differences in use of these services for parents in the *stable* and *unstable reunion* groups were observable (70% compared to 48% and 52% compared to 35%, respectively), these differences were not significant (p=0.22 and p=0.35). This was also the case for differences between the *unstable reunion* and *care* groups.

in authorities which admit a relatively small proportion of children to care or accommodation, those children who do enter tend to have very serious difficulties and are therefore less likely to be reunified with parents (Dickens *et al.* 2007; Wulczyn 1991). Our evidence suggests that, where such children with chronic and serious difficulties *are* reunified, there is a high risk that reunification may not endure.

As we saw in Chapter 3, the majority of the children in our sample had experienced multiple forms of maltreatment as well as other adversities including, in many cases, living in homes marked by domestic violence and with parents who had serious substance misuse or mental health problems. Despite the seriousness and persistence of their difficulties, many children experiencing neglect and emotional abuse had been supported in their families for a long time without decisive action. The threshold for admission appeared to have been high in these cases. In this context, in which the majority of the maltreated children who are reunified have experienced very serious difficulties over a lengthy period of time, it is perhaps not surprising that so many attempts at reunification failed.

It is also possible that the quality of planning for reunion might influence the stability of the return. In Chapter 7 we examined the circumstances in which children appeared to have remained settled at home for at least six months after the reunion occurred. In these cases, planning for reunion had been purposeful, the presenting problems that had led to the admission had improved and family-focused services had been provided. In these reunions that had endured for at least six months, the planning process had been inclusive of parents and children. It is possible, of course, that this kind of proactive planning was more readily undertaken in cases where reunion was thought likely to be successful and that it was those parents who were most willing to change who had been successfully engaged by social workers. Nevertheless, nearly one-third (11) of the children who had been settled with their birth parents six months after reunion subsequently returned to the care system.

The chance of a stable return may also be linked to the timing of reunion. As we have seen, the children who had returned home sooner were more likely to re-enter care. It is possible that they had been reunified more quickly because they were considered to be at less risk of re-abuse or neglect. Alternatively, they may have been returned to parents without an adequate assessment as to whether reunion would benefit the child or sufficient plans being made to support the return. The implication here is not that children should necessarily remain longer in care prior to reunion in order to reduce the risk of re-entry. However, where circumstances are serious enough for a child to be admitted to care, it is essential that any interventions with the family have sufficient time to achieve enduring change.

Where local authorities were more cautious about discharging children home to parents and instead made use of placement with parents, children tended to remain in care longer prior to reunification. Assessment and planning for return had typically been stronger for this group. In these circumstances, it was likely that the presence of a care order would have been helpful to social workers. Nevertheless, even where children were placed with parents on an order, 44 per cent re-entered care at some point, although it is possible that the greater surveillance of such children may have made re-entry more likely.

Finally, the likelihood of a stable reunion may be influenced by the services provided to support it. Although our evidence is not strongly in this direction, positive improvement in parent problems, effective planning and the provision of services during the initial six months after reunification had some association with home placements continuing at follow-up. As such, well-planned and well-supported returns appeared to have some positive effects. Stability, however, is only one way of measuring a 'good' outcome. Provision of services may also be associated with what the social worker thinks is best for the child rather than what the child wants. Being at home is not the same as being happy or doing well at home (the subject of our next chapter). Overall, the provision of services was associated with children and families being in difficulty. In this respect, the provision of more intensive services was likely to have been associated with shoring up home placements that might otherwise have been in jeopardy.

Our study cannot report in detail on the nature, intensity and duration of support services that were actually provided over the follow-up period. Other studies, however, have suggested that the provision of services may be inadequate. For example, a study of children in foster care found that repeated efforts were sometimes made to return children home, even when this was not in their best interests. Once they returned, the children rarely received further social work intervention (Sinclair et al. 2005). Other studies have similarly found that follow-up support after reunification may be patchy (Farmer et al. 2008; Ward et al. 2004). While good planning and reunification support are clearly a good thing, the evidence from this and other studies suggest that this is highly variable in practice. In addition, the findings here remind us that while they may help to maintain children at home, it is also important to show that they help to improve children's welfare and well-being.

Our findings on the stability of placements after reunification have a number of implications. First, where thresholds for entry to care or accommodation are high, even for children experiencing chronic and serious maltreatment, reunification may not have a high chance of success. Apart from any other risks incurred, reunification may increase instability in children's lives as they move between home and care. These findings raise important questions about decision making by social workers and the courts. Second, when it appears to be in children's best interests to reunify them with their parents, careful and thorough assessment is undoubtedly needed. Third, in the context of the serious and often chronic difficulties experienced by maltreated children, it is essential that appropriate support services are provided to children and families, that these are comprehensive and that they last as long as needed. Where children have experienced chronic maltreatment, including persistent emotional abuse and neglect, both children and parents may require long-term support if children are to remain at home successfully.

Unsuccessful attempts at reunification may increase delay in providing permanent placements for those children who cannot safely return home. An unstable reunification, or repeated attempts at reunification, may make it difficult to achieve effective permanency planning at an early enough stage in a child's life, so that some children lose their chance of adoption or a stable placement in foster care (Biehal *et al.* 2010; Selwyn *et al.* 2006; Ward, Munro and Dearden 2006).

Summary

This chapter presents data on placements, stability and change by follow-up, which was four years (on average) after the index return home of the *home* group or, for the *care* group, the decision that they should remain in care.

Although all children in the *home* group had (by definition) returned home, only just over half (53%) were known to be living with a birth parent at follow-up. Amongst those who had gone home, one-half did so within six months of admission and a majority (70%) within one year. Return within the study timeframe was less likely for children who had experienced neglect rather than other forms of maltreatment.

As expected, a majority of those who had not returned home within two years of admission (*care* group) were still living in foster or residential placements at follow-up (83%). Overall, the children in the *care* group had experienced more settled care careers by follow-up than those in the *home* group. Two-thirds had been in their placements for two years or more (65%) compared to 41 per cent of those in the *home* group.

In total, over one-half (59%) of the *home* group were known to have re-entered the looked after system at some point during the follow-up period, although some returned home again subsequently. One-fifth of children in the *home* group had experienced more than one reunification during the follow-up period. Only one-third (32%) were known to have remained with their parents throughout.

The rate of re-entry to care is higher for this sample than that found in some other studies of reunified children. While this may in part be due to the greater length of follow-up in this study, it is more likely to relate to the nature of the sample, the fact that all of these children entered care for reasons of abuse or neglect and the fact that many of their parents had problems of substance misuse, which has been found to increase the risk of re-entry to care by some other studies. The findings therefore point to the difficulties that may be associated with achieving successful reunions for maltreated children.

In total, 27 of the children (35% of those in the *home* group and 4% of those in the *care* group) had returned home while their care order remained in force (placed with parents) at some point during our follow-up period. Like the children in our *census sample*, those who were placed with parents had been in care longer prior to their initial return home (15.4 months, on average) than those who did not return home on an order (eight months).

Children who had been placed with parents were more likely to be in care at follow-up (65%) than those who had not returned home on an order (35%). This suggests that placement with parents may be used when returning children to more difficult family circumstances. However, such children may also be more likely to return to care because they are more closely monitored than those who are no longer on care orders or accommodated, so it is more likely that any subsequent maltreatment will be detected.

Child behavioural services were accessed more commonly by children at home and family support services/counsellors/education welfare services were more commonly accessed by children who were still at home at follow-up, reflecting attempts to shore up home placements.

With respect to parent services, there were few significant differences between our outcome groups. However, parents in the *stable reunion* group were more likely to have accessed help with housing and attended parenting skills training than were parents of children in the *care* group.

9

Well-Being and Progress at Follow-Up

This chapter examines the well-being of children in the *survey sample* at follow-up. Drawing on social worker assessments of well-being and progress and teacher ratings of child adjustment and educational progress, it explores whether children who returned home fared 'better' or 'worse' than those who remained looked after. As in the last chapter, the follow-up period was, on average, four years after children in the *home* group were reunified with their families or, for those in the *care* group, after the effective decision was taken.

As we saw in the previous chapter, although just over half (53%, 36) of our original *home* group were living with parents at the point of follow-up, only around one-third of them (22) had lived continuously with a parent since their index return.[1] For reasons set out in that chapter, we divided the children in the *home* group into two sub-groups. In some analyses of well-being at follow-up, therefore, we refer to three outcome groups:

- *Reunified (stable)* group: children who had returned to parents and stayed there (n=22).

- *Reunified (unstable)* group: children who had been reunified but had returned to care at some point, although some were at home again by follow-up (n=38). Just over one-third (14) of these children had returned to their parents again by follow-up and the majority of the others (19) were in care placements.

- *Care* group: children who had remained in care placements throughout or, in five cases, had left care on residence or adoption orders (n=72).

---

1   These 22 children accounted for 32 per cent of the original *home* group (n=68) and 37 per cent of those on whom information from social workers was available at follow-up (n=60).

Emotional and behavioural problems

We asked social workers about the extent to which each child displayed a number of specific difficulties at follow-up, including substance misuse, aggressive behaviour, involvement in offending, running away, eating problems, depression, self-harm and unplanned pregnancy of self or others. The only significant differences between the groups lay in three areas. Children in the *home* group were more likely to have misused alcohol (22%, compared to 5% in the *care* group), drugs (14%, compared to 4% in the *care* group) and to have committed offences (24%, compared to 8% in the *care* group).[2]

Within the *home* group, the *stable reunion* group appeared slightly more likely to be involved in offending (27% of that group) than the *unstable reunion* group (22%).[3] In contrast, reports of alcohol misuse were twice as common among young people in the *unstable reunion* group (28%) than among the *stable reunion* group (14%).

Consistent with previous research findings, children who had experienced physical abuse prior to the relevant admission were also more likely to have displayed a number of other externalizing behaviours (Cicchetti and Toth 1995; Thornberry 1995; Widom and Ames 1994), as shown in Table 9.1.

Table 9.1 Physically abused children displaying problem behaviours at follow-up (n=135) – per cent[4]

	Evidence of physical abuse	No evidence of physical abuse	Sig. p=
Misuse of alcohol	18	6	0.037
Misuse of drugs	15	2	0.015
Committing offences	22	6	0.012
Physically aggressive	46	24	0.010

Children who had experienced physical abuse were nearly twice as likely to be physically aggressive as those not known to have experienced physical abuse, a strong association previously identified in other studies (Cicchetti

---

2   Chi-square tests significant at p=0.007 for alcohol, p=0.016 for drugs and p=0.014 for offending.

3   Chi-square tests for outcome groups by offending significant at p=0.031; outcome groups by alcohol misuse significant at p=0.004.

4   Kruskal–Wallis exact test significant at p=0.027.

and Toth 1995; Manly, Cicchetti and Barnett 1994). Around one-fifth of them were known to be involved in offending and/or misusing alcohol and 15 per cent were misusing drugs.

There were no significant gender differences in relation to the above behaviours. Around one-quarter of those living with birth parents were reported to be involved in offending, compared to around one in ten of those living with relatives or in non-relative care placements. Similarly one-fifth of those living with birth parents at follow-up were reported to be misusing alcohol, compared to one in ten of those in other placements, and 16 per cent of those with birth parents were known to be misusing drugs, compared to 6 per cent of those in non-relative care and 12 per cent of those living with relatives.

We also compared the children's scores for well-being and social relationships using a measure based on one developed for the Looking After Children programme and subsequently incorporated into the government's specification for the Integrated Children's System (Ward 1995). Each item comprised a four-point scale. There were no significant differences between the groups in relation to questions about their relationships with peers (whether they had close friendships, bullied other children or were bullied or their behaviour in social situations).

However, children who remained in care had significantly better mean scores for health. They were also more likely to be reported to have close adult ties and, perhaps surprisingly, there was no significant difference in this respect between those whose reunion had been stable and those who had re-entered care. In addition, those in the *care* group were also considered by social workers and teachers to be more likely to have had a range of special skills, interests and hobbies.[5]

Progress in the past three years

At follow-up, we asked social workers to rate how the children were doing in relation to the five *Every Child Matters* outcome areas on a four-point scale ranging from 'very well' to 'not at all well'. Mean scores were more positive for the *care* group on all dimensions: being healthy; staying safe; enjoying and achieving; making a positive contribution (pro-social behaviour); and economic well-being (realizing their potential).[6]

---

5   Chi-square tests significant at p=0.013 for health, p=0.001 for positive adult ties and p=0.046 for special skills and interests.

6   Kruskal–Wallis exact test significant at p<0.001 for being healthy, p=0.001 for staying safe, enjoying and achieving and making a positive contribution and p=0.005 for economic well-being.

For all of these outcome areas and for the total score, children who had remained in care were doing significantly better than those who had returned home. The *unstable reunion* group generally had higher (that is, worse) mean scores on all dimensions compared to the *stable reunion* group, but these differences between the two groups were not statistically significant.

It was unclear from the social workers' replies precisely how many of the children had been re-abused or again neglected *after* they were reunited with their parents. However, as we saw in Chapter 7, within six months of reunification, social work concerns about child safety existed for half of the reunified children. Among those who re-entered care in this initial period, re-abuse or neglect was a factor in the re-entry of at least one-third of the children. By follow-up, over half of the children reunified with parents had returned to care. It seems likely that in many of these cases re-entry to care would have been prompted by further evidence of maltreatment.

Evidence from other studies would support this interpretation. One study, for example, found that social workers were concerned about the further maltreatment of 46 per cent of reunified children within a two-year period (Farmer *et al.* 2008), while another found that 42 per cent had again been maltreated within three years of reunification (Sinclair *et al.* 2005). Research in the US has similarly found that a slightly lower proportion of children reunified with parents (37%) were thought to have experienced further maltreatment after their return home, although not all of these reports of maltreatment had been substantiated (Jonson-Reid 2003). However, an unsubstantiated allegation of maltreatment is not the same as an unfounded allegation, as maltreatment may subsequently be substantiated and even unsubstantiated allegations have been found to be associated with behavioural problems in children similar to those among children known to have been maltreated (Jonson-Reid 2003). A recent systematic review found that the most important risk factors for the recurrence of maltreatment were neglect (as opposed to other forms of maltreatment), the number of episodes of previous maltreatment, parental conflict and parental mental health problems (Hindley, Ramchandani and Jones 2006).

We also asked social workers for an overall rating of the children's progress over the previous three years on a five-point scale ranging from 'doing very well' (1) to 'doing very poorly' (5). We advised that 'doing very well' should be indicated where children were settled at home or in placement, appeared well cared for, were doing well at school and where there were no serious concerns about the child's safety, behaviour and family relationships. In contrast, social workers were asked to indicate that children were at the opposite end of this scale, 'doing very poorly,' if they were very unsettled, frequently missed school or where serious concerns existed.

On average, children who had remained in care had significantly better scores for progress over the previous three years (1.64) than those who had returned home (2.46). Table 9.2 compares the scores for children in our three outcome groups, with lower scores indicating better progress.

Table 9.2 Overall progress during last three years
by outcome group (n=132) – per cent*

	Care group	Reunified (stable)	Reunified (unstable)
Doing very well/quite well	84	62	53
Average	11	10	22
Doing quite poorly/very poorly	5	29	25
Mean score	1.58	2.29	2.47

*Not all columns total 100 per cent due to rounding.

There was a highly significant difference between total score for the *care* group and the *unstable reunion* group. Although there was also a difference between the *care* group and the *stable reunion* group, this did not quite reach significance (p=0.069).[7] However, when we compared ratings for children living with parents at follow-up with scores for those who were not, we found that children living with parents were doing significantly worse on this measure of overall progress.[8]

A global assessment of outcome

So far, our analyses have indicated that the children in our *care* group were doing better than the *home* group on a range of measures of behavioural and emotional functioning and of social relationships. In order to keep the number of analyses as low as possible and thus reduce the risk of chance findings, we created a composite measure of outcome, which essentially measures the overall well-being of the children at follow-up. It comprises:

---

7   Mann–Whitney U exact test for progress score by *home* or *care* group significant at p=0.005. Kruskal–Wallis exact test used to compare scores by outcome group, significant at p=0.001. Tukey tests showed that the significant difference lay between the care group and the unstable reunification group (p<0.001). There was no significant difference between scores for the stable and unstable reunification groups (p=0.447).

8   Mann–Whitney U exact test significant at p=0.03.

- a measure of the extent to which the children behaved in ways likely to put themselves or others at risk of harm
- a measure of how well they were doing in terms of the five key outcomes set out in *Every Child Matters*
- a measure of school adjustment
- a teacher measure of child adjustment
- a broad measure of their behavioural and emotional well-being.

The first two of these measures were derived from social work ratings and have been described above. The next two were derived from ratings or information provided by the children's teachers. The measure of behavioural and emotional well-being is an average of both teacher and social worker ratings. Each of these scores is given the same weighting in creating the final measure. After discussion we decided to omit those children for whom we did not have a social work questionnaire.[9] We then had outcome scores for 133 children (89% of the sample). Appendix A describes the creation and validation of this measure.

This measure of overall well-being at follow-up indicated that the group who returned home had significantly worse (lower) mean scores for well-being at follow-up than those who had not, as Table 9.3 shows.

Table 9.3 Mean scores for outcome by group (n=133)

	Home group	Care group	Sig. (p=)
Mean score	8.6	10.6	0.026
Range	0.5–17.2	0.7–18	
Standard deviation	4.663	3.758	

Maltreated children who remained in care therefore did significantly better, in terms of our overall measure of well-being, than those who had returned home. This difference in outcomes was particularly marked in relation to our *unstable reunion* group, whose mean outcome score was significantly worse (8.1) than that for the *stable reunion* group (9.4). Yet despite the fact that the *stable reunion* group was likely to comprise those who had had the best

---

9   This was a pragmatic compromise. A decision to insist on the presence of both teacher and social worker questionnaires would have given a sample size of 90 and this was thought too small. The teacher questionnaires did not cover risky behaviour or the *Every Child Matters* outcomes and we judged these essential to the validity of the measure.

chance of doing well at home, the *care* group nevertheless had significantly more positive outcomes.[10] In the next chapter we will explore the reasons for these results.

Education

Our survey of teachers provided detailed information on the educational progress of these children and on the educational support and encouragement provided by parents and carers. Some information on educational progress was also collected from social workers. Where case information was available from both teachers and social workers, the teacher perspective has been given priority.

There were some differences in the education placements of the children in our three outcome groups, as shown in Table 9.4.

Table 9.4 Educational placement at follow-up by outcome group – per cent (n)*

	Reunified (stable)	Reunified (unstable)	Care	All
Mainstream primary	46 (10)	46 (17)	35 (25)	40 (52)
Mainstream secondary	36 (8)	27 (10)	46 (33)	39 (51)
Special school (day)	0	3 (1)	10 (7)	6 (8)
Pupil referral unit	5 (1)	3 (1)	0	2 (2)
Residential school	0	3 (1)	4 (3)	3 (4)
Pre-school education	5 (1)	0	3 (2)	2 (3)
Other	0	14 (5)	3 (2)	5 (7)
Not in education	9 (2)	5 (2)	0	3 (4)
Total	101 (22)	101 (37)	101 (72)	100 (131)

*Not all columns total 100 per cent due to rounding.

The majority of children in both the *home* and *care* groups were attending mainstream primary or secondary education (79% overall). A slightly higher proportion of *care* group children were attending special schools (10%

---

10   Mann–Whitney U exact test of global well-being score by *home* and *care* groups significant at p=0.026. Kruskal–Wallis test of global score by *stable reunion*, *unstable reunion* and *care* groups significant at p=0.033.

compared to 3% of the *home* group), reflecting the higher proportion of children with learning disabilities who had remained looked after. Those in 'other' education included children who were in alternative forms of education, such as provision at children's centres, bespoke one-to-one tuition and special units for behavioural problems. In comparison to children in the *care* group, those in the *home* group were rather less likely to be in mainstream secondary education or special schools and rather more likely to be in pupil referral units, alternative forms of education or, in four cases, not in education (whereas all those in the *care* group were in some form of education).[11]

Children who had gone home (whether or not they were still there at follow-up) had greater problems with attendance than did children in the *care* group.[12] One-fifth of those in the *stable reunion* group (19%) and a similar proportion in the *unstable reunion* group (18%) had a pattern of frequent non-attendance compared to just 4 per cent of children in the *care* group.

Educational progress

Two measures were devised to assess progress (rather than attainment) in education. The first asked teachers to rate the progress made by the children in the last school year relative to that for their classmates (n=78). Although only a small minority had made above-average progress (13%), over one-half were reported to have made average progress (55%). Almost one-third, however, were performing below the average for their cohort (32%). There were no significant differences in this pattern for our outcome groups (p=0.9) nor, at follow-up, for children living with birth parents, relatives or unrelated substitute carers (p=0.67).

The second approach asked teachers and social workers to rate, for the most recent relevant school year, whether the children's progress matched the expectations that they had for them. This increased the available sample size to 126, although the knowledge of social workers would have been less precise than that of teachers. Just over one-third of children (37%) were rated as having made better than expected progress; for just under half (47%) it was in line with expectations; and for less than one-fifth (17%) progress was worse than expected. Once again, there were no significant differences between our outcome groups (p=0.78).

---

11   Although these differences appear significant using Fisher's exact tests (p=0.02), it would be unwise to place too much store by them. The outcome groups did not differ significantly by age (p=0.89).

12   Mann–Whitney U exact tests comparing attendance for *care* group with *stable reunion home* group (p=0.016, n=92) and *unstable home* group (p=0.03, n=105).

Overall, therefore, the majority of children appeared to be performing at an average level both in relation to the expectations held for them and in relation to a cohort of same-age children in their local community. This did not vary significantly for those who had been reunified and those who had not. Although these findings offer some encouragement, given that the children we are considering tend to achieve poor outcomes relative to their peers in the wider population, the findings differ from those generated through the small amount of work that has so far compared looked after and reunified children. This research has suggested that those who return home tend to fare worse at school when compared to those in foster care (Sinclair *et al.* 2005; Taussig *et al.* 2001).

Support for children's education

Teachers were asked to rate, on a scale of one to four, the support and encouragement being provided by parents or carers for their children's education. This assessment covered nine areas of support that schools regard as important to home–school relationships, including encouragement of regular attendance and homework completion, support for the school's conduct code and for participation in extra-curricular activities, ensuring homework completion, attending parents' evenings and important school events, responding to school communications and providing explanations for absence.

For the sample as a whole, there was perceived to be quite a good degree of support for children's education, with over half of the children in the sample being supported in all areas. Support was particularly strong in relation to attendance and reinforcement of acceptable behaviour at school. However, there were significant differences in support for children in relation to where they were living at follow-up. The key difference, according to teachers, was in the additional support provided by unrelated caregivers. This was most marked in comparison to that provided by birth parents and the differences were significant in most areas.[13] However, in a smaller number of areas the support provided by unrelated carers was also rated as being higher than that provided by relative carers. These differences were significant in relation to ensuring attendance, explaining child absences, attending school events and, to a marginal extent, in attending parents' evenings.[14]

---

13 Mann–Whitney U exact tests comparing unrelated carers and birth parents: attendance (p=0.06), explaining absences (p=0.01), homework completion (p=0.002), attending parent evenings (p=0.000) or important school events (p=0.004), observing the conduct code (p=0.004) and responding to school requests (p=0.002).

14 Mann–Whitney U exact tests comparing unrelated and relative carers: ensuring attendance (p=0.003), explaining child absences (p=0.015), attending school events (p=0.03) and attending parent evenings (p=0.06).

Overall, therefore, teacher assessments suggest that children who were in care at follow-up received better support with their education from their caregivers. Higher-quality support was being provided for children's education by unrelated (mostly foster) carers in comparison to that provided by either birth parents or relative carers. However, as we have seen, this additional support was not reflected in the educational progress of children at follow-up. Whether it will do so as these children progress through their education remains an open question.

Conclusion

On average, children who remained in care did significantly better on measures of health, well-being, outcomes and overall progress than those who had experienced an unsuccessful reunification. They also did better on measures of health and on the total score for the *Every Child Matters* outcome areas than those whose reunification had been stable.

Progress and outcomes were also associated with whether or not children (in either the *stable* or *unstable reunion* groups) were living with parents at the point of follow-up. When we compared children living with parents at follow-up to those who were not, we found that they were doing significantly worse in relation to being healthy and staying safe, as well as on the total score for the five outcome measures and on ratings of overall progress compared to those who were not living with parents at this point.[15] However, these differences in well-being between the groups were not reflected in any major differences in educational progress at this stage in the children's lives.

When we combined these and other measures into a global outcome score measuring well-being at follow-up, it remained clear that children who remained continuously in care did significantly better than those who returned home. In the next chapter we explore whether any factors, other than returning home or remaining in care, were associated with the children's outcome scores at follow-up and discuss the implications of these findings.

Summary

At follow-up we examined progress in relation both to our *home* and *care* groups and to three outcome groups:

1. *reunified (stable)* (n=22): children who returned to parents and stayed there

---

15 Mann–Whitney U test significant at p=0.029.

2. *reunified (unstable)* (n=38): reunified children who had returned to care at some point, even though some had returned home again

3. *care group*: children who remained in the care system throughout (n=72).

Children who had been reunified at some point were more likely to be involved in offending or alcohol or drug misuse than those who had remained in care, irrespective of whether their reunification was stable or unstable.

Children who had experienced physical abuse prior to the relevant admission were more likely than other maltreated children to be physically aggressive, involved in offending or misusing drugs or alcohol by follow-up.

Social worker ratings of children's progress over the previous three years in terms of the five *Every Child Matters* outcome areas indicated that children who had remained in care were doing significantly better on all dimensions, and on their total score, than those who had returned home.

At least one-third of the reunified children were re-abused or neglected after they were reunified with their families, but it is possible that other reunified children had also experienced further maltreatment.

Social worker rating of overall progress indicated that those who had remained in care were doing significantly better than those who had returned home at any point. Children living with birth parents at follow-up were faring significantly worse, on this measure, than those who were not living with parents at this point.

On our global measure of outcome at follow-up, children who remained in care had significantly better well-being, in overall terms, than those who had returned home.

Most children (79%) were in mainstream primary or secondary education. Over one-half (55%) were reported by teachers to have made average progress in the past year relative to the cohort of same-age children, around one in eight above average progress (13%) and almost one-third (32%) below average. No significant differences in educational progress were evident for our outcome groups or for those living with birth parents, relatives or unrelated carers at follow-up.

Teachers rated the educational support and encouragement provided by unrelated (mostly foster) carers to be of higher quality than that provided by birth parents or relatives (mostly kinship foster carers). However, this additional support had not (yet) translated into improved performance.

10

Exploring Well-Being at Follow-Up

In this chapter we examine whether the differences in well-being at final outcome between the *home* and *care* groups identified in the last chapter:

- can be explained by differences in the children's backgrounds
- vary according to the type of maltreatment they had experienced
- vary according to whether children returned home to the same or a different family structure
- reflect differences in the children's safety and stability over the first six months after decision (for the *care* group) or reunion (for the *home* group).

Were differences in well-being related to the backgrounds of the children?

We began by looking at the children's basic characteristics and the reasons for the effective admission. The following factors were significantly associated (at a bivariate level) with a worse overall well-being outcome score:[1]

- greater age[2]
- experience of physical abuse and the number of types of maltreatment[3]

---

1   This overall measure of well-being was described briefly in the last chapter and is described more fully in Appendix A.

2   Pearson correlation with age at follow-up: -0.232, p=0.007.

3   Mann–Whitney U test for well-being score by any evidence of physical abuse significant at p=0.026. Pearson correlation: number of types of maltreatment by outcome score significant at p=0.051.

- child behaviour or mental health problems prior to admission to care[4]
- *not* having a parent involved in substance misuse or offending
- *not* living with a stepfather prior to admission.

At first sight, it is surprising that children with parents who had been involved in substance misuse or offending had more positive outcome scores at follow-up. A possible explanation is that where concerns about this persisted until the time of the effective decision, these children were more likely to remain in care and thus be shielded to some extent from the effects.[5]

There may be a similar explanation for the better outcomes of children living with stepfathers (p=0.011), despite the fact that all but one of them had experienced at least three forms of maltreatment. Five of the eight children in this group stayed in care and the other three only went home after their stepfather had left. As we will see later, this may be why they did better.

At this point, the best set of variables for predicting well-being outcome were where the child's behaviour had contributed to the admission (p<0.001), physical abuse (p=0.002), parental offending (p=0.012) and whether the child had lived with a stepfather prior to admission (p=0.026).[6]

However, even after these key background factors were taken into account, remaining in care, rather than returning home, predicted better outcome scores, as shown in Table 10.1.

We followed a similar process with the information available at the time of the effective decision. We found significant bivariate associations between our well-being outcome score and:

- the child's well-being at the time of decision (p=0.001)
- how well they were doing at school (p=0.001)
- the absence of behaviour problems after admission (p<0.001)
- whether the child had settled in care (p<0.001).

---

4   Mann–Whitney U test for well-being score by behaviour problems at admission significant at p<0.001; well-being score by child mental health problems at admission significant at p=0.01.

5   For 65 per cent of the *care* group, there was evidence of concern about parental substance misuse at the time of the effective decision compared to 43 per cent of the *home* group (p=0.008). For 68 per cent of the *care* group, there had been continuing concerns about parental offending at the time of the effective decision, compared to 32 per cent of the *home* group (p=0.023).

6   Linear regression: child's age was no longer significant.

Table 10.1 Background factors, *home* or *care* group and outcome (n=132)

Pre-admission factors and home/care	B	SE	Beta	t	Sig.
Child behaviour	-2.29	0.71	-0.25	-3.23	0.002
Physical abuse	-1.47	0.67	-0.17	-2.19	0.031
Parental offending	1.41	0.71	0.16	1.97	0.051
Lived with stepfather	4.14	1.48	0.22	2.80	0.006
Home or *care* group	1.72	0.67	0.20	2.57	0.011

All of these variables were significantly associated with our outcome score in predictable ways. Children whose well-being was considered positive at the time of the decision, who were doing well at school, whose behaviour did not cause concern and who were considered settled had significantly higher scores at follow-up, several years later.

At this stage, our best predictor of outcome was based on a combination of the contribution of the child's behaviour to admission and the existence of behaviour problems as assessed after admission. Even after taking these predictive factors into account, the children in our *care* group were still likely to do better than those who had returned home, as shown in Table 10.2.[7]

Table 10.2 Well-being, behaviour and *home* or *care* group (n=121)

	B	S.E.	Beta	t	Sig.
Child behaviour pre-admission	-1.66	0.71	-0.19	-2.34	0.021
Child behaviour at decision	3.78	0.69	0.43	5.45	0.000
Home or *care* group	2.53	0.65	0.29	3.89	0.000

To sum up, the children in the *care* group continued to do better when we took account of key background factors and of post-admission factors, including the circumstances that had led to their admission and their behaviour in care at the time of the effective decision.

---

7   Linear regression (n=121). Physical abuse was no longer significant (p=0.337) and parental offending did not quite reach significance (p=0.052).

Did the effects of care differ by types of maltreatment?

The natural explanation for the better outcomes of the *care* group is that these children were no longer at risk of harm. This should in theory be the case for all types of maltreatment.

Our sample was not ideal for this purpose. Many of the children had experienced two or more types of maltreatment, something others have found associated with worse outcomes (Lau *et al.* 2005), and this makes it difficult to compare the effects of one kind as against another. Furthermore, the effects of maltreatment are likely to be related to the severity and chronicity of the abuse or neglect, the developmental period in which it occurs and the perpetrator (Barnett *et al.* 1993). These are factors on which we had no reliable statistical information.

For these reasons, we used a slightly different definition of abuse and neglect from that which we had used earlier. We defined a child as 'neglected', for example, only when there was strong evidence of neglect (rather than simply 'some' evidence) and adopted a similar approach to the other forms of abuse. This made for less overlap.[8] It should also have made it more likely that the children included as neglected or abused in a particular way were more likely to have experienced severe or chronic maltreatment of this particular kind.

We first considered neglect. Our basic hypothesis was that neglected children should do better in care than at home. In other words, neglected children in the *care* group should have a higher mean well-being score. As can be seen in Table 10.3, this was indeed so and the difference was highly significant (p<0.003).[9]

Table 10.3 Well-being scores for neglected children by group (n=91)

	Home group	*Care* group
Mean score	7.63	10.9
Standard deviation	4.34	4.0

Note: This table omits children who were not neglected.

This finding was not explained by differences in the children's behaviour at the time of the effective decision. In relation to neglected children, there

8   Children, for example, were significantly less likely to be neglected on this definition if they were physically abused, whereas this was not so if the 'weaker' definitions (strong *or* some evidence) of abuse and neglect were used.

9   Mann–Whitney U exact test.

was also little difference between the outcome scores for those in the *stable reunion* (7.7) and the *unstable reunion* (7.9) groups. Even if, therefore, the home placements of neglected children had endured, their well-being was no better than for neglected children whose time at home had broken down.

A related hypothesis was that if children did go home, those who had been neglected should do worse than those who had not. This was also evident, as Table 10.4 shows.[10]

Table 10.4 Well-being and neglect for the *home* group (n=58)

	Not neglected	Neglected
Mean score	9.6	7.7
Standard deviation	4.17	4.35

Note: This table only applies to those who were in the home group.

We then tested similar hypotheses for physical abuse and for emotional abuse, first comparing those in the *home* and *care* groups. We could not do so for sexual abuse as only three of the children in this group went home. We found that:

- physically abused children in the two groups had almost identical well-being scores (an average of 8.1 for the *home* group as against 8.2 for the *care* group)
- emotionally abused children in the *home* group did worse than the emotionally abused in the *care* group.[11]

This lack of difference in the outcomes of physically abused children who did and did not go home may relate to their subsequent careers. Just over one-half of those who went home had subsequently returned to the care system and were still there at follow-up. A related reason, as we will see further below, may be that some physically abused children went back to a changed family or a different parent and, in these circumstances, subsequently did quite well. Either way, they did not have to live with the perpetrator of their abuse.

---

10 This difference was statistically significant (p=0.012) if we used as a covariate whether the child's behaviour contributed to the original admission (the main correlate of outcome in the *home* group). Neglected children seemed to benefit more than others from being in care. The interaction between being in care or not and strong evidence of previous neglect was significant in an Anova analysis using previous behaviour as a covariate (p=0.031). Being in care was also significant in this analysis (p=0.048) as was the overall model (p<0.001).

11 p=0.002 after taking account of behaviour at the time of the effective decision.

In contrast to our findings for neglected children, the physically or emotionally abused children who returned home did not do worse than others in the *home* group who had not experienced these forms of abuse.[12] It is not particularly surprising to find that these children did not do worse than others in the *home* group. They are, after all, being compared not with 'ordinary' children in the community but with others who have also been abused or neglected.

What is striking about this group of findings is that *neglected* children in the *home* group did do worse than the others in this group and that remaining in care seemed to benefit them more than it did those who had been physically abused. This finding is also in keeping with the behaviour of social workers. As we have seen, they were more reluctant to try neglected children at home, and this is consistent with other studies of reunification which have found that neglected children tend to remain in care longer (e.g. Courtney and Wong 1996; Davis *et al.* 1997; Glisson *et al.* 2000; Kortenkamp, Geen and Stagner 2004). In this study, two-thirds (67%) of those for whom there was no strong evidence of neglect were returned home, but this was true for only just over a third (37%) of the neglected children.

Does a change of family benefit those who go home?

The simplest explanation for the better outcomes among those in the *care* group is that they benefit from being away from a family that is harmful to them. If that is so, one would expect that those going back to unchanged families should do worse than those who return to families which have changed significantly in some way.

As already pointed out, this hypothesis could explain the apparently good outcomes of children living with stepfathers prior to admission. It will be remembered that five of the eight children in this group stayed in care while the three who returned to the community did not go back to their stepfathers. All were therefore separated from what may well have been the reason for their troubles.

How far did these results apply to the sample as a whole? Here we found that among the 68 children who returned home:

- 33 returned to the same 'parent(s)'

- five returned to find that a new man had moved in or their father had come back

- 14 did not return to their mothers but joined their birth father

---

12   This and the next two conclusions held if we took account of the children's previous behaviour.

- three either returned to the same parent figure (grandparent) who had cared for them pre-admission or returned to a birth parent from a relative

- 13 returned to their mother and found that their father or stepfather had moved out.

These changes are clearly of different kinds and may typically have different effects. For example, it is not obvious that a child who has been abused or neglected while with its mother will benefit from the introduction of a new adult into the family. The new adult could be dangerous and add to the risks, whereas removal to a new family should reduce those risks.

Given these uncertainties, we thought that it was best not to specify in advance which of these changes would be most beneficial but rather to test the idea that some changes would have better outcomes than others. Table 10.5 gives the average outcome scores of children returning to families according to the kind of family change they experienced.

Table 10.5 Well-being and family change for the *home* group (n=58)[13]

Nature of family change	Mean well-being outcome score	n	Standard deviation
Same parent/'parents'*	7.7	32	4.769
Same parent and new partner	6.4	3	3.425
From two 'parents' to lone mother	11.9	10	2.385
Moved from mother to birth father	9.1	11	5.005
Moved from relative to parent	6.0	2	7.042

*Parent refers to a birth parent but 'parents' includes birth parents or the current partner of a birth parent.

As can be seen from Table 10.5, three groups did comparatively badly: those who returned to the same family (mean outcome score of 7.7) and the two small groups where the children had either returned home to their parent(s) after living with a relative prior to admission (6.0) or to find that their birth father or someone else had moved in (6.4).

In contrast, two groups did comparatively well. These were those who experienced a complete change by going to live with their birth father (9.1) or those whose father, stepfather or other male figure had moved out

---

13 Kruskal–Wallis exact test significant at p=0.027.

and whose mother was now a lone parent (11.9). Both of these situations provided a clear change in that the child was removed from at least one parent or equivalent who had been with them at the time of the relevant admission. This was not the case with the other changes described above.

Unsurprisingly, given the number of different groups and the small sample size, the differences between these five groups were not significant. Nevertheless, they do suggest that when maltreated children go home to a family where one of their former parents or parent figures is no longer there, they may fare better.

There was further evidence for such an effect in particular groups of maltreated children. The differences between the five groups were not significant among the neglected, although the pattern was much the same as for the sample as a whole (p=0.12).[14] They were significant for physically abused (p=0.037) and, marginally, also for emotionally abused children (p=0.051). In both of these groups, the pattern was the same in that those who went to a new family with their birth fathers or whose family changed from two parents to one had a higher outcome score.

Although we were unable to test this hypothesis for sexual abuse, we did have some qualitative evidence that pointed to the potential benefit of a perpetrator no longer living in the home. Two of the three children where there was strong evidence of sexual abuse did go back to the same family and did very badly with outcome scores of 0.6 and 1.9. The one sexually abused child who went back to a different home with her birth father did very well with an outcome score of 16 (the second best score among those who went home and the fifth best in the sample).

So, overall, there was a similar pattern among children for whom there was strong evidence that they had been physically, emotionally or sexually abused. They tended to fare better on return home if at least one of the parents with whom they formerly lived was not there. Because of the small numbers we could not take account of the children's previous behaviour. The findings were, however, consistent with the better outcome score among children who had been removed from their parents altogether and stayed on in care.

What is the link between going home and a poor final outcome?

The most likely answer to the above question is that those at home experience further abuse or neglect through poor-quality parenting. This section

---

14   Kruskal–Wallis exact test was used in this and other analyses in this paragraph.

explores the implications for subsequent well-being of concerns about the child during the initial six months after the effective decision or the return home. We wanted to see whether these predict differences in well-being at follow-up and, if so, whether the differences between care and home at this stage were sufficient to explain the subsequent differences in final outcomes.

We used two main variables to do this: a) whether there were serious concerns about child safety at six months and b) whether there were serious concerns about the child's placement or the placement had broken down at that stage. As discussed in Chapter 7, concerns about child safety were of two kinds. In the *care* group they often centred on the children's risky behaviour. This was also true for some of the children who had returned home, but for many others in this group there were clear concerns about maltreatment.

Our first step was to see if these difficulties were more common among those who were at home. This was indeed the case, as can be seen in Table 10.6.

Table 10.6 Percentage of *home* or *care* group about whom social workers had serious concerns at six-month follow-up (n=149)

Nature of 'serious concerns'	*Home* group	*Care* group	Sig.
Placement concerns or breakdown	36	11	<0.001
Concerns about child's safety	19	6	<0.001

Our next step was to test whether these measures were associated with our well-being outcome measure at follow-up. We found that this was indeed the case.

We looked first at safety. Where social workers had had serious concerns about their safety at six months, children had substantially worse scores for outcomes at follow-up (5.9) than was the case for those about whom there had been no serious concerns (10.6). This is a highly significant difference (p<0.001) suggesting that further maltreatment or a failure to protect children from their own risky behaviour had longer-term effects on their well-being.

Can the effects of care on outcome be explained by its effects on safety at six months? If so, there should be more unsafe children at home, but they should do little or no worse than unsafe children in care. In keeping with this, we found that if we took account of safety, the association between care and outcome dropped just below significance.

Before concluding that care affects outcomes because it is safer, we need to remember that children can be put at risk through their own behaviour as well as that of others. We therefore included concerns about behaviour in our analysis but found that this slightly strengthened the association between care and outcomes. Taking account of both care and behaviour at six months returned the association between care and outcome to significance.

The most natural explanation for these findings is that care benefits children in part at least by making them safer. The impact of care on outcomes is through this variable rather than through any impact on behaviour at six months, for which in fact there was no evidence.

We looked next at placement concerns or breakdown at six months. This variable identifies those who, at six months, had had a breakdown in their placement or were remaining in a placement despite continuing serious concern. This variable was also strongly associated with outcome, with an average score of only 7.1 among those who had had such difficulties as against average scores of 11.1 among the remainder (p<0.001).

As we have seen, these concerns were also associated with being in care. If we divide the sample into those who were unsettled at six months (in the sense that they had experienced a breakdown or there were concerns about their placement) and those who were settled, we see that 64 of the *care* group (85%) were settled at this stage as against only 24 in the *home* group (41%). By contrast, 34 of the unsettled children were found in the *home* group and only 11 in the *care* group.[15]

As with child safety, we found that the effect of care on outcomes seemed to be explained through its effect on safety.

Where the reunification of children had appeared 'successful' at six months and there were no real concerns, on average the well-being of these children at follow-up (mean score 10.75) was almost as good as it was for those children who had stayed in care and about whom there had been a similar lack of placement concern at six months (mean score 11.19). Going home for most children in this group had therefore apparently 'worked', although around one-quarter of children who appeared to be settled at home at six months did subsequently experience breakdown and return to care.

The placements of only a small number of children in the *care* group had been subject to concern or had broken down during the first six months. Where this had happened, the outcome scores for these children at follow-up (mean score 7.3) were almost as poor as for children at home who had shared similar experiences (mean score 7.1). The association between

---

15   This analysis only includes those children for whom we had a well-being score at follow-up (n=133).

unsettled careers and longer-term well-being is thus similar for children in and out of care.[16]

In practice, the main determinant of whether or not there were concerns about the children at six months was whether or not there were worries about their safety. As we have seen, worries about safety were mainly focused on those in the community. The fact that concerns at six months 'explain' the association between care and well-being outcome is thus further evidence that the greater safety of those in care is a primary determinant of their better final outcomes.

A further implication of these findings is that those who were doing well or badly at six months tended to continue to do well or badly irrespective of whether they were in the *care* or the *home* group. We know that children at home had experienced more placement difficulties in the first six months. Why, then, is it that the progress of children in the *home* and *care* groups did not continue to diverge?

One reason may be that children at home who experienced these difficulties were much more likely to return to the care system – 35 per cent of those tried at home had done so within six months. Children who did so tended to differ from others in the *home* group. Their own behaviour was more likely to have contributed to the original admission and the parenting they received during the six months after return was much more likely to be the subject of concern. There was, however, some evidence that re-entering care could still benefit them. If by six months they had returned to care, they did, on average, rather better than those who had continued to live at home, despite concerns about their placement or earlier breakdowns (well-being outcome score of 7.6 for the former compared to 6.0 for the latter). This difference was not statistically significant.[17] It is, however, consistent with our earlier evidence that care can provide protection and possibly even assist recovery from maltreatment, and this is likely to have been the case for this group as well.

If difficulties at six months represent an intermediate step between being at home and a poorer well-being outcome at follow-up, is it possible to

---

16 This analysis does not take account of prior risk. The addition of placement concerns or disruption at six months to a regression equation already containing 'behaviour at the time of the effective decision' explains an additional 14 per cent of the variance in outcome. The subsequent addition of the variable 'whether in home or care group' explains only an additional 1.4 per cent of this variance.

17 $p=0.12$ (two tailed) or 0.06 (one tailed test) after taking account of behaviour before effective admission. Consistent with this, the small group of children who were known to have had a past failed reunification before the effective decision also did better if they were in the *care* group ($p=0.02$ Mann–Whitney U exact test).

prevent these difficulties occurring for reunified children? Encouragingly, the most efficient predictor of whether or not a child faced these difficulties at six months was a measure of social work planning – alongside whether or not the child's behaviour had contributed to their admission to care.[18] This suggests, as we saw in Chapter 7, that good social work planning can influence the stability of placements during the early stages of reunification.

In the long term, however, good planning was not enough. It accounted for only part of the variation in the degree to which a child was rated as being settled at home at six months. This in turn accounted for only a part of our measure of well-being outcome which was on average four years further on. As we have seen, the plans that were made were often overturned if a return to the community did not work out and this alone was likely to lessen the connection between the initial plans and well-being outcome. Good social work planning at the time of the effective decision may be an essential first step, but on its own it does not seem to be enough.[19]

Does overall career affect final outcome?

Overall these analyses provide further evidence that the children who do not have a stable experience at home tend to have a worse well-being outcome. We saw in Chapter 8 that some members of the *home* group had moved in or out of care after the six-month point. Some of those apparently settled at home six months after reunion had subsequently returned to care, while some of those about whom there had been placement concerns nevertheless continued to live at home. As we saw in that chapter, these unstable experiences over the short or longer term were associated with a poor outcome. The well-being scores were significantly higher for the *stable reunion* group (9.4) compared to the *unstable reunion* group (8.1). Both groups, however, fared worse than those who had remained in care all along (10.6).

The evidence in this chapter may help to explain how this came about. Essentially, the existence of a future difference between the *home* and *care* groups was settled in the first six months. By this point, some children had settled at home or in care and others had not, although being settled was much more strongly associated with being in care. Given the strong

---

18   We entered our two behaviour measures along with a count of the number of services received and a measure of good social work planning into a stepwise logistic regression. In the final regression, 'whether behaviour contributed to admission' was significant at $p=0.008$ and the planning measure at $p<0.001$ (Exp B=0.18). The planning measure was the only one that was significant if the analysis was confined to the *home* group.

19   It has effectively no association with well-being outcome in a regression containing our measures of behaviour (beta=0.002).

association between being settled at six months and well-being at outcome, it is not surprising that, in overall terms, children in the *care* group did better than those in the *home* group.

What is perhaps surprising amongst children at home, however, is that the gap in well-being scores between children in the *stable reunion* and *unstable reunion* groups was not wider at follow-up. Given that children in the *unstable reunion* group were far more likely to have been the subject of placement concerns at six months, we might expect their scores to have been much worse. A possible explanation is that, by definition, those in the *unstable reunion* group returned to the care system and this may have provided them with some protection. Those at home, who may or may not have been subject to similar stressors, lacked this source of safety. Continuing difficulties at home (even though these difficulties may not have been sufficient to warrant return to care) may have acted to lessen the gap between the *stable reunion* and *unstable reunion* groups, leading to the kinds of differences in final outcome that we observed. For these reasons, the overall comparisons between the *stable reunion*, *unstable reunion* and *care* groups are quite compatible with the findings of this chapter and may even help towards their explanation.

However, outcome scores were not only associated with placement disruption (or concerns) after six months but also with the stability of placements over our entire follow-up period, as shown in Table 10.7. At final follow-up, mean scores for children who had moved to their current placement relatively recently were worse than those for children who had been settled longer, and this difference was highly significant (p=0.003).

Table 10.7 Mean outcome scores at follow-up
by time in current placement (n=129)

	Mean outcome score
During last six months	7.2
6–12 months ago	8.0
1–2 years ago	8.8
2–3 years ago	10.1
More than 3 years ago	11.7

Summing up

For the sample as a whole, therefore, the factors which together most efficiently predicted children's well-being at follow-up were:

- whether evidence of neglect had contributed to the index admission to care
- whether there were concerns about the children at six-month follow-up
- how long the children had been settled in their current placement
- whether they returned home or remained in care.

On average, children who had remained continuously in care had a significantly better outcome, in terms of overall well-being, than those who returned home – whether or not this return had lasted. There was no evidence that this finding could be explained by any greater difficulties among those who went home at the point this decision was made. This suggests that, other things being equal, care is likely to enhance the well-being of maltreated children.

Our assessment of the impact of different forms of maltreatment on well-being outcome was complicated by the fact that the majority of our sample had experienced multiple forms of abuse or neglect, as well as a range of other serious adversities. Also, we were comparing children to others who had experienced different forms of maltreatment, rather than to children who had not been maltreated.

Despite these limitations, there were clear findings on neglected children. These children were more likely to stay in care, they appeared to do better if they did and, if they did go home, they tended to do worse than other reunified maltreated children.

Emotionally abused children who went home also tended to fare worse than in care but, in similar vein to physically abused children, they did not seem to do worse than other maltreated children at home. In contrast, whether physically abused children went home or remained in care appeared to make little difference to their well-being scores.

Finally, there was some evidence that maltreated children (especially those who had been physically, emotionally and probably sexually abused) who returned to a family from which a parent had moved or who moved to join a different parent were likely to fare better with respect to their overall well-being.

These results fit together. They suggest that children in care have been removed from situations that were risky for them. They are still risky for them if they go back and particularly so if the key perpetrator has not moved out.

This conclusion raises problems over the degree to which social workers can override a child's wish to return home or a family's wish to have their children with them. Ideally, this dilemma can be eased by the provision of good planning and good services for those who return. It is clear, however, that this ideal is not easy to achieve. Until it is, social workers will have to be very careful about returning children to unchanged households in which the physical, emotional or perhaps sexual abuse has taken place or neglected children to any parent who has previously been looking after them unless there is evidence of sustained change in parenting ability. In this sample, some of those who returned home did as well as those who remained in care. The majority did not.

How do these findings compare with those of others?

These findings contrast with those of many previous studies of outcomes for children in care which have compared these children to others in the general population and have found comparatively worse outcomes for those in care (Biehal *et al.* 1995; Dixon and Stein 2005; Wade 2006). These negative perceptions of the effects of care have been echoed by policy makers and practitioners and have contributed to a general view that care should be avoided at all costs (Hunt *et al.* 1999; Masson 2008; Packman and Hall 1998). Such perceptions, in tandem with other professional, policy and resource factors, have sometimes resulted in children being left in dangerous or otherwise damaging situations (see Biehal 2005). However, very few studies have, like this one, compared outcomes for children in care with those for children *in similar circumstances* who return home. Where they have done so, the findings tend to suggest, like ours, that children in care do better than those who return home.

Our findings are consistent with evidence from a number of English and American studies that have pointed in this direction. Quinton and Rutter compared scores for psychosocial functioning for 7–13-year-old girls in residential care with their scores 14 years later. Those who had returned to homes with pervasive quarrelling and disharmony were significantly more likely to have poor outcomes in early adulthood on a measure of social functioning (the Rutter B scale) than those who remained in care (Quinton and Rutter 1988). Another study compared outcomes for a younger group of physically abused children who had been admitted to care. Despite receiving intensive professional support, the children who returned home were far more likely (on a composite measure of outcome) to experience adverse outcomes than those who remained in care (Hensey *et al.* 1983).[20] Another study which assessed catch-up growth and weight in a sample of very young children who entered care for abuse also found that outcomes were much worse among those subsequently reunified with parents (King and Taitz 1985).

More recently, Forrester and Harwin followed up 186 children for whom there were concerns about parental substance misuse and who were referred to children's services. Half of these children subsequently entered care. At two-year follow-up, the group in care were found to have significantly more positive scores on a measure of welfare outcome (based on emotional, behavioural, health and educational development) than those who had returned home from care or had remained at home (Forrester and Harwin 2008). Consistent with this, a three-year follow-up of children in foster care also found a significant worsening in scores on a standardized measure of emotional and behavioural difficulties for children who returned home and who were thought to have been re-abused there (Sinclair *et al.* 2005).

In the US, Taussig and colleagues compared emotional and behavioural outcomes for 63 children reunified with their families with those for 86 who remained in care, using a number of standardized measures. At six-year follow-up, the children who had returned to home showed significantly more emotional problems, self-harming behaviour, substance misuse, risky behaviours and total behaviour problems than those who had remained in care (Taussig *et al.* 2001). Lahti similarly devised a general well-being measure constructed from ratings of health and adjustment at home, at school and in social situations, to compare outcomes for 492 American children reunified, adopted or remaining in foster care. On this measure, reunified children were found to have experienced less well-being and less stability by follow-up 15–24 months later (Lahti 1982).

In contrast, Bellamy's recent analysis of behavioural outcomes for a sample of 604 children in the US found that children who remained in care were more likely to have behavioural problems at three-year follow-up than those who returned to parents, although their behavioural problems had nevertheless declined over time. However, for children reunified with parents there was a rise in internalizing problems following reunification, and this increased with the passing of time. She argued that this increase in emotional problems was due to the reunified children's exposure to risk factors in the home environment, especially as a result of their parents' poor mental health (Bellamy 2007). Research in both England and the US has also found that children who return home from care are more likely to become

---

20   The composite measure of outcome used in this study incorporated assessments of physical development, emotional disturbance, educational progress and re-abuse.

involved in offending and other difficult types of behaviour than those who remain in care (Minty 1987; Sinclair *et al.* 2005; Taussig *et al.* 2001).

This conclusion that, on average, maltreated children who remain in care do better than those who return home does not necessarily apply to children who have not been removed to care. In relation to both behaviour and educational progress, a key study compared a cohort of 49 children in care to 58 others receiving social work services at home. Unlike the other studies cited, this one found that at two-year follow-up the children in care were doing no better on measures of educational and behavioural outcome than those receiving services at home. Neither were they doing any worse, so there is no reason to suggest that their generally poor performance was directly, or exclusively, the result of being in care (Colton and Heath 1994). However, this study did not take account of whether the children in each group had experienced maltreatment. Our positive findings regarding the well-being of those children who remained in care are therefore consistent with the findings of most of the small number of studies to date which have compared the well-being of children in care with that of others in the community who have experienced broadly similar levels of adversity.

The fact that children whose reunification with parents had broken down were doing significantly worse at follow-up than those who had never been reunified highlights the importance of ensuring that decisions about whether children may be safely reunified are the right ones. Such decisions are, of course, extremely difficult to make. Where the decision to return children home is taken, this must be based on careful assessment and the return must be carefully planned, monitored and supported for as long as this is needed. The inconsistencies that have been identified in research on decision making, planning and support for reunion are likely to mean that maltreated children who are returned home will continue to face an unacceptably high level of risk.

Summary

This chapter has used a global measure of well-being to assess final outcomes for these children at follow-up. In particular, we have tried to account for differences in well-being for children in our *care* and *home* groups.

Remaining in care continuously rather than returning home predicted a better well-being score at follow-up even after taking account of all the other background factors that were associated with children doing better or worse.

This was true irrespective of whether children had remained continuously at home after return (*stable reunion*) or had experienced a subsequent breakdown and returned to care (*unstable reunion*). However, this last group appeared to fare worst. In part, this may reflect the fact that they were in any case higher risk groups of children for reunion, but it may also reflect the damaging effects of their time at home.

While children in the *unstable reunion* group fared worst, where they returned to care, there was some evidence that the protection afforded by care could help them to catch up.

Where there had been strong evidence of neglect at admission, these children did better if they remained in care even after taking account of children's behaviour. For those who went home, even where the reunion remained stable, their well-being was no higher than was the case for neglected children who had experienced a home breakdown. Furthermore, if they went home, they tended to do worse overall than children going home who had not been neglected. For this group of seriously neglected children, 'care' appeared to be unequivocally good and reunion should be considered with caution.

Amongst children where there was strong evidence of physical abuse, there was no evidence that, on average, going home or staying in care made a significant difference to their overall well-being outcome at follow-up. This could have to do with the behavioural difficulties these children displayed in both settings. It could also reflect the fact that these children could do well if they returned to families where there had been a significant change in composition and that those who did not do well often returned to the care system.

Emotionally abused children who went home also fared worse than those who stayed in care. However, like physically abused children, they were no more likely than 'other' returned children to do badly at home. It is important to bear in mind, however, that the comparison being made is not with 'ordinary' children but with other maltreated children. In this context, the fact that they were not doing worse is understandable.

There was some evidence to suggest that certain groups of maltreated children may do better if they return to homes where significant adults have left or if they return to a different parent. While this pattern was suggested for most groups of maltreated children, it could not be evidenced for children who had only experienced serious neglect.

Children with behaviour problems six months after reunion (*home* group) or decision (*care* group) had lower well-being scores at final follow-up. Where there was evidence of social work concerns about a) child safety or b) placement concerns or breakdown over the first six months, these predicted worse well-being scores at final follow-up. This provides evidence of a link between further maltreatment, disruption or failure to protect children from their own risky behaviour and longer-term effects on children's well-being. Furthermore, our evidence suggested that the link between care and well-being outcome occurred at least in part because children in care were much more likely to be safe.

Stability was also associated with better well-being. Children who had lived in their current placement for longer also had higher well-being scores and, as we know, children in care had tended to be more stable.

11

Case Studies: From Admission to Follow-Up

In the last two chapters we have compared outcomes for children who were reunified to those for children who were not. In this chapter we use illustrative case studies to explore these outcomes in the context of children's histories and of the 'effective decision' that they should either stay in care or return home. We draw both on children's and parents' comments during interviews and on data from case files and from questionnaires returned by social workers and teachers. We conclude with some observations on the relative risks and benefits for maltreated children of reunification or remaining in care, drawing on the wider research to contextualize our own findings.

Home group
Jonathan

As we saw in Chapter 6, Jonathan came into care aged seven against the wishes of his mother, Josie, after experiencing physical (and suspected sexual) abuse and witnessing prolonged bouts of domestic violence. Although Josie did not accept the sustained nature of this maltreatment, her cooperation with plans made by children's services led to a decision being made for Jonathan to return home after four months. During this period, Josie had engaged constructively with counselling, parenting and domestic violence services.

By follow-up, four years after he returned home, Jonathan's reunion with his mother remained stable. His case had been closed by children's services over three years earlier and although there had been some contact in the previous six months, there were no concerns in relation to the care that he was receiving. There were still concerns in relation to Jonathan's sometimes disruptive behaviour at school. During the previous three years, Jonathan had accessed support from an educational psychologist, mental health services and a family support centre. It was felt that these services had some positive influence on addressing Jonathan's needs at the time. Josie had received some help from parenting support services during this four-year period, which was again thought to have made some positive contribution to her parenting skills.

At school, Jonathan was making average progress academically. Although his teacher felt that his emotional and social development was good, it was noted that he had very few friends in school, seriously lacked confidence and was frequently bullied. Nevertheless, Jonathan was enthusiastic about his school and enjoyed many of his lessons. During the previous school year, Jonathan received additional learning support, and an educational psychologist and a Special Educational Needs Coordinator (SENCO) were involved in Jonathan's schooling to review his statement of educational needs. However, it was thought that these services had made little impact due to the closure of the school, which Jonathan had found distressing.

At follow-up, his mother, Josie, reflected back on the months after Jonathan was admitted to care. She felt that she had been under close surveillance and, although she had passed these 'tests', Josie had harboured concerns about how she would manage once Jonathan had returned. In addition, although she had wanted to be free from interference by social workers, her testimony at interview bore witness to an underlying wish for some constructive help to support Jonathan's return home:

> For six months, you've lived with no kids. They've lived with other people. They give you them back and that's it, you're on your own, Jack. They'll come and see you once a month... It was really hard, because they had been gone and you're used to an empty house... It took time to adjust to them being back together... They [children's services] always felt as though I didn't really need much support.
>
> They'd come in once a month, she'd sit down, she'd have a cup of tea. I was surprised she didn't scald her mouth for how fast she drank this cup of tea and so she'd be away. She let me know that she'd shown her face and she'd be away. But that suited me fine. I didn't want them.

Laura

As reported in Chapter 6, Laura came into care when aged eight as a result of long-standing concerns about parental drug misuse, domestic violence and physical chastisement and neglect of the children. The refusal of her parents to separate, despite a written agreement to do so, finally precipitated the entry to care of Laura and her siblings.

Laura was placed in foster care separately from her sisters. Both Laura and her mother, Paula, desperately wanted a reunion. Paula was highly motivated. She worked closely with children's services to bring about the changes needed, including a separation from her violent partner and acceptance of support to improve her parenting and reduce her problems with substance misuse. As a result, Laura made a planned return with her sisters after a four-month separation.

At follow-up, just over three years later, she was still living at home with her mother, together with her new stepfather and all her siblings. She was settled at home and felt very close to all her family members. Although her case had been closed by children's services two years earlier, there had been some contact with social workers in the previous six months. Her former social worker considered that she was faring well at home and had no concerns about her safety and general well-being.

According to her teacher, Laura was a confident child and was able to maintain positive friendships. She enjoyed going to school and was enthusiastic about the subjects she was going to study when she went to high school. Overall it was estimated that she was achieving somewhat better than expected. Paula had received both housing and financial support and parenting skills training. The advice and support she had received from the local authority in relation to her parenting skills was considered to have improved her skills considerably.

Reflecting back on this period at follow-up, Paula said she had appreciated the way the changes she had to make had been very clearly set out, which had forced her to confront the problems that had led to Laura's admission. As a result, she was ready to make the changes needed.

Paula also felt that achieving these changes would have been less likely without the ongoing support that was provided before and after the children's return:

> The key worker from the Social Services, it's her who put in place like boundaries, you know, set mealtimes, things like that…I didn't have that. I didn't have a routine or anything… If it wouldn't have been for [the family worker] and the support I got from my social worker, I don't think I would have done it without their support. Basically, because of the love that I have for my kids, I didn't give in.

Care group
Becky

Becky was removed from home with her two brothers when she was just under eight years old, after a serious episode of domestic violence. Family support services had been provided to her father, Michael, and her stepmother for over a year due to concerns about persistent and severe domestic violence. Becky was subsequently diagnosed with post-traumatic stress disorder as a result of witnessing this violence. However, Michael insisted that this had been an isolated incident and that the removal of the children had been unjustified.

Six months later, the decision was made that Becky should remain looked after; but that her brothers should return home (it is unclear why). From a social work viewpoint, the core assessment had proved difficult to undertake. Michael and Becky's stepmother failed to keep appointments and were viewed as being generally uncooperative. The decision was therefore based on a risk assessment provided by the social worker and observations of parent–child interactions at the family centre. Michael had apparently refused the offer of domestic violence counselling, concerns persisted about drug dealing, his overall lack of cooperation was viewed negatively and, in consequence, he was not receiving services. It was this unwillingness to tackle the problems which had led to Becky's removal that underpinned the decision for her to remain in care.

When interviewed around six years after Becky entered care, Michael still insisted that he was unclear what changes he might need to make to secure Becky's return, and he expressed anger and resentment about his treatment by children's services:

> No, nothing was explained to me. I have applied for her several times, I've been back to court for her. I mean, they were quick enough in giving the boys back, but why weren't they giving me my daughter back? [The new social worker] says I'm no risk.

As we saw in Chapter 3, Becky was relieved to have escaped the violence at home and accepted her need for care. However, she did not settle well during her initial six months in foster care. She was struggling at school and her behaviour at home was quite challenging. At this time she was having weekly supervised contact with her father. Her original long-term foster placement lasted for three years but then disrupted. This disruption was followed by a period in which, according to her social worker, she 'put herself in grave danger sexually', experimented with drugs and showed indifference to her schooling. Following a move to a new foster placement, Becky received therapeutic support from a team within children's services, as well as respite care to support the placement. Although her social worker felt that these had a positive effect on Becky, she nevertheless experienced further placement disruptions.

In order to address the problems associated with her behaviour, she was then moved to a small children's home and a new school. At the time she was interviewed, she was living in this residential placement and appeared to be happy there:

> I love it basically. It's better than all the other places I've been...it's just like a normal house with loads of people living in it basically. It's more relaxed... I like the staff... We go out and play pool. In July, we're going to Drayton Manor. We've been to Alton Towers. We go to quite a few places actually.

After her frightening experience of domestic violence, she felt cared for and safe in this placement:

> Well, I don't really feel scared because they say, 'We're here to keep you safe, we're here to look after you, we're not here for anything else and we're here to help you get through things,'...that's what makes me feel safe.

In the two years before she moved to her current placement, Becky's attendance at school had been erratic; she had been temporarily excluded at times and consequently her educational progress was below average. However, she did not receive any additional educational support. Although Becky's foster carer at the time had been supportive and interested in Becky's schooling, her teacher felt that the social worker should have been more involved. Her social worker felt that Becky's problems at school were linked to the trauma she had previously experienced, whereas her father considered that they had been caused solely by the placement disruptions she had experienced, which had necessitated changes of school. The evidence suggests that both factors are likely to have played a part.

At the time she was interviewed, Becky had only returned to school two days previously. Although she had some anxieties about this, she felt supported by the staff in her residential placement:

> I haven't been to school for two years and when I started school I was a bit nervous, but I could talk to any of them here.

She also felt well supported by her social worker and her support worker, both of whom had been consistent, supportive figures in her life for a number of years:

> My social worker has been my social worker for a long time and basically I can talk to everyone else... [My support worker] has the same relationship that me and [the social worker] have, we talk to each other on the phone basically every day, protect each other, even at a weekend when they're off.
>
> My support worker, she's been seeing me for about five years now. And I can talk to her about anything, but we don't really talk about anything, we're just like mates more than she's my support worker.

At the time she was interviewed, therefore, Becky felt well supported by her residential carers, her support worker and her social worker. It seems that the purpose of this placement had been to stabilize her as, by the time her social worker returned our questionnaire, Becky had moved to a new foster placement, this time with her aunt.

Her social worker observed that 'she has had a traumatic childhood and continues to suffer from the result of this, which has affected her placements and her schooling' and indicated that both her well-being and progress over the previous three years had been poor. Although her health was good, her risky behaviour meant that she had not done well in terms of 'staying safe', and disengagement from school meant that her educational progress was poor. However, at the point of follow-up the placement with her aunt was going well and she was attending school.

Joe

As we saw in Chapter 6, Joe entered care aged eight as a result of long-term neglect by his mother, reinforced by substance misuse and domestic violence from her partner. When reflecting back on his admission to care, Joe indicated that he had felt relieved when he was removed from home, observing: 'I didn't really need to worry about anything.'

The decision for him to remain looked after was taken seven months later. He had settled in foster care, and although attempts had been made to place him with his father, this had not come to fruition. Meanwhile his mother's mental health and drug use had deteriorated, she had been unable to engage with agencies offering support and the prospects for return had largely been extinguished.

At follow-up, five years after his admission to care, Joe remained settled in his long-term foster placement. He was happy in his placement on a large farm and had close ties with his foster carers:

> [I like] the space. You can do a lot more things that other kids can't, like, play golf, 'cause you wouldn't be able to do that in your back garden... I like the animals as well...

> I've a relationship with [foster 'mother'] more than anyone in the house, I think. She'll probably tell me how to deal with [any problem] and, like, if it's at school, she'll tell me to tell the teacher and she'll ring up and tell 'em to make sure.

His social worker considered that Joe was settled and well cared for, and that there were no serious concerns in relation to his safety, behaviour and emotional development. She felt that this positive outcome had been achieved through the ongoing support and guidance he received from his foster carers and because Joe felt 'very much part of this family and his own family and has stated that he feels safe and secure'. Joe continued to have good relationships with his father and his siblings whom he saw fortnightly, but had chosen not to see his birth mother soon after he became looked after. As other research has shown, children who settle successfully in long-term foster placements are often those who successfully manage to reconcile belonging to two families (Biehal *et al.* 2010).

There were, however, some concerns about Joe's behaviour and progress at school. He had received a statement of special educational needs as a result of his learning and behaviour difficulties and had received support from an educational psychologist during this time, which his teacher considered to have had a positive effect on his learning. Although Joe always attended school, he was often disruptive in class and had been temporarily excluded during the past school year.

Joe's teacher noted that his foster carers were extremely supportive of his education and worked with the school to support sanctions. As well as support from his foster carers, Joe also received full-time classroom support. However, Joe had mixed feelings about this support: 'I don't like people being sat next to me when I'm trying to work, people who help me, 'cause it makes me stand out [from] the rest of the class.'

Despite some continuing problems at school arising from his learning and behaviour difficulties, Joe's social worker felt that, overall, Joe was doing very well and that he had 'thrived since coming into local authority care'.

Two other children we interviewed also commented on how they felt about their current care placements. In both cases, their comments imply that what they had experienced in their foster placements had been missing from their previous life at home.

> You get loved and stuff. I feel part of the family... It's a nice home to live in... It's close to my school and I've got lots of friends. (Andrew)
>
> There's food in the cupboards. I get clothes. I have a frisbee and all the things that I have. And they make sure it's good and they get me in school and everything, so a good education or something like that. And they just look after me properly. (Gareth)

Conclusion

Although a small selection of case studies cannot be representative of all children who enter care due to maltreatment, the histories of these children nevertheless raise important issues which are likely to have wider implications. In many respects, the issues arising from these case studies echo those that have emerged in our statistical analyses and in previous research.

First, these case studies illustrate the impact that maltreatment, domestic violence and parental substance misuse may have on children's emotional and behavioural development, even after they are removed from the environments in which these experiences occurred. Consistent with previous research, the comments of Joe and Becky, reported in this chapter and in Chapter 3, are testimony to the frightening experience of living with domestic violence, which may have a continuing resonance for children many years later (Biehal 2005). As previous research has shown, children who grow up in families where there is domestic violence or parental drug and/or alcohol misuse are at increased risk of significant harm (Cleaver *et al.* 2007). For example, they may be harmed through witnessing domestic violence or may themselves be injured in the course of it (Brandon and Lewis 1996; Humphreys and Mullender 2003). In 40 per cent of domestic violence cases, the perpetrator may also physically or sexually abuse children in the family (Itzin 2006). Apart from directly causing physical or emotional harm to children, parental substance misuse and domestic violence may also have a broader impact on parenting capacity. Furthermore, these case studies indicate that, perhaps through fear that their children might be removed or due to threats by a male perpetrator, some parents may minimize serious family problems (Cleaver *et al.* 2007). For example, like Becky's father, they may portray domestic violence as an isolated event rather than a persistent feature of family life.

Second, both this study and others have shown that maltreated children are at increased risk of developing emotional and behavioural problems (Barnett *et al.* 1993; Cicchetti and Toth 1995; Meltzer *et al.* 2003). For example, as we saw in Chapter 9, children who experience physical abuse may be more likely to display aggressive behaviour and to become involved in offending. As Becky's social worker reported, she had been severely traumatized by her experiences in her family. Her emotional and behavioural problems clearly persisted many years later and are likely to have contributed to the disruption of her long-term foster placement, risky behaviour and problems at school. Other research has found that children who experience instability in long-term care are more likely to be those with more severe emotional and behavioural problems, and that these problems may have originated many years earlier, although other factors may also play a part (Biehal *et al.* 2010).

Third, the histories of the two children successfully reunited with their parents provide evidence of the value of family support in tackling serious parenting problems. These case studies highlight the fears and doubts of some parents about their child's return and their need for support during the course of this. For example, Jonathan's mother had worried about how she would cope, about the implications of separation for relationships between her and her children and about the adjustments that would have to be made. Both she and Laura's mother needed considerable support to ensure the success of these reunions.

Given the very serious difficulties that lead to the admission of children to care, interventions by social workers, family support staff and other professionals may be needed for a considerable period of time after they return home. Ensuring that appropriate services are provided after children return home, to strengthen parenting skills and support the child, may help to increase the chance of a successful return. Provision of services may also furnish the opportunity to monitor the child's safety and general well-being until it is clear that matters have indeed improved. Reflecting on Laura's successful return home, her social worker observed: 'You can help people change with the right help and support.' A clear plan underpinning this support is also essential. For example, Laura's mother had commented that she had found the way in which children's services had set out clear expectations for her had been very helpful.

Fourth, the case studies also show that another key ingredient in decisions to reunify children, and in the success of these decisions, may be parents' willingness to accept that there are problems which must be tackled if children are to return home. Both Jonathan's and Laura's parents showed a willingness to engage with professionals and to work towards the return of their children, whereas Becky's father clearly did not. Thus, Jonathan's and Laura's parents accepted the need for change, successfully engaged with services and were reunited with their children, whereas, even six years later, Becky's father still considered the admission to have been unjustified. In some cases, however, parents may appear uncooperative or hostile when offered support and services due to threats made by a male perpetrator to the mother or child (Cleaver *et al.* 1999; Farmer and Owen 1995).

A further factor in successful reunion may be, as in the case of Laura, the departure of a violent or abusive partner. This may make the safe return of a child feasible, although such events are often beyond the control of children's services. For children who have experienced maltreatment, factors at the level of the child may also be protective. A study of over 5000 children in the US found that emotional, behavioural and educational outcomes were associated with children's social competence, adaptive functioning skills and peer relationships (Schultz *et al.* 2009).

Although the general pattern we found for the sample as a whole was that children whose reunions were stable were likely to have returned home more slowly, in the case of Laura and Jonathan reunion had taken place within only four months, as the required changes in the home had occurred by then. The rapidity with which these reunions took place may well have been related to the parents' motivation to accept that change was needed and to work with children's services.

Finally, the contrasting care careers of the two children who remained in care illustrate both the possibility of achieving positive outcomes in the context of long-term stable foster care, as in Joe's case, and the difficulty of achieving stability, as in the case of Becky. Where children accept the need to be in care, can reconcile their sense of belonging to two families and receive consistent, warm and supportive care from long-term foster carers, their placements may be settled. Such children may feel relieved to have been removed from a chaotic or frightening home and to be living in a safe, predictable environment where they experience consistent care. In these circumstances, despite continuing difficulties arising from their past experiences, children may thrive, as other studies have also found (Biehal *et al.* 2010; Forrester and Harwin 2008; Schofield and Beek 2005; Sinclair *et al.* 2005; Taussig *et al.* 2001).

However, although long-term foster care *can* provide stability, it does not always succeed in doing so, as in the case of Becky. This may be related to the seriousness of the children's emotional and behavioural difficulties, the ways in which they make sense of their experiences, their relationships with their parents, the parenting they receive in their foster placements or the quality of planning and support provided by social workers and other professionals. These factors may change over time, as may children's coping strategies, so that apparently settled placements may disrupt even after a long period of stability or previously unsettled children eventually find stability with a new carer with whom they form a strong bond (Biehal *et al.* 2010; Cleaver *et al.* 2007; Sinclair *et al.* 2005; Wade *et al.* 1998).

12

Conclusion

Introduction

Around six in every ten children in the looked after system are placed for reasons of abuse or neglect. This book has explored the experiences and pathways of these children and, in particular, it has focused on a comparison of progress and outcomes for those who remain within the system and those who return home. Decisions to separate children from their families and, later on, to reunify them once again or provide them with a long-term alternative placement are amongst the most serious taken by children's services.

Either decision involves considerable risk. On the one hand, children who enter care do not always settle, many experience further instability and some continuously yearn to be reunited with their families. As we know historically, while some young people do well, for others the outcomes of care have not been particularly good (see Biehal *et al.* 1995; Dixon and Stein 2005; Wade 2006). On the other hand, the risks involved in reunification, especially where it concerns maltreated children, are also considerable. The risk of further maltreatment is high, certainly higher than for children who remain in the care system. Furthermore, while comparative evidence has been lacking, what evidence there is suggests that those who return home have tended to fare worse against a range of psychosocial outcomes than those who stayed in public care (Biehal 2006).

Local authorities have varied in their willingness to risk reunifying looked after children. While some authorities are risk-averse, retaining a higher proportion of children within the system, others appear more willing to accept the risks of returning more children home (Sinclair *et al.* 2007). However, our knowledge of how these decisions are made, what factors influence them and what consequences flow from them has not been sufficient.

The purpose of this study has been to understand more about these decisions and their longer-term consequences for children. We wanted to know more about how the care pathways of maltreated children differed from those of other children in the looked after system. More specifically, for those who went home, we wanted to compare how they were getting on in comparison to those who had stayed in care over an average period of four years after this key decision had been made. In order to do this, we have compared these two groups across a range of outcomes, including their safety and stability, and in relation to children's emotional and behavioural difficulties, risky behaviours and progress at school.

The study

The study took place in seven of the local authorities that had participated in an earlier York study of placement stability and change (Sinclair *et al.* 2007). Our large *census sample* included 3872 looked after children who had been included in that study and about whom a large amount of information on their care careers was already known. We primarily used the councils' administrative data, complemented by social worker information collected during the previous study, to investigate the pathways and destinations of these children over a period of up to three years, comparing those who had entered for maltreatment (2291) with those who had not.

This book has focused primarily on a purposive *survey sample* of 149 maltreated children, drawn from the large sample, that provided the basis for exploring the process of reunification and comparing progress and outcomes for those who had returned home at some point during the *census* follow-up period (*home* group, n=68) with those who had remained within the system (*care* group, n=81). Outcomes were assessed four years, on average, after reunion (for the *home* group) or after the decision not to reunify (for the *care* group). Information on the progress of these children was drawn from social work case files and from questionnaires completed by social workers and school teachers. Finally, face-to-face interviews were conducted with a small number of birth parents (nine) and children (11) to understand more about how events had unfolded from their perspectives.

Thresholds, family support and admission to care

The children in our *survey sample* had come from highly troubled family backgrounds. Most children had experienced multiple forms of maltreatment, most commonly involving emotional abuse and neglect. Most had come from homes marked by a range of parental problems, including substance misuse, domestic violence and offending, and/or from homes where parents struggled with serious mental ill health. Most had therefore experienced a high number of adversities, the interaction of which would be likely to affect adversely their later progress (Rutter 2000; Rutter et al. 1998).

The vast majority of children (83%) had been known to children's services for at least two years prior to the admission decision. In most cases (79%), some family support services had been provided, although these had failed to prevent separation. In some instances, this was due to parents failing to engage with professionals, withdrawing from services or being assessed ultimately as incapable of making sufficient changes to meet the needs of their children. In other instances, however, there was evidence of services only being provided intermittently or of children being left in damaging situations without decisive action by children's services (or the courts), despite repeated reports from neighbours, police or other agencies.

These findings are not uncommon (see Horwath 2007; Stevenson 2007). The complex difficulties in families can be overpowering, making diagnosis and treatment more difficult. Cases of emotional abuse and neglect frequently lack a clear trigger around which interventions can cohere. Perceptions of the care system and its perceived inadequacies may also affect the weighting given to different risk factors, and decisions in favour of one course of action or another are quite likely to be affected by the balance of resources available to support them.

Thresholds for receipt of family support services and for admission to care tend to be high and to vary by local authority (Biehal 2005; Dickens et al. 2007; Masson et al. 2008). Decision making in cases of suspected maltreatment is unlikely to be consistent (within or) across local authorities. Depending on where children live, therefore, some children will enter care while others, in very similar circumstances, will remain at home. While it is right that children should be supported to remain at home, wherever it is safe to do so, there is little doubt that leaving children in highly damaging circumstances without a clear and time-limited plan for changes that are needed is potentially very harmful to their safety and longer-term development. Unless planning for the child is timely, it may also reduce their chances of finding an alternative pathway to permanence should one be needed.

Local authority influences on the care pathways of maltreated children

The large census study enabled some comparisons to be made between the care pathways of maltreated and other looked after children. The 2291 maltreated children in this sample differed from others in a number of respects. They tended to be younger and, as discussed above, were more likely to have come from homes marked by substance misuse and domestic violence.

They were less likely than other children to have left the care system within the *census* follow-up period; a finding consistent with wider research on maltreated children in public care (Cleaver 2000; Davis *et al.* 1996; Fanshel and Shinn 1978; Landsverk *et al.* 1996). However, they were more likely than other children to have taken alternative pathways to permanence through adoption, residence or, perhaps, long-term fostering. Furthermore, although maltreated children were less likely than others to be 'discharged' home, where they did return they were more likely to go home through 'placement with parents'. Managing children's returns through the use of care orders, therefore, appears to be an important avenue for attempting the reunification of maltreated children. Taking account of this pathway, the proportion of maltreated children who in the end went home (at 23%) was almost exactly the same as the proportion found among other children. However, the use made of placement with parents as a route home varied considerably by local authority and these differences in pattern of usage could not be explained by differences in the characteristics of the children concerned.

So not only do rates of admission to care vary by local authority, but so too do the pathways and destinations of children once admitted (see also Sinclair *et al.* 2007). For children in the *census sample*, there were local authority effects in relation to whether (and how) children went home, whether they moved on to adoption or remained in care. These variations held even when account was taken of differences in the characteristics of children and in the duration of their care episodes. Local authorities were less influential, however, in relation to whether children who returned home stayed there or returned to the system after breakdown, or whether children who stayed in care had a stable placement. In these respects, the levers available to local authorities were weaker and outcomes of placement were more dependent on the quality of care provided by social workers, carers and parents.

There was also evidence that social work teams had an influence on these pathways over and above that exerted by local authorities as a whole. Not only did teams appear to influence children's pathways, but they also had some influence over the stability of children's destinations, at home or in care. Although these findings are not conclusive, they do fit with other recent research that has found a similar local authority effect in relation to overall care pathways (Sinclair *et al.* 2007) and in the use made of adoption (Biehal *et al.* 2010), kinship care (Farmer and Moyers 2008) and special guardianship (Wade *et al.* 2010). They suggest that both local authorities and the teams within them exert an independent influence on these pathways and point to the policy levers that do exist by which the range of permanence options for maltreated (and other) children can be expanded and made more consistent and equitable.

Which maltreated children do or do not go home?

The *census study* identified a number of factors associated with whether or not maltreated children returned to their families within the follow-up period, although none predicted return as strongly as did the local authority responsible for their care. Reunification was significantly less likely where children had been looked after for a longer time, they accepted the need to be in care, they were considered to have a disability and if they had come from families marked by substance misuse and domestic violence.

The detailed *survey* of 149 children provided more nuanced evidence from children's social work files. Consistent with the *census* findings, children reported as having a learning disability were less likely to have been reunified within the follow-up period. This was also the case where there was file evidence that children did not want to go home and where their contact with birth parents was infrequent. Wanting to go home was the only child-level factor that appeared to influence a return decision strongly. Although most forms of maltreatment were not associated with the return decision, where neglect had contributed strongly to a child's admission, these children were significantly less likely to have returned, were less likely to have wanted to return and were rather more likely than other maltreated children to be rated as having settled well in care.

Families that maltreat children are often beset by complex and multilayered difficulties. At the time of the return decision, 'serious' social work concerns persisted about birth parents in relation to the likely safety of children if returned, their parenting capacity and their willingness to cooperate with agencies and, to a slightly lesser extent, in relation to quite deep-seated parental problems such as substance misuse, domestic violence, offending, presence of other adults at home and parental mental health. Of these, only mental health was not significantly associated with a decision for children to remain within the looked after system.

The most important predictors of return, however, were a) whether the assessed risks to the safety of the child were considered to be acceptable and b) whether the problems that had led to the child's admission were seen as having improved during the child's period of care. Amongst older children whose views were perhaps more often consulted or who were in a position to make their own decision (with or without permission), there was also some evidence that a strong desire to return home carried weight.

From a social work perspective, therefore, risks to the safety of the child appear to form a central strand of thinking when decisions of this kind are being taken. Where there were no evident concerns about child safety, the vast majority of children (87%) went home. Alongside this, where there were signs of some improvement in family problems, this provided separate evidence about the potential for reunification and, in these circumstances, 88 per cent of children returned home. Given the known risks attached to reunifying maltreated children, it seems right that a focus on child safety and evidence of change should be of central importance in reunification decisions.

Planning and decision making

Evidence was collected from case files about the degree of planning that was associated with the decision for children to go home or remain in care. Historically, the literature has highlighted a tendency for poor reunion planning, emphasizing drift arising from lack of planning and returns frequently occurring through happenstance, from the direct actions of children or parents or from placements breaking down (Bullock *et al.* 1998; Farmer and Parker 1991; Millham *et al.* 1986; Sinclair *et al.* 2005). It has also emphasized the importance of purposeful and inclusive planning, detailed assessments, clear goals and targets in relation to the changes that are needed and agreed timescales and support to achieve them as features of positive reunification practice (Biehal 2006; Cleaver 2000; Farmer *et al.* 2008).

The case files revealed that, in overall terms, there was a reasonably good degree of social work planning in a majority of these cases (67%) that was broadly inclusive of birth parents and children. In most cases, the core decision had been taken by children's services, perhaps supplemented by reports from external agencies. Although multi-agency planning has been linked to more effective assessments and services to tackle identified problems (Farmer *et al.* 2008), external professionals appeared to have a central role in decision making in less than one-third of cases. However, written reports by children's guardians, paediatricians or psychiatrists outlining the impact of maltreatment on children or assessing the potential for change in parents appeared to be influential.

The planning process also varied by local authority. It was evident in all aspects of planning and in the kinds of evidence that were used in reaching a decision. For most local authorities, this pattern was not consistent. Some had strengths in one area of planning (e.g. involvement of external professionals), but weaknesses in another (e.g. inclusion of children). In one area where planning was weaker overall, there was more evidence of parents removing children at will, of planning drift requiring the intervention of children's guardians to get cases back on track, and of reunions occurring by default without any sign of clear plans having been made. At this micro-level, therefore, differences in case management, assessment and planning connect with our *census study* findings on the influence of local authority policies and procedures in shaping children's care pathways and point to some of the ways in which this effect may come about.

The existence of a care order gave social workers greater control over the planning process and the timing of reunion. For those who went home through 'placement with parents', every dimension of assessment and planning was stronger than for children who were 'discharged' home. Of course, limited planning may occur for a number of reasons. Some children go home very quickly, leaving little time for planning. Many children are accommodated voluntarily, giving parents the right to remove them suddenly. Older children may vote with their feet or fail to return from a home visit. Around one in ten children went home in this way. Abrupt or unplanned returns may also occur through crises. Around one-quarter of the children went home as a consequence of placement breakdown (or the threat of it) and/or in circumstances where suitable alternative placements were lacking. It is the prevalence of these kinds of examples within the 'discharge' group that led to the overall finding that planning for them was generally weaker. However, as the literature suggests, the findings also point to overall inconsistencies that continue to exist in planning for reunion.

Children's safety and stability

An initial assessment of children's progress was made at six months after reunion (for the *home* group) or at six months after the decision not to return a child was made (for the *care* group). Final outcomes were assessed four years, on average, after this key decision had been made.

Most concerns about children were already evident at the six-month assessment and quite clear patterns had emerged by this point. It was no great surprise to find that, over this period, children in the *care* group were faring better. Amongst those who went home, concerns about child safety and the quality of care provided by parents were significantly higher. This is consistent with findings from similar studies which have highlighted a heightened risk of re-abuse or neglect amongst those who return home (Biehal 2006; see also King and Taitz 1985; Sinclair *et al.* 2005). Within the *home* group, however, these concerns were less evident for children who had returned to a different parent.

Children in the *care* group were also more settled at six months. Although similar proportions in both groups had changed placements, the moves for children in the *care* group were more likely to have been planned moves occurring for broadly positive reasons – for example, from short- to long-term placements or from stranger to kinship placements after assessments had been completed. In contrast, virtually all moves by children in the *home* group had resulted from arrangements at home disrupting and over one-third (35%) had re-entered the care system by this stage. For around one in five of the *home* group, there was evidence that they had never settled, moving instead between relatives or family friends before eventually returning to care.

By final follow-up, only one-third of children in the *home* group had remained continuously at home since their index return. Well over half of them (59%) had made at least one return to care (although some were back home again) and one-fifth had experienced more than one attempt at reunification. Children in the *care* group also continued to be more settled. Two-thirds of this group (65%) had been settled in their current placement for two or more years, compared to just two-fifths (41%) of those at home. Although reunification is recognized as a desirable outcome for children and may be insisted on by the courts before alternative permanence plans are accepted (Biehal *et al.* 2010), amongst these maltreated children it had not provided stability for well over half of the children who went home. The evidence on concerns about child safety suggests that further maltreatment, exposure to inadequate parenting or failure to manage children's own risky behaviour accounted for most returns to care.

Social work concerns about children at home meant that, during the first six months (and over the follow-up period as a whole), more services were devoted to shoring up home placements. Although contact with social workers was quite frequent across the whole sample during the first six months, it was higher for children at home. These families also tended to receive more family-focused social work interventions and parents accessed significantly more services, especially in relation to housing, financial assistance and parenting guidance. Over the course of the follow-up period, more services were also devoted to children at home. Some were addressing behavioural difficulties (offending, substance misuse or problems at school), while others (such as counselling) may have been addressing the effects of maltreatment. In overall terms, provision of services was associated with home placements lasting. The evidence also certainly points to the long-term commitment to services that may be needed if maltreated children are to be supported successfully at home; services which the existing literature reports as being patchy (Farmer *et al.* 2008; Sinclair *et al.* 2005; Ward *et al.* 2004).

In Chapter 7, we identified factors associated with home placements continuing at six months. Stability at home was not associated with children's personal characteristics, the reasons for their admission, including the types of maltreatment they had experienced, or with most aspects of their care careers. However, home placements were more likely to be continuing where:

- children had gone home more slowly
- planning for reunion had been purposeful and inclusive
- the problems that had led to the child's admission had improved
- more family-focused social work interventions had been provided
- parents had accessed more services.

These factors continued to have resonance for stability at final follow-up, although not all reached the threshold for statistical significance. In addition, by this stage re-entry was more likely where parents had continuing difficulties with substance misuse, a common finding in the literature (Brook and McDonald 2009; Shaw 2006) or where children had been tried at home on a care order. This may reflect social workers using court orders to attempt reunification where family circumstances are more difficult or, perhaps, the greater surveillance that may occur in these cases over time.

These findings on stability make sense and are consistent with the literature on planning and support for reunion identified above. Going home slowly gives more time for well-managed planning and proper consultation. Evidence of change, support to achieve it within an acceptable timeframe and provision of services to support return appear important to the likelihood of returns lasting. However, stability is only one way of measuring a 'good' outcome. Provision of services may be associated with what the social worker thinks is best for the child and not with what the child wants. It could derive from a determination by social workers to keep the child at home and may not necessarily equate with the child 'doing well'. To understand more, we needed to consider factors associated with child well-being.

Child well-being at follow-up

A global outcome measure was constructed to assess children's overall well-being at final follow-up and to identify factors associated with children doing better or worse at this stage.[1] Given what has been said so far, it was

---

[1] The outcome measure included ratings by social workers and teachers in relation to children's risk behaviours, overall progress in line with *Every Child Matters* outcomes, emotional and behavioural development, school adjustment and well-being (see Appendix A for details). Each of these was significantly associated with outcome in the direction expected.

no surprise to find that children in the *care* group scored more favourably. This difference applied even in comparison to children in the *home* group whose returns had remained stable throughout the follow-up period. There was no evidence that this finding could be explained by greater difficulties among children who went home and suggests, all other things being equal, that being in care is likely to enhance the well-being of maltreated children. These findings are also consistent with those from the limited number of studies that have made similar comparisons (see Hensey *et al.* 1983; King and Taitz 1985; Minty 1987; Sinclair *et al.* 2005; Taussig *et al.* 2001).

Across the sample as a whole, stability was associated with well-being as those settled in placement for longer tended to have better well-being. Furthermore, children in the *unstable reunion* group, who had experienced a breakdown, had a significantly worse outcome score than children in the *stable reunion* group. Yet, despite this latter group containing children who had the best chance of success at home, those continuously in care still had a more positive outcome.

Some variation in outcome was evident for children who had experienced different types of maltreatment. This comparison was complicated, however, by the fact that most children had experienced multiple forms of abuse or neglect. The clearest findings concerned neglected children. Where there had been strong evidence of pre-admission neglect, and even after taking account of other factors that predicted the well-being outcome, these children did best if they remained in care. Amongst those who went home, the stability of the reunion had little impact on their overall well-being and they tended to fare worse at home than other maltreated children who had not been neglected. Where children have suffered chronic and/or severe neglect, therefore, the potential for reunification should be viewed with great caution. This was generally recognized by social workers through their greater reluctance to return these children home.

Emotionally abused children who went home also fared worse than similarly abused children who remained in care. However, with respect to physical abuse, there was little evidence, on average, that being in care or at home made much difference to overall child well-being. These children were more likely to display externalizing behaviour problems, such as physical aggression, substance misuse and offending (Cicchetti and Toth 1995; Manly *et al.* 1994; Widom and Ames 1994). It is therefore quite likely that for many of these children their difficulties had negative effects on well-being in either setting.

However, there was some evidence to suggest that certain groups of maltreated children (including those who have been physically abused) may do better if they return to homes where significant adults have left or if they return to a different parent. In either case, it is likely that the person primarily responsible for the maltreatment is no longer living in the household. While this pattern was suggested for most groups of maltreated children, it could not be evidenced for children who had only experienced serious neglect. This may relate to the pervasive and chronic nature of this form of maltreatment which occurs, as we have seen, as much by omission as commission (see Iwaniec 2006; Stevenson 2007).

Finally, problems in the early stages of reunion predicted a poor well-being outcome at follow-up. Behaviour problems at six months predicted poor well-being and this was also the case where serious social work concerns existed about the child's safety or where placements had broken down (or were subject to serious concerns) at that stage. These experiences, as we have seen, were much more common for children at home. These findings are not surprising but they do point to the link between further maltreatment, disruption of placements at home or the failure to protect children from their own risky behaviour and the continuing legacy of these some years later with respect to children's well-being.

Conclusion

The evidence we have presented should not lead to the conclusion that maltreated children should not go home. In any event, where parents and children strongly want this, it may prove extremely difficult to resist. It does, however, suggest that reunification of these children involves a high risk of failure and that decisions of this kind should be taken with caution. The longer-term risks to children's well being arising from further maltreatment, breakdown and disruption are evident.

Most children had had a relatively long exposure to risk before admission to care and had suffered multiple forms of maltreatment and a high number of other adversities. Although most had received some family support services, these often appeared intermittent and were insufficient to prevent separation. High thresholds for access to preventive services and for admission to care are influenced by resources, public and professional attitudes towards the care system and local authority and team-level policies and practices. Where admission rates are low, the difficulties of children within the care system will be higher. In these circumstances, the potential for reunification is less (see also Dickens *et al.* 2007; Wulczyn 1991). Where children with a chronic exposure to maltreatment are reunited, our evidence suggests there is a high probability that these reunions will not endure.

If lower numbers of children in care are desirable, then much greater priority needs to be given to early intervention strategies to support (and significantly reduce harm to) children in the community. Given the difficulties of engaging parents in treatment programmes, this will need to be enforced through written agreements (specifying goals, timescales and consequences) perhaps supported by court involvement and agreed sanctions.[2]

Once children do enter care, their pathways to permanence are greatly affected by the local authorities and social work teams responsible for their care. Differences in gatekeeping, decision making and planning are important, perhaps more important than any differences in children and families themselves. We need to know much more about the levers that are available to local authority policy makers if we are going to be able to improve and make more consistent the permanence options available to children through reunification, special guardianship, long-term fostering or adoption. Whether placements last, however, has much more to do with the quality of parenting and relationships and the role of social workers who support them. There is no real substitute for high-quality placements.

Reunification of maltreated children should not occur without careful assessment and evidence that sustainable change in parental problems has taken place. It will help, wherever possible, for returns to take place slowly, giving time for a well-managed and inclusive planning process and for sufficient services to be available to help parents make the changes that are needed. These factors appeared to be important for home placements that endured. Of course, it is likely that this kind of proactive planning was more readily undertaken in cases where the potential for success appeared good and where parents were more willing to engage in a change process. This appeared to be an important message from some of our more 'successful' case studies. However, it was also the case that the placements of around one-third of children who were rated as settled with their parents at six months subsequently broke down. This suggests that well-managed and supported transitions in the early stages of reunification may not be sufficient.

Services of the right type and of sufficient intensity for the problems being addressed should be provided for as long as they are needed. Many children and parents had received services over the course of the follow-up period, although we are unable to report on their nature, duration and intensity. In overall terms, provision of services reflected the difficulties of children and parents. Concerns were much higher about children at home and these families received more services in an effort to prevent further deterioration and maintain home placements. Our findings suggest they were probably

---

2   We found that engaging parents in substance misuse programmes appeared especially ineffective (see also Farmer *et al.* 2008). The pilot being undertaken by the Family Drug and Alcohol Court may therefore offer a helpful way forward for some parents prepared to commit to treatment for addiction.

insufficient. Although there was some evidence of effect on stability, we were unable to find evidence that they helped to promote children's well-being.

Repeated attempts at reunification should be avoided to prevent children oscillating between care and home (see also Farmer *et al.* 2008; Sinclair *et al.* 2005). This message, though not new, bears repeating. The children in our *unstable reunion* group were amongst those to have the worst overall outcomes and around one-fifth had made two or more returns. Not only is this unsettling and potentially destabilizing for children, but it may also entail the risk of them losing the chance of finding an alternative pathway to permanence. Where changes in the homes of reunified children are not sustained or parents fail to comply with treatment programmes, an early assessment of the likely impact on the child should be made to prevent drift and further deterioration. These messages are important not just for social workers but also for the courts, which not infrequently insist on further trial periods at home before approving a permanence plan.

Where children have experienced chronic and serious emotional abuse or neglect, extreme caution should surround a decision for reunification. These children did significantly worse if they went home. For neglected children, in particular, remaining in care was an almost unequivocal good. Returns for these children, therefore, should only occur in circumstances where there is evidence of sustained change in parenting capacity and where long-term resources are committed to monitoring and supporting subsequent progress.

Finally, while many reunions proved problematic, the findings have provided some important messages about the potential of substitute care for many maltreated children. Although children generally do not want to be wrenched away from their parents, the small number of children we interviewed frequently expressed considerable relief at being removed from families marked by violence, addiction and chaos. Most also spoke fondly of the relationships they had established with foster carers and the improved quality of care they were experiencing. In overall terms, most children had settled quite well in care, had good relationships with those supporting them, were doing averagely well at school and were not getting into great difficulty. Compared to children who then went home, they were also more likely to have remained settled and to be doing well at follow-up.

The care system is rightly criticized for its weaknesses. In particular, as a corporate parent it has struggled to provide some children with precisely this sense of stability and permanence. It has not always managed to compensate children adequately for their past disadvantages (although most do make progress) and, in comparison to the wider non-care population of children and young people, outcomes on leaving care have been relatively poor. However, this study has shown clearly that for many maltreated children it has provided an important shelter and an opportunity for children to refashion their lives and take advantage of opportunities that had erstwhile been closed to them. Overall, therefore, the balance sheet was broadly positive.

Appendix

A Global Outcome Measure of Child Well-Being

We created our global measure of child well-being by combining the following measures:

1. *Risky behaviour score*: This was based on social worker ratings of the degree to which the child was involved in risky forms of behaviour including offending, risky sexual behaviour, running away, misuse of alcohol and misuse of drugs (available on 132 children).

2. *Every Child Matters score*: This was based on a set of five ratings from the social worker questionnaire on how far the child met the five outcomes identified in *Every Child Matters* (being healthy, staying safe, enjoying and achieving [education and life skills], making a positive contribution [pro-social behaviour] and economic well-being [realizing potential]). Each rating was from 1 to 4 and the overall score ran from 5 to 20 (available on 124 children).

3. *Combined emotional and behavioural development score*: This was the average of two four-point ratings of the child's emotional and behavioural development. One of these was made by a teacher and the other by the child's social worker (available on 143 children).

4. *Teacher's well-being score*: This was based on the average of 12 four-point ratings made by the teacher and covering the child's emotional well-being, social skills and behaviour in school (available on 90 children).

5. *School adjustment score*: This was based on adding teachers' ratings of whether the children enjoyed school, had no problems over attendance and had not been temporarily excluded over the past year (available on 87 children).

We considered that these components of the score would all be regarded as having a high face validity and that a score that was based on adding them would thus also have internal validity.

Before forming the overall outcome score, we tried to normalize the component scores by transforming them to natural logs.[1] We then reversed the signs of those scores where a high score would suggest a poor outcome. Finally we transformed them to a standardized form so that each would have a mean of 0 and a standard deviation of 1. We then took the average of the various scores to create our outcome measure. The purpose of these various steps was to create a score to which each measure had contributed the same amount and where a high score was clearly a 'good' outcome.

The outcome score, as we had it, still did not pass the Kolmogorov–Smirnov test for normality and, in particular, it had an undesirably large 'skewness'. A further transformation dealt with this problem and ensured that the final score was approximately normally distributed.[2] The new distribution had a mean and median of 9.7. The measure of skew was -0.25 with a standard deviation of 0.21. The measure of Kurtosis was -0.35 with a standard deviation of 0.41. The measure does not differ significantly from Normal as judged by the Kolmogorov–Smirnov test and while it is still not perfectly normal (the Shapiro–Wilk test is significant at 0.03) we judged that it was sufficiently so for our purposes. Figure A.1 gives the 'Q-Q' plot which compares the actual distribution with the one that would be probable if the data were truly normal. Again, it can be seen that the deviations from normality are small.

Table A.1 shows that the correlations between the variables that make up this score and their correlation with the overall outcome score are all positive and highly significant, features which suggest that the measure has internal validity. A measure of the internal reliability of this scale is given by Cronbach's alpha which is 0.79. This reduces if any item is omitted, although never by more than 0.06.

---

1   The combined emotional and behavioural adjustment score was already approximately normally distributed and so we did not transform it in this way.

2   The original score had a minimum score of -2.4. We first added three to all the scores, thus ensuring that none were negative. We then squared the result.

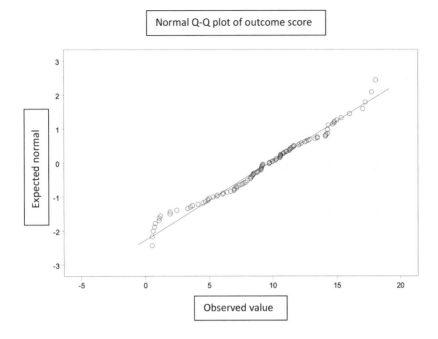

Figure A.1 Cumulative distribution of outcome score and predicted distribution

If this measure is valid, we would expect it to relate to others in predictable ways. To test this, we looked at correlations between this measure and ratings that were made by the case file reviewer which related to the child's well-being at the time of the effective decision. The results are shown in Table A.2. All these correlations were negative. This fact reflects the scoring – high well-being and adjustment were scored low on the reviewer ratings and a negative association is to be expected. The table therefore provides strong evidence that children seen as having good adjustment and well-being by the reviewer at the time of the effective decision tended to be seen in a similar way by their teachers and social workers around three years later. This in turn provides strong evidence for the construct validity of the outcome score.

Table A.1 Correlations between variables composing the outcome score

Correlations		Emotional and behavioural development score	Absence of risky behaviour score	ECM score	Teacher well-being score	School adjustment score	Outcome score
Emotional and behavioural development score	Pearson	1	0.456	0.456	0.772	0.362	0.809
	Sig. (2-tail)		0.000	0.000	0.000	0.001	0.000
	n	143	131	123	90	87	143
Absence of risky behaviour score	Pearson	0.456	1	0.632	0.302	0.464	0.804
	Sig.	0.000		0.000	0.007	0.000	0.000
	n	131	132	123	78	75	132
ECM score	Pearson	0.456	0.632	1	0.280	0.319	0.768
	Sig.	0.000	0.000		0.016	0.007	0.000
	n	123	123	124	73	71	124
Teacher well-being score	Pearson	0.772	0.302	0.280	1	0.473	0.788
	Sig. (2-tail)	0.000	0.007	0.016		0.000	0.000
	n	90	78	73	90	87	90
School adjustment score	Pearson	0.362	0.464	0.319	0.473	1	0.714
	Sig. (2-tail)	0.001	0.000	0.007	0.000		0.000
	n	87	75	71	87	87	87
Outcome score	Pearson	0.809	0.804	0.768	0.788	0.714	1
	Sig. (2-tail)	0.000	0.000	0.000	0.000	0.000	
	n	143	132	124	90	87	144

Table A.2 Outcome score and reviewer ratings
of child well-being at time of decision

Correlations		Child's mental well-being good	Child's behaviour pre-admission	Child few behaviour problems	Child doing well at school·
Outcome score	Pearson	-0.346	-0.403	-0.473	-0.393
	Sig.	0.000	0.000	0.000	0.000
	n	116	133	122	103

Conclusion

This appendix has described the creation of an overall child well-being outcome measure. We would see it as having the following advantages:

- Its component measures have face validity and correlate with each other in ways that suggest the measure has internal reliability.

- It is approximately normally distributed.

- It is available on a high proportion of the follow-up sample (133 out of 149).

- It correlates with other measures in ways that suggest it has construct as well as face validity.

References

Aldgate, J. (1980) 'Identification of factors influencing children's length of stay in care.' In J. Triseliotis (ed.) *New Developments in Foster Care and Adoption.* London: Routledge and Kegan Paul.

Arad-Davidzon, B. and Benbenishty, R. (2008) 'The role of workers' attitudes and parent and child wishes in child protection workers' assessments and recommendation regarding removal and reunification.' *Child and Youth Services Review 30,* 107–121.

Ayre, P. (1998) 'Significant harm: Making professional judgements.' *Child Abuse Review 7,* 330–342.

Barnett, D., Manly, J. and Cicchetti, D. (1993) 'Defining Child Maltreatment: The Interface between Policy and Research.' In D. Cicchetti and S. Toth (eds) *Child Abuse, Child Development and Social Policy.* Norwood, NJ: Ablex.

Barth, R. and Berry, M. (1994) 'Implications of Research on the Welfare of Children Under Permanency Planning.' In R. Barth, J. Berrick and N. Gilbert (eds) *Child Welfare Research Review, Vol. 1.* New York, NY: Columbia University Press.

Barth, R.P., Snowden, L.R., Ten Broek, E., Clancy, T., Jordan, C. and Barusch, A. (1987) 'Contributors to reunification or permanent out-of-home care for physically abused children.' *Journal of Social Service Research 9,* 31–45.

Barth, R.P., Weigensberg, E.C., Fisher, P.A., Fetrow, B. and Green, R.L. (2007) 'Reentry of elementary aged children following reunification from foster care.' *Children and Youth Services Review 30,* 353–364.

Bebbington, A. and Miles, J. (1989) 'The background of children who enter local authority care.' *British Journal of Social Work 19,* 349–368.

Bellamy, J.L. (2007) 'Behavioural problems following reunification of children in long-term foster care.' *Children and Youth Services Review 30,* 216–228.

Belsky, J. (1980) 'Child maltreatment: An ecological integration.' *American Psychologist 35,* 320–335.

Berliner, L. and Elliott, D. (1996) 'Sexual Abuse of Children.' In J. Briere, L. Berliner, J. Bulkley, C. Jenny and T. Reid (eds) *The APSAC Handbook on Child Maltreatment.* London: Sage.

Berridge, D. and Cleaver, H. (1987) *Foster Home Breakdown.* Oxford: Blackwell.

Biehal, N. (2005) *Working with Adolescents: Supporting Families, Preventing Breakdown.* London: BAAF.

Biehal, N. (2006) *Reuniting Looked After Children with Their Families: A Review of the Research.* London: National Children's Bureau.

Biehal, N. (2007) 'Reuniting children with their families: Reconsidering the evidence on timing, contact and outcomes.' *British Journal of Social Work 37,* 1–17.

Biehal, N., Clayden, J., Stein, M. and Wade, J. (1995) *Moving On: Young People and Leaving Care Schemes.* London: HMSO.

Biehal, N., Ellison, S., Baker, C. and Sinclair, I. (2010) *Belonging and Permanence: Outcomes in Long-Term Foster Care and Adoption.* London: BAAF.

Brandon, M. and Lewis, A. (1996) 'Significant harm and children's experiences of domestic violence.' *Child and Family Social Work 1,* 33–42.

Brandon, M., Belderson, P., Warren, C., Howe, D. *et al.* (2008) *Analysing Child Deaths and Serious Injury through Abuse and Neglect: What Can We Learn?* London: Department for Children, Schools and Families.

Brandon, M., Thoburn, J., Rose, S. and Belderson, P. (2005) *Living with Significant Harm: A Follow-up Study.* London: NSPCC.

Brook, J. and McDonald, T. (2009) 'The impact of parental substance abuse on the stability of family reunifications from foster care.' *Children and Youth Services Review 31,* 193–198.

Buckley, H. (2000) 'Beyond the rhetoric: A "working" version of child protection practice.' *European Journal of Social Work 3,* 13–24.

Bullock, R., Gooch, D. and Little, M. (1998) *Children Going Home: The Reunification of Families.* Aldershot: Ashgate.

Bullock, R., Little, M. and Millham, S. (1993) *Going Home: The Return of Children Separated from Their Families.* Aldershot: Dartmouth.

Cawson, P., Wattam, C., Brooker, S. and Kelly, G. (2000) *Child Maltreatment in the United Kingdom: A Study of the Prevalence of Abuse and Neglect.* London: NSPCC.

Cicchetti, D. and Toth, S. (1995) 'A developmental psychopathology perspective on child abuse and neglect.' *Journal of the American Academy of Child and Adolescent Psychiatry 34,* 541–565.

Cleaver, H. (2000) *Fostering Family Contact.* London: The Stationery Office.

Cleaver, H., Nicholson, D., Tarr, S. and Cleaver, D. (2007) *Child Protection, Domestic Violence and Parental Substance Misuse: Family Experiences and Effective Practice.* London: Jessica Kingsley Publishers.

Cleaver, H., Unell, I. and Aldgate, J. (1999) *Children's Needs – Parenting Capacity: The Impact of Parental Mental Illness, Problem Alcohol and Drug Use and Domestic Violence on Children's Development.* London: The Stationery Office.

Colton, M. and Heath, A. (1994) 'Attainment of children in care and at home.' *Oxford Review of Education 20,* 317–327.

Courtney, M.E. (1994) 'Factors associated with the reunification of foster children with their families.' *Social Service Review 68,* 81–108.

Courtney, M.E. (1995) 'Reentry to foster care of children returned to their families.' *Social Service Review 69,* 226–41.

Courtney, M. and Wong, Y.I. (1996) 'Comparing the timing of exits from substitute care.' *Children and Youth Services Review 18,* 307–334.

Courtney, M., Piliavin, I. and Wright, B. (1997) 'Note on research. Transitions from and returns to out of home care.' *Social Service Review 71,* 652–667.

Creighton, S. (2004) 'Prevalence and incidence of child abuse: International comparisons.' *NSPCC Inform,* April 2004.

Davis, I., Landsverk, J., Newton, R. and Ganger, W. (1996) 'Parental visiting and foster care reunification.' *Children and Youth Services Review 18,* 363–382.

Davis, I.P., Landsverk, J.A. and Newton, R.R. (1997) 'Duration of Foster Care for Children Reunified within the First Year of Care.' In J.D. Berrick, R.P. Barth and N. Gilbert (eds) *Child Welfare Research Review, Vol. 2.* New York, NY: Columbia University Press.

Department for Children, Schools and Families (2009a) *Children Looked After in England Year Ending 31 March 2009.* London: Department for Children, Schools and Families.

Department for Children, Schools and Families (2009b) *The Protection of Children in England: Action Plan: The Government's Response to Lord Laming.* London: Department for Children, Schools and Families.

Department for Children, Schools and Families (2009c) *Referrals, Assessments and Children and Young People Who Are the Subject of a Child Protection Plan, England – Year Ending 31 March 2009.* London: Department for Children, Schools and Families.

Department for Education and Skills (2004) *Every Child Matters: Change for Children.* London: Department for Education and Skills.

Department for Education and Skills (2007) *Care Matters: Time for Change.* Norwich: The Stationery Office.

Department of Health (1995) *Child Protection: Messages from the Research.* London: HMSO.

Department of Health and Social Security (1985) *Social Work Decisions in Child Care.* London: HMSO.

Dickens, J., Howell, D., Thoburn, J. and Schofield, G. (2007) 'Children starting to be looked after by local authorities in England: An analysis of inter-authority variation and case-centred decision making.' *British Journal of Social Work 37,* 597–617.

Dixon, J. and Stein, M. (2005) *Leaving Care: Throughcare and Aftercare in Scotland.* London: Jessica Kingsley Publishers.

Dixon, J., Wade, J., Byford, S., Weatherley, H. and Lee, J. (2006) 'Young people leaving care: A study of costs and outcomes. Final report to the Department for Education and Skills.' York: Social Policy Research Unit, University of York.

Egeland, B., Sroufe, L. and Erickson, M. (1983) 'The developmental consequences of different patterns of maltreatment.' *Child Abuse and Neglect 7,* 459–469.

Ellaway, B.A., Payne, E.H., Rolfe, K., Dunstan, F.D. *et al.* (2004) 'Are abused babies protected from further abuse?' *Archive of Diseases of Childhood 89,* 845–846.

Fanshel, D. and Shinn, E. (1978) *Children in Foster Care: A Longitudinal Investigation.* New York, NY: Columbia University Press.

Farmer, E. and Moyers, S. (2008) *Kinship Care: Fostering Effective Family and Friends Placements.* London: Jessica Kingsley Publishers.

Farmer, E. and Owen, M. (1995) *Child Protection Practice: Private Risks and Public Remedies.* London: HMSO.

Farmer, E. and Parker, R. (1991) *Trials and Tribulations.* Norwich: The Stationery Office.

Farmer, E. and Pollock, S. (1998) *Sexually Abused and Abusing Children in Residential Care.* Chichester: John Wiley and Sons.

Farmer, E., Sturgess, W. and O'Neill, T. (2008) *The Reunification of Looked After Children with Their Parents: Patterns, Interventions and Outcomes.* Bristol: University of Bristol.

Fisher, M., Marsh, P. and Phillips, D. (1986) *In and Out of Care.* Batsford: British Agencies for Adoption and Fostering.

Forrester, D. and Harwin, J. (2008) 'Parental substance misuse and child welfare: Outcomes for children two years after referral.' *British Journal of Social Work 38,* 1518–1535.

Frame, L., Berrick, J.D. and Brodowski, M.L. (2000) 'Understanding reentry to out-of-home care for reunified infants.' *Child Welfare LXXIX,* 339–372.

Fraser, M.W., Walton, E., Lewis, R.E., Pecora, P.J. and Walton, W.K. (1996) 'An experiment in family reunification: Correlates of outcomes at one-year follow-up.' *Children and Youth Services Review 18,* 335–361.

George, M. (1990) 'The reunification process in substitute care.' *Social Service Review 64,* 422–457.

Gibbons, J., Conroy, S. and Bell, C. (1995) *Operating the Child Protection System.* London: HMSO.

Gibbons, J., Gallagher, B., Bell, C. and Gordon, D. (1995) *Development after Physical Abuse in Early Childhood: A Follow-Up Study of Children on Protection Registers.* London: HMSO.

Gibbs, I., Sinclair, I. and Stein, M. (2005) 'Children and Young People in and Leaving Care.' In J. Bradshaw and E. Mayhew (eds) *The Well-Being of Children in the UK.* London: Save the Children.

Runyan, D. and Gould, C. (1985) 'Foster care for child maltreatment: Impact on delinquent behaviour.' *Pediatrics 75*, 562–568.

Rutter, A., Giller, H. and Hagell, A. (1998) *Antisocial Behaviour by Young People.* Cambridge: University of Cambridge Press.

Rutter, M. (2000) 'Children in substitute care: Some conceptual considerations and research implications.' *Children and Youth Services Review 22*, 685–703.

Rzepnicki, T.L., Schuerman, J.R. and Johnson, P. (1997) 'Facing Uncertainty: Reuniting High-risk Families.' In J.D. Berrick, R.P. Barth and N. Gilbert (eds) *Child Welfare Research Review, Vol. 2.* New York, NY: Columbia University Press.

Schofield, G. and Beek, M. (2005) 'Risk and resilience in long-term foster-care.' *British Journal of Social Work 35*, 1283–1301.

Schuerman, J., Rzepnicki, T. and Littell, J. (1994) *Putting Families First: An Experiment in Family Preservation.* New York, NY: Aldine de Gruyter.

Schultz, D., Tharp-Taylor, S., Haviland, A. and Jaycox, L. (2009) 'The relationship between protective factors and outcomes for children investigated for maltreatment.' *Child Abuse and Neglect 33*, 684–698.

Seaberg, J.R. and Tolley, E.S. (1986) 'Predictors of length of stay in foster care.' *Social Work Research and Abstracts 22*, 11–17.

Selwyn, J., Sturgess, W., Quinton, D. and Baxter, C. (2006) *Costs and Outcomes of Non-Infant Adoptions.* London: BAAF.

Shaw, T.V. (2006) 'Reentry into the foster care system after reunification.' *Children and Youth Services Review 28*, 1375–1390.

Sidebotham, P. and Heron, J. (2006) 'Child maltreatment in the "children of the nineties": A cohort study of risk factors.' *Child Abuse and Neglect 30*, 497–522.

Sinclair, I. and Gibbs, I. (1998) *Children's Homes: A Study in Diversity.* Chichester: Wiley.

Sinclair, I., Baker, C., Lee, J. and Gibbs, I. (2007) *The Pursuit of Permanence: A Study of the English Care System.* London: Jessica Kingsley Publishers.

Sinclair, I., Baker, C., Wilson, K. and Gibbs, I. (2005) *Foster Children: Where They Go and How They Get On.* London: Jessica Kingsley Publishers.

Smith, B. (2003) 'How parental drug use and drug treatment compliance relate to family reunification.' *Child Welfare 82*, 335–366.

Stein, T.J.A. and Gambrill, E.D. (1977) 'Facilitating decision making in foster care: The Alameda Project.' *Social Service Review 51*, 3, 502–513.

Stevenson, O. (1996) 'Emotional abuse and neglect: A time for reappraisal.' *Child and Family Social Work 1*, 13–18.

Stevenson, O. (2007) *Neglected Children and Their Families.* Oxford: Blackwell Publishing.

Taussig, H.N., Clyman, R.B. and Landsverk, J. (2001) 'Children who return home from foster care: A 6-year prospective study of behavioral health outcomes in adolescence.' *Pediatrics 108*, 10.

Terling, T. (1999) 'The efficacy of family reunification practices: Reentry rates and correlates of reentry for abused and neglected children reunited with their families.' *Child Abuse and Neglect 23*, 1359–1370.

Thornberry, T. (1995) 'The Prevention of Serious Delinquency and Violence: Implications from the Program of Research on the Causes and Correlates of Delinquency.' In C. Howell James (ed.) *A Sourcebook: Serious, Violent and Chronic Juvenile Offenders.* London: Sage.

Trickett, P., Mennen, E., Kim, K. and Sang, J. (2009) 'Emotional abuse in a sample of multiply maltreated, urban young adolescents: Issues of definition and identification.' *Child Abuse and Neglect 33*, 27–35.

Wade, J. (2006) 'Support for Young People Leaving Care in the UK.' In C. Mcauley, P. Pecora and W. Rose (eds) *Enhancing the Wellbeing of Children and Families through Effective Interventions: International Evidence for Practice.* London: Jessica Kingsley Publishers.

Wade, J., Biehal, N., Clayden, J. and Stein, M. (1998) *Going Missing: Young People Absent from Care.* Chichester: Wiley.

Wade, J. and Dixon, J. (2006) 'Making a home, finding a job: Investigating early housing and employment outcomes for young people leaving care.' *Child and Family Social Work 11*, 199–208.

Wade, J., Dixon, J. and Richards, A. (2010) *Special Guardianship in Practice.* London: BAAF.

Wade, J., Mitchell, F. and Baylis, G. (2005) *Unaccompanied Asylum Seeking Children: The Response of Social Work Services.* London: BAAF.

Ward, H. (1995) *Looking After Children: Research into Practice.* London: HMSO.

Ward, H., Holmes, L., Soper, J. and Olsen, R. (2004) *Costs and Consequences of Different Types of Child Care: Report to the Department for Education and Skills.* Loughborough University, Centre for Child and Family Research.

Ward, H., Munro, E.R. and Dearden, C. (2006) *Babies and Young Children in Care.* London: Jessica Kingsley Publishers.

Webster, D., Shlonsky, A., Shaw, T. and Brookhart, M.A. (2005) 'The ties that bind 11: Reunification for siblings in out-of-home care using a statistical technique for examining non-independent observations.' *Children and Youth Services Review 27*, 7, 765–782.

Wells, K. and Guo, S. (1999) 'Reunification and reentry of foster children.' *Children and Youth Services Review 21*, 273–294.

Widom, C. and Ames, M. (1994) 'Criminal consequences of childhood victimisation.' *Child Abuse and Neglect 18*, 303–317.

Wilding, B. and Thoburn, J. (1997) 'Family support plans for neglected and emotionally maltreated children.' *Child Abuse and Neglect 22*, 343–356.

Wulczyn, F. (1991) 'Caseload dynamics and foster care reentry.' *Social Service Review 65*, 133–156.

Wulczyn, F. (2004) 'Family reunification.' *The Future of Children 14*, 95–113.

Zimmerman, R. (1982) 'Foster care in retrospect.' *Tulane Studies in Social Welfare 14*, 1–119.

Subject Index

Author Index